To Tom & Monique
With all good
wishes that you will
enjoy the good things
that have happened
this past century.
Cordially,
Al Connable

Feb 20, 1998

A Michigan Man:

The Life & Times of Kalamazoo's Al Connable

as told to

Tom Thinnes

Eight year old Al, his pal Prince and their first automobile ca. 1912.

A Michigan Man:

The Life & Times of Kalamazoo's Al Connable

as told to

Tom Thinnes

The Priscilla Press
Allegan Forest, Michigan
1998

ISBN   1-886167-09-5

This record of my heritage, life and times is dedicated to my hometown, Kalamazoo, Michigan, and all of its citizens, past and present, who have made it such a remarkable place.

Alfred Connable II

TABLE OF CONTENTS

FOREWORD

Our memories are those of Al Connable. After all, he's 93, going on 94-years-old, and he's actually seen most of what any of us think we recall or have heard our progenitors recall. But it is not just that Al has outlived most of the events and triumphs and tragedies of his era, though, that is indeed an achievement worth celebrating. No, it is a lot more: our memories really are those of Al, and his memories are of us, the Kalamazoo community.

History is not just a list of sequenced facts. Actually, a dry chronology — if such ever exists — is probably the least important part of any communal record. What is important and what lasts is the active telling of those moments by which we collectively mark the significance of our lives. What is important is the people with whom we identify ourselves because they are a part of that memory. Memory is not just a receptacle, but an actively engaged dialogue between each of us and all of us, a dialogue through which we construct for ourselves the definition of what we mean when we say "We."

Al Connable is central to the dialogue of Kalamazoo in a way that almost no one else has ever been. He has been a happy presence in and around our community and most of its institutions for most of this century. He has never been an interferer. Nor has he been a wallflower. One always knows that Al is there. His is the voice of encouragement. His is the voice urging that we do a bit better. He is called "Admiral" by some because he used his famous Gull Lake pontoon boat to float legendary parties. He is called "Senator" by some because of his political career and especially because of his joyous statesmanship. Most of all he is the Great Encourager. Whether it is a concert or a play or a political movement, Al finds a way to be there and cheer on those who have the courage to extend themselves.

Al has little patience for pessimism and none for mean-spiritedness. He has scant time for what our ancestors

11

called "cant"—pious platitudes and cliches that obscure the very subject that they ostensibly refer to. Getting to the heart of any matter and figuring out what is good for the community are what Al is about.

Any community can go out and hire technicians and specialists. People who form the bonds that hold communities together, people who are "the glue" of a town are either grown there or they do not exist. Al with his memories, his encouragements, and his insistence that we can do a bit better is the "glue" of this community. We are immensely blessed to have him as one of our own.

Timothy & Joy Light
Hickory Corners, Michigan

PREFACE

My hope in undertaking this biography is that it may inspire people to experience the wonders of volunteerism. Looking back on my lifetime, I truly believe that my most satisfying moments came from activities associated with the University of Michigan Board of Regents, the Western Michigan University Board of Trustees, and the community organizations with which I have been involved. All have been "labors of love."

Living our lives one day at a time, few of us ever think our meager existence is worthy of capturing for posterity. No doubt humility plays a role in our reticence. Also, most of us stay pretty busy.

But it was a person's death that invigorated me to relive my life. When my dear friend Irving Gilmore died in January of 1986, the tragedy was not only losing a truly wonderful colleague, but that his life and times were never put down on paper chapter and verse. Many of his remarkable and little-known contributions to this community were lost. Worse yet, his great stories about those events were stilled.

With Irving's passing, my wonderful wife, Tenho, suggested the idea of writing my memoirs. Her sentiments were echoed by Dr. Valdis Muiznieks just about every time that I paid a visit to my friend's office for chiropractic services. Similar rumblings were sent to Kalamazoo from Ken Scheffel of the Bentley Library on the Michigan campus.

Well, I finally paid some heed and began the process via taped interviews with Russell Strong of Western Michigan University in 1986. But the "of mice and men" syndrome set in and the project fell dormant.

When Encore magazine published a cover story on me in February of 1994, the juices started to flow again and a long-time journalistic friend, Roger Kullenberg of The Kalamazoo Gazette, convinced me to rekindle the project. He suggested Tom Thinnes, which seemed like the perfect

13

match to me since he had written the articles for Encore. Tom, a former Gazette reporter/editor himself and whom I regarded as a brilliant storyteller, accepted the challenge. He then directed me to Larry and Priscilla Massie as publishers.

We've all formed an effective team — Tom with his writing skills, Roger with his editing talent and extensive knowledge of our community, and Larry, who, as Michigan's premier historian, filled in so many blanks with facts and figures.

Tenho and I joined in to make certain we were all on the same page and presented as many angles as we could recall. But 90-plus years is a long time to recount and I'm certain we've omitted some worthy people and accomplishments. We'll just have to chalk that up to a fading memory and a goal to produce a readable, unencylopedic account.

Some of the memories came back too late to be included in the main text by deadline, but since it's my book I can add a short anecdote here about my acquaintance with actress Margaret Sullavan whom I first met as a Harvard graduate student in the late 1920s. She was a member of the same university theatrical troupe that included Jimmy Stewart and Henry Fonda, the Cape Cod Players.

Because of her husky, sultry voice, subtle talent and unique, magnetic charm, Hollywood beckoned and Margaret scored an immediate success in motion pictures. She made 15 films from 1933 to 1943. However, she was her own person and voiced a critical disdain for the Hollywood establishment, which didn't put her in the good graces of movie moguls. With her screen output significantly reduced, she returned to her true love — Broadway. That's when our paths crossed again as she did a pre-Broadway stint in Buffalo. Later, when I was a Monroe Calculator director, she was the guest of honor at a dinner party I staged in New York.

Margaret married three times — to Fonda, famed film director William Wyler and producer-agent Leland Hayward. Why do I bring this all up? Well, Margaret died

Tenho, Jack Moss and Al at his 92nd birthday celebration.

of a drug overdose on New Year's Day of 1960 at the age of 49. Her daughter later published family memoirs titled "Haywire." All of us have a little haywire in our lives. The secret is to face those challenges head on, and then move on because life can offer so much more as this volume portrays.

Others who have supported this project with their best wishes and encouragement include: Dr. Robert Hume, perhaps my best friend and who as my surgeon knows me inside and out; James Westin of The Connable Office and president of The Irving S. Gilmore International Keyboard Festival; Gazette sports editor Jack Moss, one of the kindest fellows I've ever known and who has been around here almost as long as I have; and Karl Sandelin, a longtime colleague of mine in Rotary and a person who epitomizes the spirit of volunteerism.

I am especially pleased that two people I highly respect took time from their busy schedules to add their comments to this publication — Dr. Timothy Light, the son of one of my best friends as a boy, and former Gov. William G. Milliken. In my mind, Bill Milliken is unparalleled as a selfless public servant and citizen statesman. His character is completely matched by his wife, Helen. On second thought, Congressman Fred Upton Jr. ranks right up there as a voice of moderation, rational thinking and common sense. Our community and our state have been fortunate to be served by these three fine individuals.

Al and long time secretary Florence Vander Molen at her retirement party. Beginning in 1943 she served as his entire staff for many years.

Before closing, let me say that I have been privileged to serve as a volunteer because many in my office down through the years so ably assisted me. I've had secretaries — Lewisa Hogg (who transcribed those first tapes), Florence VanderMolen, Evelyn Somers, and Lori Bridgeman — who helped me keep track of where I was going, when I was supposed to be there, and what I had to do upon arrival.

Tenho and I say thanks to all of you. We hope you have fun reading the book and you learn something new about a wondrous community and some of its outstanding people.

Al's current secretary Lori Bridgeman and her husband Tim.

17

WELCOME TO THE LIFE AND 20TH CENTURY TIMES OF AL CONNABLE

The Kalamazoo City Commission chambers were packed as the community pondered tampering with tradition by writing an end to its chapter in American urban history as "The Mall City."

Emotions were high on both sides of the issue as pro-and-con debates echoed off the hallowed halls of municipal government where many a community leader had volunteered his or her time as civic leaders and decision-makers.

Suddenly, a grey-haired, elderly man, sitting in one of the back rows of the commission chambers, raised his hand and was acknowledged to speak.

"I was privileged to be born in Kalamazoo. I live in Kalamazoo and continue to work in Kalamazoo. And I will die in Kalamazoo."

For those so-called Kalamazoo "Newcomers" who may not have recognized the stately gentleman, that preamble established his credentials for being listened to and for delivering what he hoped was sage advice.

He talked about his part in the revolutionary initiative that in the late 1950s proposed to rip up one of the major streets serving the central business district and replace it with a pedestrian plaza. Yet, he testified, nearly a half a century later, the bold and brash move had served its purpose and it was time to move on.

"Move on!" Wow! Had Alfred Barnes Connable Jr. experienced a lot of that in his nine decades of life. As Kalamazoo's "20th-Century Man," he has been a person of vision, action, courage, compassion and humility. Some say Latin is a dead language. If that's true, the "status quo" is a death sentence for a community.

To a man of Connable's perspective, the "good old days" were just that - - "good" and "old." They were "good" because people came forward with ideas and had the courage to back their dreams with their financial and personal resources.

The Kalamazoo Mall looked like this in 1962.

It's a brave new world out there, one that is changing at warp speed. In Connable's way of thinking, for Kalamazoo to remain a beloved and a "good" place to be born, live, work and die, it must keep up with the pace. It must solicit new and collaborative ideas and cultivate them.

He's been a man with a mission and, like the rest of us, sometimes a man of mistakes and miscues. Yet, he's always had the courage to "move on," to cut the losses, to learn from the errors, and to strive for new horizons. "Keep a happy outlook," he says. "You'll live a lot longer if you see the bright side." He saw the bright side of double-bypass heart surgery in the 1970s and negative thoughts have been few and far between since then.

Alfred Barnes Connable Jr. has sampled life's zeniths and nadirs, and lived to tell about them. In surviving the peaks and valleys of daily existence, not too many breaths have escaped the essence of Al Connable without a hearty, healthy laugh, a positive attitude, and a let's-press-on approach to life.

From going nose-to-nose with Joe McCarthy at the height of the Commie-hunter's power to almost becoming a flaming marshmallow at 10,000 feet while aboard an in-trouble U.S. Air Force jet, Alfred Barnes Connable Jr. followed the philosophy of the Paul Anka-composed song, "I Did It My Way," yet not at the selfish exclusion of his community and those whose lives he's touched. More than always being available to answer the call of service with all his heart, mind and soul, he's been in the forefront. His lifetime is a chronicle of a creed that it was better to light one little candle than to curse the darkness.

With the exception of Ishmael, you can just about call Al Connable by any name. He answers to "The Admiral," "Chief Hollow Thunder," "Alligator Al," "Tailfeathers," "Big Al" and "Senator."

Generically, he has answered to entrepreneur, city-statesman, presidential and political confidant (and one who was never afraid to challenge the party line when integrity was at stake), true-blue Kalamazooan, friend of higher education, local historian, a comedian at heart, and a good-time Charlie... make that Good-Time Al.

To say he's been a gregarious soul is to say the sun rises in the east and sets in the west. Take his encounter with Marcia Clark, the lead prosecutor in the murder trial of O. J. Simpson and who was booked to speak before the Economics Club of Southwest Michigan. Connable, as one of the organization's founders decades earlier, was invited to a small, pre-event supper party with Clark.

He only knew her from watching the trial's proceedings on television. She didn't know him from, well, Alfred. Yet, his introductory greeting was a huge hug, which took her somewhat aback. Her post-dinner comment, even without any wine, was that Connable was "just about the cutest man I've ever met."

Larry Schlack, Al and long time friend Julius Frank at a Kalamazoo Rotary Club meeting.

At a black-tie gala in honor of Timothy Light, a conversation at the Connable table drifted to the value of physical exercise, especially among senior citizens. Connable said he practiced what he preached by doing a certain number of push-ups each day to start his regular routine.

21

A younger co-diner challenged his veracity and the two agreed to a friendly wager. The bet would be won or lost the next day in Connable's sweatsuit, Right? Nope. It would be settled right then and there. The tuxedo-clad Connable went to the floor, performed the winning number of push-ups and collected as the working waiters and celebrants at the gala gazed in amazement.

"A cat may have nine lives, but Al's had four or five that anybody would be proud to have lived," said business colleague James Hilboldt. "The investment life, the education life, the political life, the love-of-music life, the downtown life. And he's lived all of them possessed with a great sense of humor. Rare has been the time when an inkling of temper has shown. He has always looked for the bright side and has always encouraged the people around him."

A score of companies tapped his talents to help steer a course through the minefields of business and investment. "I think I brought a good knowledge of what kind of people it takes to make an organization tick," he said. "I have been complimented that I am a catalyst in bringing people together and spotting the right person for the right job. That was above and beyond my training and experience in education and finance."

"What's more important in a business operation?" he asked. "Finances or people? I think it has always been people. In judging an investment. one should find out about the people in the organization and the quality of the management. I've found that it's the people who make or break a company. That's not to say that finances aren't important, too."

Al Connable has been cast in the starring role of being regarded as one of an organization's most important resources - - a dependable and loyal person. Just ask the University of Michigan where he served on its governing board from 1942 until 1958 and compiled a career-long record of avid support and undying interest.

In June of 1996, the university acknowledged that level

This steel engraving of the Detroit Observatory appeared in the 1855 University of Michigan Catalog.

of respect by naming the conference room in the newly retooled and updated Detroit Observatory in Connable's honor. The oldest building on campus, the observatory dates to 1854.

The restoration included bringing in the latest in star-tracking equipment so that the Ann Arbor campus could host global conferences of astronomers and space scientists - - an appropriate and symbolic gesture in the name of a U of M graduate known for seeking clear pictures of situations and the truth.

From biplanes to man on the moon, from mechanical calculators to computers, from silent movies to digital television, from World War I to the Gulf War, from street cars in Kalamazoo to the return of cars to Burdick Street, from The Upjohn Co. going public to the arrival of Pharmacia & Upjohn Inc., from a pristine Kalamazoo River to a milk shake meandering westerly to a better stream once again, these are "The Life and 20th Century Times of Al Connable."

Join us for a trip into the past and for a glimpse into our collective future.

Al and Tenho enjoy a rare gusto for life.

GENESIS

Born in Kalamazoo on Feb. 20, 1904, Alfred Barnes Connable Jr. can trace his maternal ancestry to the first white settlers of Kalamazoo County. Thanks to the historical bent of an uncle, the paternal roots were tracked back to mid-17th century England.

While the surname has evolved from various forms, his direct link is to a London joiner (carpenter), John Cunnabell, who was born in 1650. The woodsmith made the big jump across the puddle in 1673, missing a booking on The Mayflower by about 50 years. The head of the now-Connable clan must have landed very near Plymouth Rock because many family gravestones dating back to the early 1700s can be found in the Boston area.

Lines of the family headed off for upper New York State, Nova Scotia and eventually Illinois, where, along the way an "N" was dropped out of the name. For example, there is the family of cousin Barber Conable in upstate New York. Barber represented his region in Congress for many years and served as the president of the World Bank. Another link is to south-of-the-border Tomas Garrido Canabal, the governor of Tabasco and the minister of agriculture in the Mexican government in the early 1930s.

The "two N" Connables, to whom "Big Al" pays homage, for the most part stayed put in New England for several generations. The glossy, bound genealogy, published by his Uncle Ralph prior to World War II, contains photos of one vintage Connable homestead, a former tavern along the Connecticut River near North Bernardston, Mass.

Another photo is of a historical marker erected in 1930 by the Massachusetts Bay Colony Tercentenary Commission. It reads: "Connable Fort — site of the second fort and building in Fall Town. Erected in 1739 by Samuel Connable."

Such private forts, hewn from 13-inch logs and impregnable to attacks from the traditional weapons of unfriendly

Indians, were generally built as the first line of defense by settlers moving west out of "civilized" Boston. Timbers from Fort Connable were then used for homes, one of which still exists today.

Connable's paternal grandfather, Ralph Connable Sr., was born in Bernardston, Mass., two days after Christmas in 1835, but his parents moved to Xenia, Ohio, within two years and the boy grew up as a Midwesterner. At the age of 15, he called Jackson, Mich., home, which is where he met his wife, Mary Stanton. She too, had been born in the East, the daughter of an Albany, N.Y., doctor. Grandfather Ralph also tried higher education, attending Albion College for two years.

The Depot in Jackson, ca. 1870.

Ralph's pursuit of success took him first to Chicago and connections with other "Conables," engaging in milling, the ice business and processing of tobacco products. He returned to Jackson, Mich., where Al's father, Alfred B. Connable Sr., was born on Aug. 18, 1871. Manufacturing sewer pipe, drain tile and fire brick fed his family.

Ralph Sr. had very bad hay fever and asthma. So in 1877 he moved his family to Petoskey, which in those days was free from ragweed. There, he practiced mercantilism, served as the postmaster, and diversified into Great Lakes fishing. According to the family history, his inventive nature fashioned a mechanized lifter of fishing nets that was utilized throughout the industry. A building and street in

Petoskey carry the family name.

Shortly after the family relocated in northern Michigan. Al's father learned the ways of work early, starting as a mail sorter in the Petoskey Post Office as an 8 year old and then at his father's fish house, breaking ice with a maul to package the odoriferous and tasty product.

Lumber laden bob sleighs were a common sight in Petoskey in the 1880s.

The youngster also learned about the fragile line between life and death. Mary gave birth to 12 children, but only four sons reached adulthood. A first-born son died within four months. Two daughters didn't make it to a second birthday. Alfred Sr. was the seventh in line. No. 8, Albert, died at the age of 10. The others were buried as infants or toddlers, with the 12th living only one day in August of 1881.

Mary Stanton Connable was steeped in the value of fine arts, particularly music. She gave singing lessons to Indian youngsters and handled choral duties at Sunday School. Her four sons were raised to appreciate music and took piano lessons.

The senior Connable was sent south to Ann Arbor to complete high school in 1890 and prep for his entrance into the University of Michigan, where he earned his bachelor's in 1894. Two years later, he added a Northwestern

University law degree to his credentials. He was to marry his first client, the former Frances Peck, and that's how the Kalamazoo branch of the Connable clan started.

Frances Peck Connable just prior to her marriage to Alfred Connable, Sr.

Frances' grandfather, Horace M. Peck, was born in Watertown, Conn., in August of 1814 to a prominent farm family in the Nutmeg State. At the age of 22, Horace M. tried Michigan on for size for a short stay but returned to Connecticut. He moved for keeps in the spring of 1838, choosing the village of Yorkville as his first homestead.

**Al's Great Grandfather Horace M. Peck,
born 8/17/1814 died 4/24/1894.**

Peck became related by marriage to Col. Isaac Barnes, who had arrived in the area from Medina, Ohio, in 1832 five years before Michigan entered the union as the 26th state. Barnes was one of the first white homesteaders to farm the spacious 2,800-acre Gull Prairie. His original home was a log cabin that he built about a mile north of Richland where the Stage Coach Inn restaurant is now located at the intersection of M-89 and M-43.

Barnes built his main house probably in 1837, adjacent to that first cabin and in the center of what was supposed to become the platted village of Geloster. Named after Barnes' three sons — George, Carlos and Lester — Geloster never materialized as a community. After serving as the area's first township supervisor, postmaster and probate judge, Barnes moved on to Allegan County in 1841 because economic prospects seemed the brightest there for Southwest Michigan.

But the colonel's brother, Tillotson Barnes, stayed in the area. He was the first white pioneer to settle on Gull Lake. Tillotson built the dam at the foot of the lake and installed a grist mill. One of his daughters, Mary Barnes, married into the Little clan, another pioneer family in the Richland area whose combination of farming and mechanical skills led to grist and lumber-mill operations on Gull Lake as well as the grain-elevator business. Direct from that family line came Alvin Little and his daughter, Mary Little Tyler, as well as a future mayor of Kalamazoo, Caroline Ham.

Ownership of the original Isaac Barnes homestead eventually passed to Horace M. Peck, who earned his living marketing livestock and real estate, and had married Amelia "Emily" Barnes, another of Tillotson's daughters. In 1869, Horace M. left the Gull Prairie and moved to the village of Kalamazoo where he became a founding investor in the Kalamazoo Savings Bank that incorporated in 1884. A daughter ended up in Washington as the spouse of a Michigan congressman, while two of his four sons grew to be mirror images.

The sons — Horace B. and his brother, Charles — were certainly not Peck's bad boys. They were enterprising ones who evolved from being thrifty farmers to industrious entrepreneurs and financiers. As young men, they saved their money and then started loaning it out. Charles and

Horace B. initially followed the Isaac Barnes clan north-
westward and established the Allegan City Bank in 1868.
In 1875, Horace B. was elected "president" of Allegan, the
community where Connable's mother, Frances Peck, was
born three years earlier. Her only sibling, sister Luella, was
also born there.

Al's Grandfather Horace B. Peck, born 7/20/1841 died 6/14/1903.

Al's Great Uncle Charles A. Peck, born 12/23/1852 died 7/23/1923.

The Peck brothers were reunited in capitalism and investment in 1890 when Horace B. moved his family, including 18-year-old Frances, into Kalamazoo. Allegan's predicted economic potential had actually landed farther up the Kalamazoo River in the form of regular railroad service, higher-education opportunities, an international reputation for producing the best celery in the world, an industrial base that promised to grow with the development of paper-making technology, and an enterprising physician who had devised an interesting way to deliver medication in the form of "friable" pills.

Peck money helped capitalize a number of ventures — Star Brass Co., Kalamazoo Sled Co., Kalamazoo Vegetable Parchment Co. and Monroe Calculating Machine Co., among others — and also investments in enterprises around the state.

That the Pecks were a part of the Kalamazoo establishment is almost an understatement. For years, Charles Peck's home on South Street (the site of the Kalamazoo Institute of Arts' expansion) hosted the community's elite.

Horace B. Peck's home was at the corner of Rose and South streets, where the refurbished Kalamazoo Public Library is now situated. After Grandmother Peck died, the

The Horace B. Peck home at the corner of Rose and South streets shown just prior to its demolition in the late 1950s.

family donated the building to the community and it served as the home of Kalamazoo's first museum for 30 years until being demolished in the late 1950s. Surviving as a core exhibit in the Kalamazoo Valley Museum is the stained glass window that was designed to grace the stairway of the new Peck quarters more than a century ago.

By the time of his 1896 graduation from law school, Connable's father had already chosen to begin his career in Kalamazoo. Certainly, the community's economic potential had something to do with the decision. But the move was more a matter of the heart. Alfred Sr. had first spotted 24-year-old Frances Peck on a tennis court near Petoskey as she vacationed with her family in northern Michigan. It was six-love, six-love, six-love, point, set and match made in heaven. In November of 1896, they swore ultimate allegiance to each other at the altar.

Alfred Barnes Connable Sr.'s law career was short-lived. Within a year, he joined the Pecks' investment business, which was first housed in what is now called the Park Building on South Street. About midway through the first decade of the 20th century, the Peck firm moved to its own quarters at the southeast corner of Burdick and South streets, where Standard Federal (nee Fidelity Federal Savings and Loan) is now situated. The firm eventually purchased what was then known as the "Brown Block. The Peck Building was razed in 1975. Over a four-generation period, "The Peck Office" evolved into "The Connable Office," as it shifted from providing venture capital to estate planning and trust management.

Horace B. died in 1903, the year prior to grandson Alfred Jr.'s birth, while Charles lived another 20 years.

So what happened to the original "Barnes House?"

Col. Barnes' settlement acted as the local rallying point for those who, like future American presidents Zachary Taylor and Abraham Lincoln, wanted to fight in the Black Hawk War. That 1832 skirmish was organized to push the Sauk and Fox Indians across the Mississippi River, out of what was the state of Illinois and the future state of Wisconsin. While Taylor was able to earn a few combat ribbons, the Geloster detachment got as far as Niles because the "war" lasted only from April through September.

The 1880 History of Kalamazoo County included this lithograph of Col. Barnes' homestead near Richland.

The Barnes House served as the area's post office, stagecoach stop, tavern and lodge hall. Potawatomi Indians frequently came down from Barry County for swapping sprees at that crossing of trails. Some never left, as existing Indian mounds and burial sites can attest to.

As the decades passed and a new century dawned, ownership changed several times. The inn fell into disrepair, especially after it was vacated when a fire drove the last residents out. Improperly protected from the elements, the structure suffered the tolls of weathering, time and termites.

In 1971, Alice Tigchelaar, a 35-year veteran of the food-service business, saw that a "For Sale" sign had been planted in the front yard of the place she had always dreamed of owning. A collector of antiques, she envisioned the old homestead to be the perfect vehicle for a restaurant that dripped with local lore.

Her dream began taking on nightmarish proportions when restoration efforts revealed significant and potentially dangerous deterioration to major beams. The work crews also learned that the Barnes estate originally faced to the north. Sometime, somehow, it was picked up and turned to face the west.

Her toughest decision, but one she had to face in order to make the Stage Coach Inn a dream come true, was to raze the original structure, salvage as much of the termite-free stuff as possible, and build a replica.

Col. Barnes would have been proud. Al Connable certainly was.

The Stage Coach Inn restaurant, 1997.

CHILDHOOD —
FROM COLIC TO A COW IN THE
FRONT YARD TO CULVER

Sunday gatherings for dinner, a presidential visit, the treat of a ride in an electric car, the pride of reaching a storied mountain's summit, and the eerie feeling of climbing the back exterior steps of a stately family mansion fill the childhood memories of Al Connable.

A philanthropic gift to the community in its final years, the stately home of his grandparents, Mr. and Mrs. Horace B. Peck, now exists only in vintage photographs, giving way to "progress" in the 1950s to make room for a new library/museum building at South and Rose.

The electric car is supposedly making a comeback as part of a planet's environmental concern, and so did Connable's childhood memories as he scanned his recollections for these memoirs.

"Big Al" was one of five children — three brothers and two sisters — all born in Kalamazoo to Alfred and Frances Connable. He was first of the three sons. Some infants come into the world "yellow" suffering from jaundice. With his stomach talking to him, Al entered Feb. 20, 1904, on a noisy note — with colic.

His older sister, Virginia, was born in 1897, two years before sister Josephine. Brothers Horace (H.P.) and Harold joined the family in 1907 and 1914, respectively.

"My parents moved out of the Peck house shortly before I was born in 1904 and took up temporary residence farther west on South Street across from what is now the Marlborough Condominiums. The house where I was born was torn down and the land is now a parking lot."

The ultimate destination was a pillared home on Prospect Hill near the Henderson Castle. Connable was raised in that almost idyllic western part of Kalamazoo. The area was still quasi-rural, beyond what is now

Kalamazoo College and the prestigious "new" neighborhood pioneered by U.S. Sen. Charles Stuart, a local host of Senate colleague Stephen Douglas of Illinois.

The majestic edifice on Prospect Hill where Al grew up.

"My mother was a very fine woman and understanding of her children. She was quite remarkable in being able to cope with five lively youngsters because my father was very active in the community and in many companies. Those public duties frequently took him away from home."

Because of one of those public duties, a sitting president of the United States came to the Connable house on the hill and etched a memory in a young boy's mind. William Howard Taft, sworn into office in March of 1909, came to Kalamazoo two years later to dedicate the new YMCA building at the corner of Michigan Avenue and Park Street. As mayor of Kalamazoo, Alfred Barnes Connable Sr. was

Taft's official host.

"My father met President Taft at the railroad station. Taft was an immense man. Some of his critics called him obese. We had a Pierce Arrow, the kind of car with headlights on the fender and very wide seats. Well, when A.B. brought him up to our house to give him a view of the city, President Taft took up the whole rear seat.

"Naturally, we kids were awed by the visit and the fact that the president of the United States was in our house. From then on we all vied with each other as to who could sit in President Taft's seat. Turns out we all could."

One must remember that the Connable-Peck union was not too far removed from when folks lived almost totally from "the land." A family cow, "Brown Betty," grazed on the front lawn during the first decade of the 20th century. She had three acres of grass to chew.

**Brown Betty provided the Connable family milk
and doubled as a lawn mower.**

"Our home had four two-story pillars that faced south down the hill. At Christmas, we put up candles in the windows and it took around 40 to do the job. The children in our family were fairly congenial with each other. Sure, there were ins and outs, but nothing very serious. My two younger brothers complained I picked on them, but that's par for the course."

During Al's toddler years, summers were spent where his father enjoyed his boyhood — on Little Traverse Bay at Harbor Springs near Petoskey. Little Al had a propensity for collecting worms in a tin can, towing his bait box on a short rope and entering the dining hall of the resort where the family was staying — much to the disgust of those enjoying a meal. After all, they preferred white fish, not nightcrawlers or even escargot.

Cars were still something of a luxury. Michigan's network of roads and highways were still a glint in some traffic planner's eye. A gas station? What was that? Driving from Kalamazoo to Petoskey was a two-day endeavor, mostly on dirt roads What must have been a pain in the posterior for the two parents was nothing but thrills and adventure for the kids, especially when the family's White

The Connable family posed before Grandma Peck's cottage on Gull Lake, ca. 1909. Al is third from left in front.

Steamer became stuck in the sand and had to be pulled out by farmers who thought that such a mechanized contraption would never replace dependable, flesh-and-blood horse-power.

Gull Lake also beckoned during the summers, especially Grandmother Peck's cottage on the island. The cottage still exists. The Connable kids would travel there by the electric Interurban, catching the train at the downtown station that in later years housed Vermeulen's Furniture Store and now has been restored by First of America as part of Arcadia Commons. The Interurban carried both a legacy of family fun and tragedy. Mary Barnes Little, then the mother of three, died from internal injuries after a car she was riding in stalled on the tracks and was struck by the train near Richland.

The Battle Creek-bound Interurban dropped off passengers at the south end of the lake in the vicinity of what is now the Bay View Gardens and the former Anchor Inn.

Gull Lake recreationists at Midland Park, ca. 1910.

In the era of silent movies, that location was the first outdoor theater in Michigan. It was a walk-in, not a drive-in. Movie fans sat on benches scattered across the hillside to watch the antics of Charlie Chaplin, the perils of Pauline and the heroics of William S. Hart and Tom Mix. When the talkies arrived, that was the last word for Gull Lake's outdoor theater. Early in the 1930s, an enterprising woman converted the lone house near the hillside and opened "Ma Norton's Cottage Inn," the forerunner of the Anchor Inn.

"Ma's significant other," who in Al's childhood recollection was known as "Captain Norton," was equally opportunistic. He ran a ferry system to the island with seaworthy craft called "The Michigan" and "The Brownie."

While the boat ride was a means to an end for adults, especially those responsible for food, rations and other supplies on the power-less island, it was "Treasure Island" time for youngsters. The power of winter provided the energy for surviving the summer. Packed in sawdust in the island's ice house were huge blocks that were cut from the lake's frozen surface. They kept the chill on perishable food transported from shore.

Capt. Norton's Gull Lake ferry boat, the Michigan.

"You could consider my family as being fairly well-to-do. Remember, that was really before The Upjohn Co. registered the tremendous growth that created so much wealth and has done so much for this community. The Peck broth-

42

ers were regarded as pretty wealthy people in their days and my mother was a Peck. When one of the brothers died, the headline in a local newspaper was `Peck, Richest Man in Town, Dies.' That might have been something of an exaggeration, but in those days sending daughters to private schools in the east was not too common, and my father did that." The Connables were also wealthy enough to do some substantial sightseeing with their children.

When "Little Al" was 7 years old, his father organized a three-week camping expedition to Yellowstone Park, which in 1911 was a remote, primitive area. Accompanying the Connable clan were "Uncle Charlie" Peck and his daughter, Dorothy, and her best friend, Genevieve Upjohn, daughter of Dr. William E. Upjohn. Also in the party was "Auntie" Bessie Dayton, a trained nurse.

The family changed trains in Helena, Montana, during their 1911 trip to Yellowstone. Shown are Al, his parents, sisters and Genevieve Upjohn Gilmore (2nd from right).

43

A two-day train trip took them to Cody, Wyo., where they stayed at the Irma Hotel while being outfitted for the camping expedition. A bus took the Kalamazooans to a lodge operated by Buffalo Bill Cody's sister at the east edge of the park. They stayed there for a week getting acclimated to the altitude and polishing camping skills.

Because no autos were allowed, "roughing it" describes the experience well — tenting in Indian tepees, riding into the bush by horseback, and eating out of a chuck wagon. Seared in his memory is watching park rangers shoot Roman candles at bears to scare them away, as opposed to using bullets.

There was also the Pikes Peak adventure, which could be a young boy's desire to be with his father, or a metaphor for setting one's sights high in life — like 14,000 feet up. For whatever reason, he convinced his father that he belonged on the Sunday-afternoon adventure. That feat made the 7-year-old Kalamazooan the youngest person at the time to reach the top, which merited an Associated Press wire story and created a lifetime mountain climber and trail hiker in the Rockies. The Kalamazoo Gazette printed the July 1911 dispatch.

"I was the youngest to climb to the top by way of the cog railway right-of-way. At the halfway house, I asked my father if we could keep going. I was so young I didn't know any better, but he agreed because the view was spectacular. I guess you could call it euphoria. That wasn't too smart because we hadn't planned for the full trip and at about the 12,000-foot level, it got more than chilly. We weren't dressed for it.

"When we reached the summit, we were mighty appreciative when the railroad men up there allowed us to stay in the warm bunkhouse. We got there just before dark and they took us in. It was kind of embarrassing because we didn't have any money to pay for the lodgings. They must have trusted us because we were allowed to stay. The next day we rode the cog railroad down the mountain and sent some money back on the return trip."

After joining the Boy Scouts troop sponsored by the First Presbyterian Church in 1912, "Little Al" would be better prepared for the thrills of the outdoors. He fondly recalls campouts in two-boy puptents at Bonnie Castle Lake west of the city and treks northward to Cooper's Glen, the present home of the Kalamazoo Nature Center.

He worked his way up from tenderfoot to first class scout and, with 20 merit badges, was one away from scouting's pinnacle — the rank of Eagle. However, with prep school in the offing, he forever remained one badge short — until about 80 years later when the Southwest Michigan Council of the Boy Scouts of America presented him with a special Eagle award in recognition for what he had done to help his community and its citizens soar to new heights.

Less testing than Colorado hiking but just as exhilarating for a son was a long train trip that took junior and senior in 1915 to Chicago and across country to San Diego and

The Connable home on Prospect Hill often hosted important gatherings such as this DAR meeting, ca. 1910.

San Francisco to the Panama-Pacific Exposition . Many of the Moorish and Spanish Renaissance-style exhibition halls built for the fair remain and Connable visited them each time he returned to San Diego because of the fond memories he had of that trip as an 11 year old. The itinerary took

**Five-year-old Al posed with his nanny and sled
proudly lettered "Alfred."**

the pair up the coastline to San Francisco, Seattle and Vancouver before heading homeward via the Canadian Rockies.

As more and more people moved to the west side of Kalamazoo, the Connable home on the hill became quite the gathering place, especially after he built the first private tennis court in Kalamazoo in 1904.

"Many of the town's best tennis players had their early training on that 'neighborhood' court. That's where they learned the game. People like Wildie and Fred Fischer, Bill Walsh and the Hodgeman kids. Their father, Dr. Bert Hodgeman, was a great tennis coach and his children played there."

The court served Al Jr. well, too. For years, he enjoyed Sunday-morning tennis with his racquet-swinging pals. When more than 100 of his friends gathered for a weekend party in Palm Springs, Calif., to help mark his 80th birthday, a reunion tournament was staged. Point, set, match to "Birthday Boy Al."

Sister Josephine later played for a state championship and was Ann Arbor's best player during her days at the University of Michigan. Both Connable daughters were destined to marry ardent tennis players whose court abilities were as adept as their courtship skills.

When the "t" in tennis stood for tobogganing, sledding became the favorite sport of the hilly neighborhood. Even though vehicular traffic was not even close to rush-hour standards in those days, the sledders took turns guarding the hill at the bottom of Prospect Street because on a good, slick day, a sled could easily make it to the park below by crossing the street.

Horse-drawn streetcars started carrying Kalamazooans in 1884. Nine years later, electric power was pushing the travelers over the rails. As a teen-ager, Connable can remember the five-cent fare that took his friends downtown where they'd get a transfer for another cent and head south on Burdick Street for one of those great ice cream cones at

As a teenager Al rode trolleys such as this to downtown adventures.

The Chocolate Shop that opened in 1917.

He and many of his pals attended the Woodward Avenue School, hence their collective name — The Woodward Avenue Gang. One of the hangouts was Dunwell's Drug Store, next door to the Jones Gift Shop and what is now the Burger King parking lot at the confluence of West Michigan Avenue and West Main Street. It was probably here that "a gang" conceived the caper, that if perpetuated in these times, would bring them to the attention of the local prosecutor.

Even though the statute of limitations has long since expired for this deed, the memory remains fuzzy — who did it? Al Connable's crew or Richard Light's legion.

"Well, Dick always claimed that I led the gang that did it, but I think he did. Regardless, like all kids did back then

Al and his goat powered cart cruised the Prospect Hill neighborhood.

49

and do now, we had gangs. Dick and our pal in this west-end gang, Lawrence Pierce, were both better teen-age engineers than me or anyone. `Piercey' did become an engineer. He was one of my first chums.

"There was also Bill Stone, Scott Field and Frank Supple. Frank was the grandson of the fellow who built Henderson Castle. I guess Frank was my best friend because we were next-door neighbors. We both learned Morse code and had a grand time sending messages to each other on our home-built telegraph sets.

**Prince assisted Al in his first business venture,
a lemonade stand, ca. 1909.**

"Bill Stone went to Yale and became an architect. He lived across West Main from Stowe Stadium. His house was torn down when the street corners were widened. Bill

Recuperating from his broken femur, Al posed with brother Harold on the family home's porch in 1918. Henderson Castle is in the background.

liked to have fun, but he sometimes had a tough time escaping his mother's apron strings to let off a little steam on our escapades. I guess we all did at times.

"My brother, H. P. (Horace) Connable, was very a much a part of the gang until he went away to school. There was 'Sev' (Severens) Balch, who had a bright mind and a bent for curiosity. He organized the National Waterlift Co. that provided important materials to the government during World War II. Sev became a great yachtsman, too.

"Another neighborhood pal was Stu Irvine, whose family owned the Saniwax Paper Co. We played lots of tennis together and later were part of a University of Michigan travel group to Europe as underclassmen. He became a military pilot and often flew me to Wolverine football games.

"Together, we were often the mischievous bunch. We thought it was much fun to mix a little gunpowder in an empty shell casing, strap it to the streetcar track and see what would happen. Most of the time — nothing. Except once. The explosion lifted the trolley car off the tracks. Nobody was hurt and nothing was damaged. But it was a darned nuisance for the city to place the trolley back on the track. In today's world, we would have been picked up and thrown in jail. And probably we would have deserved it.

"I really enjoyed school. We always walked to Woodward from home, picking up our buddies along the way and planning what we were going to do next, what great adventure was down the road. Those were happy days."

About this time, the family's tongue-in-cheek genealogy had this to say about Alfred Jr.:

"His early life overflowed with the boyhood that brings premature gray hairs to all parents, but they took on much hope when, at the age of 16, he could milk their one cow and practice his two hours per day on the piano, with loud pedal, 'so he could hear his mistakes,' and always at the hour that most annoyed and startled."

After spending his grade-school years at Woodward

Elementary and preferring to stay on the local scene, Connable was scheduled to be separated from his chums in 1917 and be sent south to the Culver Military Academy in Indiana. However, he got a one-year reprieve, and not the most pleasant one, either.

"I decided to try to play football my first year at Culver and broke the femur bone in my right leg the first day of practice. Other than tennis and swimming, that's been my only venture into competitive athletics, and it cost me a year in rehabilitation. From then on I stuck with extra-curricular things, like the school newspaper and helping with the base-ball team.

"The femur was badly twisted and the technology wasn't close to what's available these days. Dr. Homer Stryker wasn't even in Kalamazoo back then. He was serving in France as a 'doughboy.'"

After two weeks, doctors had to rebreak the leg because the broken bone had slipped in traction. Even though X-ray pioneer Dr. Augustus Crane of Kalamazoo had been advancing his see-through technology for nearly 20 years, all of its ramifications and potential had not yet entirely per-meated the medical profession, and wouldn't have helped anyway. Starting over again with a new break was fairly common practice during World War I, and was still the practice through the Vietnam War.

After three months in Borgess Hospital and an equally long period at home on crutches during which he was tutored for his first year of high school studies, Connable was begrudgingly ready for Culver and a three-year hitch that was not of his choosing. If the experience was designed to prep the 14 year old for the rigors of the University of Michigan, then the sour medicine he had to swallow was definitely worth it.

Culver's enrollment in Connable's final year of 1920-21 was about 740, with cadets hailing from nearly all of the 48 states. With World War I still fresh in the American psyche, military training was pretty serious stuff. In his scrapbook

IN RECOGNITION
OF THE HEROIC AND
MAGNANIMOUS SERVICE
RENDERED OUR CITIZENS
BY THE
CULVER CADETS
DURING THE FLOOD
MARCH 26.27.1913
THIS GATEWAY IS ERECTED
BY THE
CITY OF LOGANSPORT
MCMXIV

**Cadet Connable stood at attention before the
Culver gateway in 1918.**

is a 1921 Culver brochure depicting "A Modern Camelot" as cadets, protected a la the Knights of the Round Table, engaged in bayonet practice in a mini-trench warfare situation.

When Connable wasn't watching a swimming meet to cheer his cohorts on in the "fancy diving" and "plunge for distance" events, he was studying for the "gunner's examination," or researching such topics as the causes of Puritan emigration to America, the careers of Joan of Arc and Garibaldi, the history of relations between the United States and Cuba, and the components of a good short story for "Lt. Hubbard's final examination in extemporaneous speaking."

While the Army life was and never would be his bag, Connable was buoyed by Culver's curriculum that catered to "the complete boy." There were ample opportunities in the creative and fine arts as well as chances to follow his bent for the spirit of journalism as a member of the academy's student newspaper, the Vedette.

"I was a solid `B' student. I might have been even better if I hadn't enjoyed doing those other extra-curricular things — working on the school paper, singing with the glee club and managing a baseball team. My studies suffered a bit because I spent a lot of time doing other things.

"I don't think that is all bad. There is more to education than just books, lectures and classrooms. Those other activities teach discipline, teamwork, responsibility and other positive traits. That's the value of the arts. That's what they teach. I'm glad I did all of those things.

"Another great teacher for me was travel and I'm very grateful to my parents for taking us kids along. We owe so much to them for healthy outdoor summer experiences and being able to see so many places. For example, my father took me to several world expositions where I saw `the future.' In San Francisco, I also saw `the past.' Grandmother Peck was there in April of 1906 when the earthquake and fire killed 452 people and did $350 million in damage. I went to the St. Francis Hotel where she had

The Prospect Hill home, ca. 1950.

been staying. Talk about history coming alive."

While his brothers followed him on many of these trips, neither followed him to Culver. If there is an ironic ending to this chapter in Connable's life, it's this:

For years, the Indiana military academy had hosted what was then known as the National Junior and Boys Tennis Tournament. Japan's greetings at Pearl Harbor and Hitler's Third Reich ended the string. With Culver unable to serve as sponsor, Dr. Allen Stowe, a Kalamazoo College chemistry professor who doubled as tennis coach, brought the games in 1943 to within shouting distance of Connable's homestead. When the fathers of American tennis informed Stowe that Kalamazoo could retain the tourney if facilities were upgraded, a town-and-gown partnership was formed and the rest is history.

The Prospect Hill house remained in the Connable family into the second half of the 1950s. In its latter years, the occupants were sister Josephine and her husband, Dr. Paul Rood, who later served as chair of the Western Michigan University Department of Physics from 1952 to 1965. They lived there with Al's widowed father after Frances Connable died in 1929 of cancer.

"The house and property eventually were given to Kalamazoo College. They originally had some good ideas for it — the concept of a second campus with the house serving as a school of music or as a dormitory for women. That would have been ideal to our way of thinking. While the college's board of trustees was deliberating on a decision, vandals did significant damage to the house. It was razed. I have an idea the college came out well on the sale of the land and I hope it did."

College for Al Connable came out just fine, too.

UNCLE RALPH'S
CANADIAN CAPER AND
HANGIN' WITH HEMINGWAY

The 72-point headline of a Toronto newspaper said it all in red ink: "Germans Land in Canada"

Was this shades of John Belushi's character in "Animal House?" "Over! Over! Was it over after the Germans bombed Pearl Harbor?"

No, this was 1917! And it was no joke. The panic this authentic-looking newspaper set off in Toronto predated the chaos caused in the United States 21 years later when Orson Welles' radio adaptation of "The War of the Worlds" sounded so real that people committed suicide.

The mastermind behind this well-intentioned ruse was one of Toronto's leading citizens, Ralph Connable Jr., who was described by a reporter later recounting the incident as "a man noted for his startling if not revolutionary ideas." In Kalamazoo, he was known as "Uncle Ralph" to Alfred Barnes Connable Jr., destined to be quite an iconoclast in his own right.

The streamer's subheads continued the numbing tale: Halifax and St. John in Ruins, German Navy Bombarding Montreal, Enemy Headquarters Established in Hamilton, Prominent Toronto Citizens Killed When Buildings are Demolished by Bombs Dropped from German Aeroplanes, Half Million Huns Take Quebec, Entire British Fleet Is Sunk, 2,000,000 German Troops Land, Ottawa in Flames.

Supposedly, this was to be a harmless take-off on a routine edition of a daily newspaper, but it set off something of a firestorm, and here's how it all came about:

World War I was grinding along in its third year. Legions of foot soldiers sacrificed themselves at the altar of trench warfare as they exchanged sprints across No Man's Land. Back home in Canada, the citizens were dragging their feet in the support of "Victory Bonds" to maintain a strong war effort against the Huns.

Ralph Connable Jr., president of F. W. Woolworth's store operations in Canada, was serving as the chairman of the Toronto Victory Loan Publicity Committee. The campaign needed a little shock therapy, a shot in the arm, and it turned out to be a shot heard all over Canada.

Uncle Ralph Connable's 1917 newspaper spoof nearly
caused a panic in Canada.

His "revolutionary idea" this time was to publish an eight-page fake newspaper, dated Nov. 23, 1921, that would chronicle the story of the Germans invading Canada because Canadians had not purchased enough Victory bonds four years earlier.

Connable reasoned that the newspaper's bogus name, "The Victory Telegraph," the fact that it was dated four years into the future, and that the front page contained a boxed-off section in large type that read "None of These Things Has Happened Yet —" would deliver the message loud and clear that this was all fun-and-games with a message.

As ESPN sportscaster Chris Berman would say, "Ahhhh, no!"

"All hell broke loose at 9:30 on the morning of publication," according to one "authentic" news report. Women fainted at the "news."

The publication looked too much like the Toronto World, one of the community's legitimate dailies Even back then, many people only read the headlines. The caveat-emptor warning, as they say in the newspaper trade, "was below the fold." Few people saw the bottom half of the paper and the disclaimer before being launched into varying degrees of panic.

Written mostly by Connable in an obvious tongue-in-cheek style that required a much closer inspection to catch the real message, the copy contained some fairly grisly stuff — German conquerors announced that 40 citizens would be shot at sunrise each day, while the ears and noses of 20 children would be whacked off daily. "Tightwad" citizens who had penny-pinched back in 1917 and had not bought the war bonds, hanged themselves

Although he was the "Head Cheese" according to the publication's masthead, Connable was not riding solo in presenting this shocker, a Canadian version of Gomer Pyle's "Surprise, surprise!" His committee contained some of Toronto's major industrialists, who helped sell advertisements for the special edition.

Commented one Toronto journalist 36 years later: "I think it possible that if the astonished campaign committee had not bowed before the first storm of protest, this plan (for promoting the sale of bonds) would have succeeded. Certainly everybody would have read it. Mixed with the horrific items were telling advertisements putting strongly the case for the war bonds and as strong articles."

But the other members of the committee panicked as much as the citizenry. They overruled Connable and his vice chairman, J. Allen Ross. They insisted that distribution stop, that every copy be recalled, and that the legitimate newspapers, "in the interests of the pubic peace of mind, be induced to say nothing." Commercial radio was not even a force in those days. For example, John Fetzer didn't launch Kalamazoo's first commercial radio station until 1931.

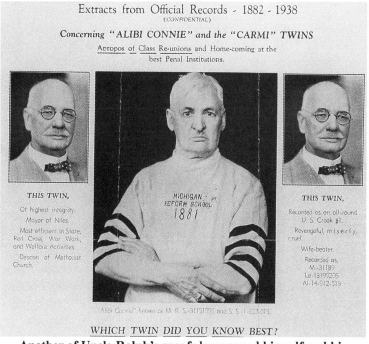

Another of Uncle Ralph's spoofs lampooned himself and his
Albion College friend, Carmi Smith.

Consequently, as the journalist reported in his column on April, 8, 1953, in The Globe and Mail: "And so it happens that today there are not many people even in Toronto who know about this `First and Last Edition of The Victory Telegraph, Volume 1, No. 1'. . .The sale (for five cents each) was stopped at noon after 14,000 papers had been sold and the balance were ordered burned in the furnace of the World newspaper."

Did it work? Well, yes and no. Connable and his cohort took the brunt of the criticism. Bond sales did spurt, but was that caused by the publication? Or by Canadian patriotism, a 5.5-percent interest rate, or by a tax-exempt status? Whatever the reason, the Victory Bonds were oversubscribed. And the Germans never did invade Canada, just as, despite "Mr. Bluto's" version of history, they never dropped a few salvos on Pearl Harbor.

"Ralph had a crazy sense of humor," says his Kalamazoo nephew, "and like many people like that, he sometimes went a little astray. He wasn't afraid to go a long way to get across a joke. In the family genealogy that he wrote, you sometimes couldn't tell where the facts ended and his imagination began."

Uncle Ralph was born in the last year of the Civil War near the stockyards in Chicago. After a family move to Jackson, Mich., the clan ended up in Petoskey where it engaged in many enterprises, including mercantilism and commercial fishing.

That's where he returned after giving Albion College a try for a couple of years. When the smell of dead fish became too much for him, Ralph Jr. sampled the laundry business and then moved his family to Traverse City where he managed a bookstore.

When the ways of the big city beckoned, Uncle Ralph returned to Chicago where he went to work for a five-and-dime store, moving up to being the main buyer for the 22-outlet chain. After its 1911 consolidation with the F. W. Woolworth Co., Uncle Ralph was sent to Canada in 1915 to blaze the trail and became chief of its operations north of the border.

Two years after the Canadian newspaper caper, Uncle Ralph was introduced to a young writer named Ernest Hemingway and then opened a few doors that helped lead the author to fame and fortune.

Ernest Hemingway was given a journalistic boost by Uncle Ralph Connable.

Hemingway was born in 1899 in Oak Park, Ill. After World War I broke out, he sought to enlist in the U.S. Army but was rejected because of an eye injury suffered as a child. Undaunted, Hemingway signed on as an ambulance operator for the Red Cross. While he couldn't see well enough to shoot, his vision was good enough to drive. Figure that out.

Severely wounded in Italy, Hemingway came home from the war with a slight limp that would stay with him for years. He found a source of income in 1919 as a newspaper reporter for the Kansas City Star. As a child growing up near Chicago, Hemingway spent many a summer in Michigan's north woods near Petoskey where Uncle Ralph had notched many a fine memory himself.

Who says serendipity doesn't work? According to his biographers, Hemingway gave only three public speeches in his lifetime and one of them was in the summer of 1919 before the Petoskey Art Club. Uncle Ralph and his wife were vacationing nearby on Walloon Lake. For some reason, Mrs. Connable decided to take in the lecture by a young Kansas City reporter.

No more than 20 years old, Hemingway was certainly not a polished public speaker, much less an accomplished writer. But he came across to Mrs. Connable as a strikingly handsome, intense and intelligent fellow. They struck up a conversation and Hemingway indicated he was looking for another newspaper job. She introduced him to Uncle Ralph and the two developed a fast friendship.

The Connables were planning to head for Florida for the winter, but Uncle Ralph told Hemingway that, as soon as he returned to his base in Canada, he would contact some friends at the Toronto Star. In the meantime, the Connables invited Hemingway to winter at their palatial home in Toronto where he could be a companion for a son who had been lame since birth.

As soon as the train fare arrived in the mail, Hemingway was off for Toronto. After all, money was tight for the budding journalist and prospects looked brighter for him in Canada. The fact that the Connables lived in something of a mansion convinced the young man that he might have made the right decision.

When the family returned from Florida, the interview was arranged. The tallish Hemingway, attired in a leather coat and carrying a walking stick, impressed the editors who hired him as a "space" correspondent. No, not "Star Trek" stuff. He was to be paid so much a word for everything that he wrote and The Star published. That first year, Hemingway earned only $150, but he was happy because he was writing and being paid for his work.

Mrs. Connable also became a beacon of hope and support for the fledgling writer, who collected a bounty of rejection slips from book publishers. She constantly restored his confidence. He also struck up a friendship with the couple's daughter. The effects of World War I were still part of his essence. He slept with the lights on in his room.

The pieces he wrote for The Toronto Star were features as opposed to news stories. They often came couched in bitter and ironic tones, such as the article he wrote about a Toronto mayor who, despite not serving in the war, surfaced as the chief spokesman for the nation's veterans. After about 100 of his articles had been published, The Star sent him to Paris as a foreign correspondent. That's where he met Gertrude Stein and Ezra Pound, who became major influences in his writings.

By 1923, he returned to Toronto and again moved in with the Connables. He had been published in book form once in France, but he was a changed fellow for another reason. Toronto was no Paris in his eyes. With the prospects of one of his short stories being sold and published, he contacted Stein, shucked journalism and returned to the French capital. In 1926, Hemingway produced "The Sun Also Rises" and followed that up with "A Farewell to Arms" in 1929.

He was on his way to the Nobel Prize for Literature (in

1954) and all because Mrs. Ralph Connable decided to take in a lecture in her vacation hometown in northern Michigan, probably because her husband had gone to the links for the day.

Uncle Ralph, who was a scratch golfer and a member of the Canadian senior team, played on some of the greatest and most famous courses in the British Isles. Much credit goes his way for mainstreaming the game of golf in his adopted homeland.

"Uncle Ralph was a fortunate man and had the financial assets to be able to play golf wherever and whenever he wanted," Connable recalls. "It bothered him that many immigrants, particularly those who came to Canada from Scotland, the birthplace of golf, couldn't afford to join a country club and play the game they loved."

He organized a consortium of Toronto business leaders, who agreed to donate some of their property in order to develop a public golf course.

That made him something of a beloved figure among Canada's "tee-totalers." His bogus publication about an invading army of Germans was quickly forgotten by an ever-growing army of bogey golfers.

"AL" COLLEGE

Was the 17-year-old Kalamazooan ready for the University of Michigan?

Well, as with fraternities, he was one of those legacy situations. Since his father was a member of the Class of 1894, he had an "in."

Academically, it looked as if he could hold his own, as illustrated by an essay test Cadet Connable took while at Culver. His chosen topic was: "Milton — the Man and His Writings." To compose with any veracity, he had to know some British history — the mid-17th century civil brutality between Parliamentarians and Royalists, Milton's siding against the throne, and the poet's thin-ice status with the restoration of Charles II as king of England in 1660.

". . .With the Restoration, Milton was allowed to live in a modest home on condition that he would stop his political writings. So the poet who for twenty years had been championing the rights of the people was silenced. He retired to the small house and there lived in his blindness for the rest of his life, for he had become blind before the Restoration, getting his only joys from memorys (Oops).

". . .Milton's great qualities are sublimity and harmony. He has a wonderful selection of words and he seems to be able to not only pick the write (another Oops) ones but to write the ones that are also the most harmonious. That is why his poems are so easy to read."

Those two academic faux pas cost him 10 points on the way to a score of 83 on the paper.

Socially, there was no doubt that higher education was in his future. Sisters Virginia and Josephine had both prepped for college by heading east, attending the Bennett School in Milbrook, N. Y.

"Those were the World War I years and some people's knowledge about geography was just as bad then as it is today. Anybody who lived east of the Hudson River knew there wasn't anything out in the Midwest except Indians.

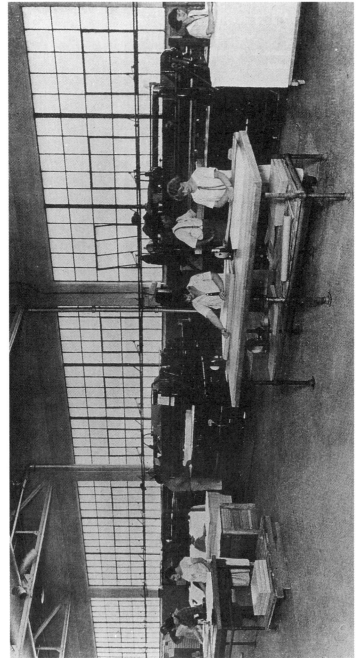

The finishing room at the KVP mill in the 1920s employed guillotine-like trimmers that Al dreaded to sharpen.

My sisters were once asked by some socialite where they were from. When they reported they were from Kalamazoo, the questioner replied, `Oh, that's in Africa, isn't it.'"

Not quite. After returning to their "Timbuktu," "Ginny" chose marriage to Lorence Burdick while Josephine tried the University of Wisconsin for a year before transferring to her father's alma mater where she was inducted into Phi Beta Kappa, the national honorary society, before graduating.

After his graduation from the Culver Military Academy in 1921, Al worked that summer for Jacob Kindleberger at the Kalamazoo Vegetable Parchment Co., an enterprise that the Pecks and his father had helped capitalize. Working for Uncle Jake catapulted him to college with great zest and in the proper frame of mind to tackle the rigors of academia.

"I worked from 7 a.m. to 5 p.m. with Jake's son, Joe, in the machine shop. It was great experience and good hard work. One of our jobs was sharpening the heavy trimmer blades that cut through thick piles of paper. Taking those long blades off the guard boards and carefully lifting them on to the sharpening machine was a nervous experience. I remember I was scared to death of them because they were monstrous enough to chop off a foot if we dropped them. I certainly had enough bandages on my hands that summer. I knew that I didn't want to do that kind of work for the rest of my life."

He recalls Kindleberger stopping by frequently to check on the duo. The paper baron would say something like: "Hey, you guys! There you go cutting off your fingers again. If you do that one more time, I'm going to fire you."

That summer was another one of those valuable outside-the-classroom learning opportunities for Connable from a Horatio Alger-like mentor who carried the image of being both a tough taskmaster as well as a softie.

Born in Alsace-Lorraine in 1875, Kindleberger immigrated with his family to the United States as a 10 year old, settling in West Carrollton, Ohio. He joined his father, working at a local paper mill to help feed five siblings. He earned a quarter a day sorting rags for 10 hours. On the way home, he hunted for chunks of coal along the railroad tracks to keep his family from freezing.

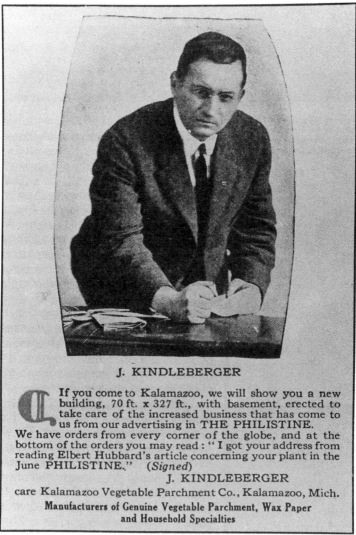

J. KINDLEBERGER

If you come to Kalamazoo, we will show you a new building, 70 ft. x 327 ft., with basement, erected to take care of the increased business that has come to us from our advertising in THE PHILISTINE. We have orders from every corner of the globe, and at the bottom of the orders you may read : " I got your address from reading Elbert Hubbard's article concerning your plant in the June PHILISTINE." (*Signed*)
J. KINDLEBERGER
care Kalamazoo Vegetable Parchment Co., Kalamazoo, Mich.
Manufacturers of Genuine Vegetable Parchment, Wax Paper and Household Specialties

"Uncle" Jake Kindleberger, master salesman.

In spite of poor vision that had him working by touch, his hard-work ethic earned a promotion to paper-machine hand and a raise in pay when he turned 13. A hard life was forging a hardened teen until the night he and a gang of fellow mill hoodlums decided to do some heckling at a local Methodist revival meeting. It was like the lightning-quick conversion of an agnostic Saul of Tarsus to the apostolic St. Paul on the road to Damascus.

Kindleberger's first formal education came when church members taught him how to read the Bible. Better yet, he literally saw the light for the first time when he was given a pair of glasses at the age of 19. He recalled the event this way: "I sobbed when I first saw it all. I hadn't dreamed there was so much beauty. For days I just wandered about, drinking in the loveliness of the earth."

The staunch convert focused on becoming a man of God, enrolling at nearby Ohio Wesleyan University. To pay his way to the priesthood, he stumbled upon an innate knack — salesmanship. From door to door, he hawked all kinds of gadgets. When a physician told him the strain of book-learning could render him blind, Kindleberger hit the road full time as a salesman, earning as much as $100 a week while his old chums at the paper mill brought home $10 on a good week.

But paper pulp was in his blood and Kindleberger returned to his West Carrollton roots as a salesman. He thought the industry had great potential as the century turned and he was right, gaining the reputation as one of the best marketers in North America.

In 1909, Kindleberger and a brother-in-law reached a career critical mass. They wanted to launch their own paper-making venture. Their target was a town called Kalamazoo, then regarded as one of the nation's leading production centers of paper. Kindleberger's plan was to specialize in vegetable parchment, a water-resistant product made by applying sulfuric acid to formula. The Peck brothers and Alfred Connable Sr. were among the group of investors who liked what Kindleberger had to say and how he said it.

Kindleberger, his brother-in-law and a charter work-force of 15 spent the winter of 1909-10 converting a former sugar beet factory along the Kalamazoo River north of the city and installing equipment. Production at the Kalamazoo Vegetable Parchment Co. began in April of 1910. A machine for waxing paper arrived the following year. Kitchen aids, bread wrappers and waxed food containers became the product line. The coating material was furnished by the Saniwax Co., which was owned by the family of Al's boyhood friend, Stu Irvine.

Hard work, long hours, and a dependable product for the money pointed Kindleberger's enterprise in the right direction, but a dose of national publicity from a fellow "super salesman" he had befriended prior to coming to Kalamazoo didn't hurt. Elbert Hubbard had become something of a molder of opinion and a popular philosopher who reached the American middle class through his publications.

This is what he wrote after a 1914 visit to what Uncle Jake had wrought along the Kalamazoo River:

"I found the home of the Kalamazoo Vegetable Parchment Company delightfully situated on the river road, two miles north of Kalamazoo. It is an unusual institution saturated with the spirit of mutual helpfulness and good will.

"The executives are alert, able and sanguine; the employees happy and contented and efficient. The whole place breathes the spirit of the hive — busyness, business and cooperation, activity and intelligence.

"A cleanliness and order prevail that mirrors the mind of the institution. For the main idea upon which the Kalamazoo Vegetable Parchment Company was formed was that of hygiene, and time and labor saving. What Lincoln was to the slave, the Kalamazoo Vegetable Parchment Company is to the housekeeper."

In contemporary terms, that would be like receiving the

The KVP Company sprawled along the Kalamazoo River in the late 1930s.

endorsement of Consumer Reports, The Wall Street Journal and Ralph Nader, all wrapped up in the Good Housekeeping Seal of Approval. Business boomed for the company, which expanded into paper production and package printing. More and more employees built houses. The company town of Parchment was born.

Hubbard and Kindleberger were truly strange bedfellows. While both were self-made men, crack marketers, people with vision, and apostles of the work ethic, they were the antithesis of each other in so many other aspects. Uncle Jake was a stern Sunday-School preacher of the Methodist ilk. He practiced a pushy style of piety that never lost the opportunity to harvest someone in the darkness.

The young Culver graduate remembers the sayings on the walls of Uncle Jake's office: "Push. If you can't push, pull. If you can't pull, then please get out of the way." And: "To avoid criticism, do nothing, say nothing, be nothing."

"Uncle Jake kept a close eye on everything and everybody, but he set a terrific example of hard work. His was a unique, pioneer operation and he did an outstanding job building it up. As I recall, to produce a waterproof paper required a high cotton content from old rags and a chemical treatment. Yet he was also devoted to what he called the golden rule of business — being fair to his employees."

Uncle Jake might have brought that commitment to the table himself, or he might have learned the lesson from Kalamazoo's First Citizen of Business, Dr. William E. Upjohn. Spurred by his only son, Harold, "Doctor Will" fostered advanced ideas about human relations, which by 1902 translated into employees working only eight-hour days and having half of Saturday off long before that kind of "radical thinking" infected other industries.

As Upjohn's style of civic philanthropy illustrated, the quality and creative use of leisure time among people meant better and more-rounded employees, more productivity among the job force, and a healthy cultural climate. Like his paper-making colleague, "Doctor Will" never tolerated mediocrity, believing that settling for "the good" was often the enemy of getting "the best."

With Harold's inducements, the Upjohn company installed one of the nation's first company-paid, life-insurance benefits that covered both office staff and factory workers. Employees thus received more than a week's pay for a week's work. There were paid vacations and Christmas bonuses. Upjohn's reasoning was simple: "If I'm going to look after my community, why shouldn't I look after my employees."

The corollary went like this — better employees meant a better community. If employees didn't have to be like slave labor for a pittance of a wage, they could have more time to devote to their families and to the volunteerism that feeds a community's vitality.

Said Dr. Upjohn: ". . .There must be better wages even for shorter hours of labor. We can never have real and permanent prosperity in this country until there is more work available and more people working. Our prosperity depends on the prosperity of the working classes. They are the ones who spend their money and that means more business for everyone."

Uncle Jake went Kalamazoo's pharmaceutical king one step better. He created his own community. With his paper production expanding to new plants along the river and a workforce growing to nearly 1,500, Parchment became its own village in 1930 and a "model city" nine years later. The company provided water service, street maintenance and fire protection. The price for that was a zealot's religious fervor and paternalistic approach about residents matching his high moral, ethical and neat-and-tidy standards.

"He was a very religious man. Because the church was very important to him, he wanted it to be that way for all the people in his town. He provided a very fine community house for people to use and during the Great Depression, he donated 38 acres of land for a park, using his workers to

Uncle Jake, second from left, posed before the Christmas Tree
in the Community House he built for employees in Parchment,
ca. 1925.

develop it in those lean years. In that vein, he was very
much like W. E. Upjohn.

"For their financial support, the Pecks and my father
served on the company's board of directors. That's how I
was able to get that summer job while waiting for my first
semester in Ann Arbor. While they provided some wise
counsel, it was Uncle Jake who really was the driving force.
He hired some outstanding people, like Alfred 'Doc'
Southon as vice president, Frank Mossteller from
Cincinnati as sales manager, and Ben Morris as manager of
the fine-paper department."

That hands-on proximity to captains of capitalism,

Al, 5th from left, posed with other members of the U of M Student Council he presided over in 1925.

along with a summer full of "fingers-please-stay-on" encounters with giant cutting blades prepared him well for the University of Michigan, launching a love affair for Alfred Connable Jr. that is as torrid today as it was back in the fall of 1921. He did more than major in history on his way to a bachelor of arts degree in 1925.

"I loved campus activities. I got involved in student government and became president of the student council my senior year. Since I had always loved to write from my days on The Vedette at Culver, I worked for the student newspaper, moving up to the role of night editor at the Michigan Daily. At one time, I harbored thoughts of being a journalist."

Following his sophomore year in 1923 came more educational travel with another dose of international flavor under the auspices of the university's bureau of travel. His parents and sister Josephine were part of that contingent led by William Frayer, a professor of history. With scars from World War I still visible, the mobile classroom explored the art, architecture and history of cathedrals and their towns in England, Scotland, France, Switzerland and Italy. They lived on trains, boats and buses for two months.

Despite his Uncle Ralph's ribbing about having a tin ear as a kid, Connable's piano and vocal lessons bore fruitful results on the Ann Arbor campus when he auditioned for the University of Michigan Glee Club in his freshman year and made the team as a tenor in the back row. The real star of the show was a 19-year-old fellow from Owosso — Thomas Edmund Dewey.

Dewey had enrolled at Michigan to study music. Instead, he ended up in law, continuing his studies at Columbia University. By 1933, Dewey had become a U.S. district attorney for the southern district of New York and served as a special assistant to the U.S. attorney general.

In 1935, the former Michigan music man was appointed special prosecutor for a grand jury investigation of vice and racketeering in New York City. As he sought to make mobsters sing about the likes of Lucky Luciano, Bugsy Siegel and Meyer Lansky, Dewey gained national prominence as a crusader against the rackets. Three times (1941, 1945 and 1949), he was elected governor of New York.

Thomas Dewey, Al's U of M classmate, unsuccessfully campaigned for president in 1944 and 1948.

Political pundits considered Dewey to be the Republican Party's sacrificial lamb for blocking Franklin Roosevelt's fourth term in the 1944 presidential election, but Dewey did surprisingly well, collecting 22 million votes to FDR's 25 million even though the electoral results were 432 to 99.

With President Harry Truman swimming in a sea of controversy and discontent, the Republicans thought that

Dewey was their man in 1948 to regain the White House after 16 years. So did the so-called experts. Dewey went to bed, as did many Americans that election night, thinking he had been the 28th man elected president of the United States. That was the same thinking of The Chicago Tribune, which put its first edition to bed with the banner headline — "Dewey Defeats Truman."

Truman won the popular vote 24 to nearly 22 million, and the electoral tally 303 to 189, with third and fourth-party candidates syphoning off 2.2 million votes and 39 in the Electoral College. One of those "spoiler" candidates was U.S. Sen. J. Strom Thurmond of South Carolina, who plans on becoming the first member of Congress to be serving on his 100th birthday.

In 1952, Dewey swung his political support to Dwight Eisenhower and retired from active Republican affairs three years later. He died in 1971. While this Michigan man would never serve in the White House, Connable would have the distinction of personally knowing an American president with state ties years later.

Connable was such a BMOC (Big Man on Campus) that when Michigan's president, Marion LeRoy Burton, died of pneumonia in February of 1925, the Kalamazooan, as the president of the student council, was one of the pallbearers. He's personally known every U of M president since then.

High cheek bones notwithstanding, his closest tie to a Native American heritage was induction into the university's prestigious senior honorary society, Michigamua. "It used to be a big deal back in those days and a lot of fun. About 20 were inducted each year. It was a real initiation. You were stripped, painted and given Indian names. Mine is Hollow Thunder. Bob Brown, a member of the Class of 1926, was Big Bellows. Other inductees who I've known are Jerry Ford, Julie Franks, Bob and Ross Hume, Paul Goebel, Bob Matthews, and Bob Brown's son. I think they've done away with all that now. Too bad."

Connable wrapped up his student days at Ann Arbor

80

The tribe of Michigamua in 1924, included Al, fourth from right in front.

with a third voyage to Europe that involved a little entrepreneurism.

"In the summer of 1925 after my graduation, the University Travel Bureau in Newton, Mass., offered a special three-month package tour. You could go steerage to Europe, travel third class on trains, stay in fourth-class hotels, and do a lot of walking. I signed up to be an agent for the tour. For each $500 tour I sold, I received a $25 commission. I convinced 17 friends — Stu Irvine and the Boyd brothers — and alumni to sign up so my trip only cost me $75. We went to Italy, Switzerland, The Netherlands, Belgium and England."

At the Leaning Tower of Pisa, the Michigan travelers got a glimpse of the future. Benito Mussolini, former editor of a Socialist Party newspaper who had done an about-face in political allegiances, expanded his Fascist ranks to more than four million members. His march on Rome three years earlier had put him on the path to dictatorship. Mussolini's youthful followers became carbon copies of Hitler's "Blackshirts" in Nazi Germany. They were an accident looking for a place to happen. But this time, it didn't happen.

"We were near the tower when some young Mussolini `Blackshirts' approached. We weren't wearing the maize and blue, but maybe we should have been. They started singing their national anthem. Instead of `Hail to the Victors Valiant,' we responded with `The Star-Spangled Banner.' Instead of big trouble, there was big laughter and back-slapping. Of course, that was only 1925.

"After that, we went by train as far as Naples. One side excursion took us along unbelievably dusty roads around the bay to Sorrento where we saw the hotel where Enrico Caruso often sang from the balcony."

Back up the boot-shaped country, the travelers headed north out of Milan bound for Italy's lake district. The destination was the Great St. Bernard Pass east of 15,781-foot Mt. Blanc in the Alps. Shades of Pikes Peak!

"We started the climb in light clothing and it was very cold by the time we reached the top where the famous pass into Switzerland is located. We were headed for the 10th century monastery of St. Bernard because it is famous for taking in travelers. That's where the St. Bernard dog breed evolved with its powerful sense of smell and direction. The Augustine monks used them to find people stranded in the snow.

"The monastery's spirit of hospitality hadn't suffered in its thousand years. We were given hot soup, bread and some red wine. Naturally, before departing the next morning down the steeper slope into Switzerland, we left a tidy contribution so that those who followed could receive equal treatment. Many years later, my stepson, Dan, sent us a postcard from the monastery. Things still haven't changed."

Carefree college days were coming to an end. So was Al's bachelor status. At Ann Arbor, he had met Dorothy Malcomson, whose father, Alexander, had a similar talent for wise investments in enterprises as did the senior Connable. Malcomson was one of the principal backers of Henry Ford when he launched his car company in 1903.

"Dorothy and I were engaged at the time my group went to Europe. We were all passengers on the ship Mauritania. But the only trouble was that she was traveling first class with her mother and sister while our group was down in steerage. Working our way up from the bottom of the ship to first class to see how the other half lived was quite the challenge."

Just the latest of many challenges for A. B. Connable Jr.

OFF TO RIO, BUENOS, QUITO AND A RESCUE AT SEA

Sandwiched between those three treks to Europe was a university-sanctioned trip to South America that supposedly was the first of its kind and allowed Al Jr. to once again sample the excitement of journalism.

He was able to report on a rescue at sea, student unrest in unstable "banana republics," and encounters with people who were about to embark on Indiana Jones-like adventures.

As a University of Michigan junior, Connable was selected to be among the 11-student delegation that represented the university on a three-month tour of South America in the summer of 1924 to promote international relations. The delegation included the president of the stu-

Al (right) and a traveling comrade Norman Vissering posed along the Panama Canal in 1925.

dent council, the editor of the Michigan Daily, the presidents of two top fraternities, and other campus and athletic leaders.

There is no such thing as a free lunch, and this was no free trip, either. They had to chronicle the industrial, commercial, political and educational conditions in the visited countries as the basis of reports they would deliver upon return to Ann Arbor. Because letters from the president of the university to the U.S. embassies and to the ministers of education in each country preceded the entourage, the red carpet was frequently rolled out at each of the multi-nation stops.

"We did a little studying along the way," he says, "learning Spanish and learning about the cultures in different countries. It was a great educational experience. We went

Al's travel articles were posted to the Kalamazoo Gazette in 1925 when the headquarters looked like this.

through the Panama Canal in a banana boat, trekked into Inca country, visited famous ruins, and traveled over the Andes by narrow-gauge railroad.

"It was billed as the first-ever goodwill trip of North American students to South America and I've got the newspaper clippings to prove it. I sent five articles back to Kalamazoo Gazette editor Jack Walsh and he paid $5 for each one. He probably overpaid me. Each one I typed out took about two weeks to reach Kalamazoo. We got a heck of a lot of press and so did the University of Michigan.

"Our guides were two young Spanish instructors at the university. They hailed from Bogota, Colombia, but had been outside of their own country very little so it was a learning experience for them, too. Our ship carried mostly freight and fewer than 100 passengers. Sailing down the west coast of South America, our first stop was Ecuador and then Lima, Peru, where we were greeted in the harbor by a man wearing tux and tails. He was the minister of education. Because he took his role very seriously, so did we. We were escorted to the presidential palace where all those we met seemed genuinely glad to see a group of American students."

Under the headline of "South American Students Play Real Role in Politics," Connable filed this dispatch — a combination report and commentary — from Lima as students protested the Peruvian president's action to have the non-reelection clause in the constitution annulled so he could serve another term:

". . .These students (at San Marcos University) who, unlike their North American contemporaries, play a real role in the political life of the country, have stubbornly fought what they term the `tyrannical rule of a dictator.' They issued formal protests to the Peruvian congress, circulated manifestos and have held indignation meetings in the streets where the guards have broken up their radical demonstrations.

"The afternoon when our party was at San Marcos (the oldest educational institution in the western hemisphere), they were gathering for another meeting to protest the action of the government in throwing the president of the Student Federation into jail. They asked us to attend but we declined, and did not regret that we had done so when a cavalry troop galloped up in the street and stationed itself outside of the gate.

"From there we went to the government buildings and met President Leguia — from one hostile camp to the other — about whom all the fuss is being made. The impression he made was excellent. He speaks perfect English and fits exactly the term current in North America — a `live wire.' The details of his re-election may be a little shady but a better man for the position could hardly be found in South America.

"And then with 75 percent of the population native Indians, most of them still illiterate and unfit for civic duties, an election such as is held in the United States is impossible. July 7 was the first time that riots didn't occur around the ballot boxes.

"The student attitude may be explained by first the lack of college activities such as athletics, publications, dramatics, etc., in which the student may devote his energy, and secondly the temperament of the Latin type, which is a suspicious one by nature and, when idle, a dangerous one. Youthful skepticism runs to politics and soap-box orators abound."

Connable and two other Wolverines expressed an interest in visiting Inca country. One was Norman Vissering, who would serve in Italy during World War II as a general and earn a series of decorations. The arrangements were made and the trio left the main party for two weeks to roam the high ground of Peru and Bolivia. They would rendezvous at Valparaiso in central Chile.

"The excursion into the land of the Incas was a highlight. From Lima, it was a two-day train ride to an elevation of more than 12,000 feet to the Andes Mountain plateau. That would be about an hour's plane ride now."

Passing before their eyes was Peru's hacienda system, a

Al's party boarded this train in Lima, Peru, for a two day ride to the land of the Incas.

serfdom in which people are sold with the land, not much unlike what had disappeared from Western Europe back in the 13th century.

"Cuzco, capital of the ancient Incan empire, was so primitive there was only one bathtub in the entire city, even though it is the oldest continuously inhabited community in the western hemisphere. But the museum there was full of the archeological findings that were being uncovered at the famous lost ruins at Machupicchu, considered one of the wonders of the world today, since it was first discovered in 1911. We felt privileged to see them."

Cuzco was the center of the highly organized Incan dynasty before it was subjugated by the Spaniards in 1533. The secret of how the Incas built their stoneworks, each piece so perfectly fitted that mortar was not needed, remains yet undiscovered in the ruins of Machupicchu.

Some of the blocks at Machupicchu, located 2,000 feet above the V-shaped canyon of the Urubamba River, weigh

In Bolivia Al and his friends posed alongside a motorized railroad inspection car made by his hometown's Kalamazoo Manufacturing Company.

200 tons. How did they move them around, other then as explained by the classic answer of "very carefully?" Scholars believe that Machupicchu was one of a chain of fortified cities that the Incas built after they began their conquest of the Andean people during the 10th century and as a line of defense against equally hostile Amazon tribes.

What the Incas built over the millennia has survived the erosion of time and shattering earthquakes. The Spanish-constructed masonry has crumbled. No classroom lecture could make the same impact as seeing this splendor in person in the shadow of what at the time registered as unparalleled poverty among the majority of the people who then occupied that region.

Connable and his companions sailed to La Paz, the capital of Bolivia, via an overnight steamboat ride across Lake Titicaca, which at an elevation of more than 10,000 feet is the highest steam-navigable body of water in the world.

"We took in a bullfight, but there wasn't too much action, at least for the natives. The crowd finally began to boo and throw straw hats at the matador. The bull didn't seem to mind, though."

Another train ride to the Peruvian seaport town of Mollendo connected them to a southbound cruise to Chile. About this time, a border dispute between Peru, Bolivia and Chile that had been making headlines took on realistic proportions for the Michigan students as they got up close and personal with international and diplomatic relations.

The global issue involved the capability of the United States to mediate South American disputes in the light of the fact that the U.S. Senate had embarrassed President Woodrow Wilson by refusing to join the League of Nations. The "little picture" issue, however, predated World War I, "the war to end all wars" that the league was supposed to prevent in future years. The origin of the three-way border dispute can be traced to the 1820s with the birth of the Republic of Bolivia.

The most recent fate of the provinces of Tachna and

Arica, rich in resources ranging from valued ores and minerals to alpaca wool to chinchilla skins and to the coca plant that produced a medicinal substance known as cocaine, had been argued for 43 years since "The Nitrate War of 1883." Called "the Alsace-Lorraine of South America" for its ability to prompt war-like actions between nations, the provinces were about the size of Massachusetts.

Peru declared war on Chile over the national rights to the provinces' nitrate fields and to their harbors. After the short-lived war, a treaty placed Chile in military possession of Tachna and Arica under the provision that a plebiscite would make the final decision within 10 years.

Four decades later, the people had still not been asked to render an opinion on what country they wanted to pay allegiance. The involved countries waffled, pointed fingers at each other, and refused to take responsibility for staging the referendum. Commented one diplomat who had a way with words: "The Tachna-Arica controversy reminds me of a fight between two bald-headed men for the possession of a comb."

Not escaping the attention of American capitalists was the advice from World War I hero Gen. John "Black Jack" Pershing that British and German companies, financiers and investors were hauling in some tidy profits from South American operations. President Warren Harding suggested that the negotiations be brought to Washington for arbitration by Secretary of State Charles Evans Hughes.

As Connable was traveling through South America, reports circulated that Hughes was leaning in the direction of siding with Chile's case, even though the United States' relations were much friendlier and less abrasive with Peru than with the country that looks like a stringbean on a world map. Carrying the reputation of being a renowned jurist, Hughes seemed to be favoring an arbitration decision based on justice instead of politics.

So what happened? Long after Connable had returned to Kalamazoo, Tachna was ceded to Peru, Arica to Chile, and Bolivia was shut out, and, along with Paraguay, remains the only South American country without direct access to an ocean.

"Some of the characters we encountered were just as interesting as the sights. One fellow, dressed in a white robe decorated by a large sunburst and wearing sandals, claimed he could restore the Inca civilization and its sun worship. I thought he was German, but he liked to hang around us and was a delightful nut."

Under the erroneous byline of "Fred Connable Jr." in the Gazette, he reported this encounter datelined Arica, Chile:

"Way up in the mountains of Peru in the heart of what some anthropologists say is the oldest civilization in the world and near the unexplored lands of reported head-hunting Indians, we met a man who is a vegetarian.

"Theosophist and founder of what he calls Incaism, he says he has reformed his soul there, far away from the present order. And there he will help other people do the same thing, all modeling their lives after the old Inca kings and living together in a perfect, communistic state. . .

"His name is Adolph Diehl and, although he is looked upon by the natives as 'poco loco' in their language, they all respect him for his devotion and knowledge of the numerous wonders all around them left by a civilization vastly superior to theirs and concerning which many of them are totally ignorant.

"As a beginning he has purchased 300 acres from the Peruvian government for about $50. To this land he will proceed next summer dressed in a tunic, wearing sandals and carrying a staff as the apostles of old. A long, flowing beard will complete the effect, while on his chest he will bear a sun. He expects to be followed by disciples from throughout the Western Hemisphere, who will herald him as the modern prophet and follow him to this new Garden of Eden.

". . .Houses will be built and all will live together in perfect harmony. It is the same old idea that man has studied for ages only worked out on a new basis for Diehl in going to reincarnate the spirit of the Incas in his model village. As with those historic people, there will be no private owner-ship. Every man will be given his share of the work to do. Every man will have to learn every profession.

Al visited the eccentric Adolph Diehl in Peru.

"A carpenter will teach a poet to drive nails and the poet will show the carpenter how to write verse. The entire community will be one great university of learning. There will be no poor or no rich, for the community will take care of all.

"Such a system was similar under the old Inca rulers. They held their people under absolute subjection but they gave them the benefits of good government and healthy living. It was their very despotism that made a success of the agrarian commission. With the heavy stick that they wielded, they saw that every man did his share of the work and that those physically unfit were supported by the rest.

"It was a system of leveling. The average standard of living was undoubtedly high, while ambition and initiative were discouraged because after a man had done his share of the community's work, he was through and the returns for additional labor were taken away from him.

". . .The success of Diehl's scheme is therefore very problematic from this standpoint alone. If human selfishness and laziness could be done away with, such a community then could be used. But then, with these two factors removed, such a change in living orders would not even be necessary."

Connable's last paragraph was something of a tongue-in-cheek solicitation because Diehl told him he needed $50,000 in seed money to launch his utopia. He even listed the prophet's Peruvian address. Ironically, while Upjohn and Kindleberger back in Kalamazoo would never sympathize with Diehl's socialistic methods, in their own way all three were searching for the same outcome.

Landing in Santiago and reuniting with the other Michiganders, the Connable party met Chile's minister of education, exchanged pleasantries with the U.S. ambassador, and sampled Chilean culture for several days. He filed a column with the Gazette based on his impressions of taking in a silent movie in a small town.

"The air between the mud walls is damp to a North

94

American and you wonder if you are really entering a cinema house or buying tickets to see the Mammoth Cave or some other subterranean wonder of the world. . .A player piano, with many sighs, starts in to butcher Paderewski. It hesitates but struggles on."

Wondering why the action on the screen was coming at a less than slow-motion pace, he wrote that "glancing at the program, the truth dawns. The film is scheduled to last for two full hours and with only five reels, the manager is doing his best to give the audience their money's worth (Connable paid 42 cents for the best seat in the house; five cents bought a place in "the peanut gallery.") Snap! The film has broken. Well, one is in need of fresh air now and then."

Next came a day-long ride over the Andes via a narrow-gauge railway during what he called a "spectacular" journey to Argentina. The capital city of Buenos Aires was reached by another train trip across the pampas.

"Back then, that city reminded me a lot of Paris but it sounded more like Rome because they said there were more Italians in Buenos Aires than in any city of the world outside of Rome. There was plenty of excitement the week we were there because the King of Italy had just arrived for a royal visit. There were all kinds of Italian warships in the harbor.

"For some reason, the crowds seemed to resent us being around. We were walking down a boulevard and were approached by a bunch of people. They wanted to know what time it was and then asked to see our watches. When they questioned our intentions, it became obvious that somebody was looking for a fight and it wasn't us. We all had the same look on our face — `Let's get the heck out of here before we create an international incident.' We hailed cabs and took off. They were shaking their fists at us as we left."

The theory behind sending the Wolverines down to South America in the first place was to promote social contact between the young blood of the two continents and build stronger ties of friendship. The incident in Argentina had all the trappings of bad blood.

Bidding Buenos Aires a good riddance, the Michigan contingent sailed up the coast to Santos, the No. 1 coffee port in the world, for a short trip inland to Sao Paulo, then a comparatively small city on the Brazilian scene and far from being the metropolitan mecca that it is today.

How big is Brazil? Well, in today's terms, once you cross the Amazon River, which is said to contain one-fourth of the planet's fresh water, there is still more than a three-hour flight of 1,600 miles south to Rio de Janeiro. Before the systematic harvesting of the rain forest, Brazil's plant life supposedly produced one-fourth of the fresh air in the world. Giant forests meant giant ant hills and mountainous nests of termites, which frequently could be seen along the train tracks.

In Rio, the contingent met Brazilian officials and American businessmen. While the picture-postcard mountains, white silver sands, azure-blue lagoons, and black and white mosaic sidewalks were there, this was years before "The Girl from Ipanema" went walking in her G-string bikini and the pre-Lenten "Carnival" (when translated literally means "farewell to flesh") soiree was not yet attracting "The Jet Set."

"The National City Bank of New York (now Citicorp) was, I believe, the first American bank to establish branches in South America and had headquarters in Rio. The president, Boise Hart, came from Adrian in our home state. When we were introduced as students from the University of Michigan, he couldn't do enough for us. Coincidentally, we learned that Mr. Hart was returning to New York City on the same ship we were. He became our fine friend and host while on board, regaling us with some great stories about South America.

"Before we sailed home together, Mr. Hart arranged an overnight rail trip for our group to a famous gold-mining town in the Brazilian interior. Because of the remote location, few ever saw the shaft mine that was said to be more than a mile deep, the deepest of its kind in the world. It was owned and operated by a British company that didn't cater to visitors.

"We had to sleep on wooden berths on the train with one blanket and no sheets. The track was all curves so we did our share of rolling around. Our greeting was friendly because we posed as mining students from Michigan Tech. That little white lie was needed for the bank to get permission to send us. We played the part and evidently were good actors, asking all the right questions and not disclosing our ignorance. We parted company with smiles all around."

Connable departed Brazil agreeing with a news article he had read in a major American daily — that this was what the United States promised for those Europeans who came at the end of the 19th century: "A Place for Beginning Again."

In a piece Mike Royko would have been proud to write, Connable reported his observations on how Peruvian dock workers, who had developed the tactics of strikes into a science, also used Einsteinian reasoning to figure out rates of pay. Working on Sunday was double pay and rightfully so. If Sunday was a special biblical holiday as well, then pay quadrupled and again, maybe rightfully so.

When the work stretched into the evening hours, along came another boost to six times the normal rate because it was now dark. It was time for a rest. Maybe rightfully so, too. But not a "free" rest, as Connable wrote:

"'Señor,' said the leader of the gang to the captain, `we have worked hard for you and pay is not much. We now want a rest, but our pay should not be stopped while we rest. Ordinarily, you see, we receive no pay for loafing hours, but this is when we work for single pay. Today we work for six times the usual pay. Shouldn't we then be given double pay for resting?' The captain regained consciousness two days later."

Early in the journey, during a quick stop in Quito,

Ecuador, the Michigan Daily editor wrote about how the attitude among residents in that city is status quo, contentment, and an appreciation of inertia. He stumbled upon something of a town slogan that translated this way: "I wish to go from Quito to heaven and in heaven to have a peep hole through which I may gaze down upon Quito."

"Fancy," he wrote to the Gazette, "a Kalamazooan saying this about our town. One sees our cute little (railroad) station and courthouse enough without wanting to admire them further after life."

Connable also became fascinated by the exploits of the Quichuan Indians, Ecuador's original inhabitants who were conquered by the Incas despite an advanced technology that gave them the ability to melt copper, build houses of heavy masonry, embalm bodies, and treat gold like any other pretty metal instead of going crazy over it.

Yet, they were known most for their exploits as long-distance runners. When the reigning Inca ruler wanted to dine on fish, it had to be the freshest so relays of Quichuan runners conducted their version of a two-legged Pony Express from seaside to palace hundreds of miles inland. Belonging in Ripley's "Believe It or Not" is the legend that a Quichuan slave, to deliver the news that a revolution had been quashed, ran 297 miles in 24 hours.

Whether that was fact or fable, Connable witnessed some real-life heroics on the sail home from Rio, and that account constituted his final report to The Gazette. Gale-force winds had battered the Atlantic Coast and his cruise ship rescued six survivors of a four-masted schooner, "Samuel W. Hathaway," that had gone down off of Cape Hatteras five days earlier.

While the sailors had spotted several ships during their ordeal, only Connable's "Southern Cross" came within hailing distance and saved their lives about 250 miles southeast of New York City. As the six were being fed small amounts of food and water, Connable played reporter: "The old sea dog wiped his lips badly swollen by salt and gave me the story of their fight for life.

". . .The hurricane hit us and spilled several tons of water down the fo'c's'le companionway. Then it was all hands to the pumps. By and by the wind went down a bit and we tried to lower a boat, but it got smashed by the sea. 'Bout noon the ship was sinking and we all stood on the poop deck. The captain yelled 'jump' and we jumped. The water was cold.

"We had life belts and that was all — no food, no water. Every man got hold of a piece of wreckage and held on. Finally six of us got together on the roof of the cabin. I saw the captain and three others and yelled for them to come over. After a while I could see the captain, but I couldn't

Al's ship, the Southern Cross, rescued these shipwrecked sailors en route back to New York City.

see the other two. The wind had died down but the sea was still rough.

"From then until you just now picked us up it was a fight to the finish. We became hungry and thirsty. The sharks began cutting the water all about the raft. They gave us an idea and we rigged up a fishing outfit with a bent nail and string made from one of our shirts.

"The first fish bit on a piece of white cloth. We pulled him in, split him in two and sucked the blood to our parched lips. These fish — little black ones — were our only food."

Connable reported that their only source of water was the rain they could trap in their hands, a task made nearly impossible by bouncing seas. Their "island," tossed around like a cork, was about 15 feet wide, too small to lie down on. Even if they did, chances are they would be tossed off and become chum for the sharks.

Their weakened voices were not able to hail down the passing ships, and they would have perished, like their captain, if fortune had not placed them in the path of the Southern Cross. Passengers and crew passed the hat and raised $900 for the rescued seamen and the captain's widow. The story was front-page news in the New York dailies.

Connable knew the outcome of that adventure, but not the one that possibly rated a Stephen Spielberg epic. An acquaintance he had made while exploring Inca country with his two college pals wrote him about a mysterious man, a will, letters and a map that supposedly led to "a mine with an iron gate" somewhere in the wilds of Peru. Near the entrance were two huge flat stones that had obviously been transported there for grinding and cracking whatever was being extracted from the mine. They were not indigenous to the region because only small rocks and pebbles were in the vicinity.

Strangest of all, Connable was told, was the fact that nowhere could be found traces or particles of anything that looked as though it might have been brought out from the mine. Obviously, whatever came from the mine was of great enough value that its location must remain a secret and "hidden."

Now here comes the intrigue. The man who stumbled upon this mystery knew enough about mining not to enter one that had been dormant for possibly centuries. He pocketed his curiosity, checked his bearings, made some maps and returned to Lima with the intention of preparing himself with the right equipment to explore and exploit.

But he suffered a stroke and was never able to return. Because his only son had died, the paralyzed man decided to keep his secret until a grandchild reached his 20th birthday. As with any good novel, two weeks before the magic date, the man died, taking with him his personal knowledge of where the iron-gated mine could be found. All that remained were his letters and drawings with no definite bearings. The grandson had found those papers and had asked Connable's Peruvian acquaintance to join him on the treasure hunt.

Connable never read or heard anything about the outcome — whether it was a wild goose chase or whether the party became trophies for headhunters. He had another year of college and then he'd be out on his own treasure hunt. He'd learn that capitalism had its own special breed of cannibalism.

OUT ON HIS OWN

The ink was hardly dry on his 1925 diploma and his English just back to normal when Connable first tested what he had learned at Michigan as a sales assistant under Jake Kindleberger's stewardship at KVP back in Kalamazoo.

Newspapering was not going to become his forte. He'd worked his way up to night editor on campus and was in line for the next move up to the hierarchy — managing editor. However, he had already been nominated for the presidency of the student council. When he won that position for his senior year, he dropped out of the competition at the newspaper. Phil Wagner got the job and went on to become editor of The Baltimore Sun. Ink was in Wagner's veins, but grapes were in his blood. He became a well-known wine connoisseur.

During his two years in the papermaking business, Connable signed an important piece of paper — a marriage license — exchanging vows with Dorothy Malcomson in April of 1927.

By then, Al had enriched his business acumen by hearing about conversations between his new father-in-law and various associates, including the likes of attorney Horace Rackham in Detroit. He learned it's likely that one can make some bad decisions, especially when ego gets in the way of wisdom.

"Everybody called Dorothy's father `A. Y.' just like folks around here called my dad `A. B.' He induced several people like the Dodge brothers and Mr. Rackham to invest in Henry Ford's enterprise at the turn of the century. He became one of the principal financial backers himself. The Dodges traded their engines for stock, while Horace Rackham bartered his legal services.

"A. Y. and Ford were the majority shareholders. Mr. Malcomson was known around town for being a `canny Scot' but not in this instance. Because of differences of opinion about how the car company should develop,

The father of Al's first wife Dorothy, Alexander Y. Malcomson, shown to the left of his coal yard, was at one time a majority stockholder in the Ford Motor Company.

Dorothy's father sold his large interest to Henry Ford for $275,000. That was a tidy figure, but 20 years later it was worth in the millions of dollars. Both men had strong personalities and in this case, Ford had the right vision.

"Horace Rackham was a very humble person and very appreciative of what he called `his luck.' We had some great conversations in his Detroit law office. Horace once told me he swapped his legal services for Ford stock because he really didn't want to invest his own money. He never thought it would ever be worth a nickel. Horace became a great philanthropist, especially regarding the University of Michigan."

Meanwhile, the Connable siblings had moved on as well. The sisters were married and had started their families. Josephine, through her husband's position at Western, moved in academic circles, but "Ginny" through her husband was closer to the business community. In the spring of 1922, she married Lorence Burdick, the younger (by 10 seconds) of the twin sons born to Willis Burdick, who in 1897 had founded the Fidelity Building and Loan Association. It evolved into the Fidelity Federal Savings and Loan Association by the time "Larry" held office in the family business.

"The Burdick twins were so identical that I couldn't tell which one was courting my sister. At the wedding, I learned it was Larry. I can remember their father as being a very

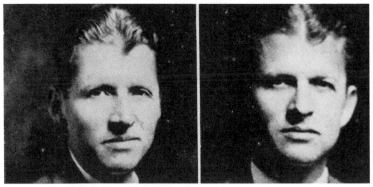

Twins L.B. (left) and W.B. Burdick were like two peas in a pod.

distinguished gentleman with a finely groomed beard. Their mother was the former Florence Bushnell, but everybody called her `Prissy` for some reason. She was a smallish woman who looked like a Dresden doll. Her size belied how feisty she was."

When the Burdick boys were at Kalamazoo College as members of the Hornets' baseball and tennis teams, Dr. Herbert Stetson, then the president, stood up in chapel and delivered a stirring appeal for the men of "K" to enlist and drive back the evil and wicked Huns. Just short of their 20th birthdays, the twins swallowed the pep talk and enlisted in the Coast Guard. When something about an "air force" was being hashed around, they applied for a transfer. The move was approved, but the twins, for the first time in their lives, were separated — until Prissy boarded an eastbound train and talked to some high-powered general in Washington. They'd be split up later when they went "over there" but were able to link up a few times in Paris. After Armistice Day, they came home and continued their education at the University of Michigan.

"My younger brother Horace was quite sickly when young because of a bout with pneumonia so he attended a ranch school in Tucson in Arizona. That built up his health. He graduated from Stanford and in 1933 married Genevieve Wildermuth, a 1928 graduate of Kalamazoo College. Her mother, Edna, was a nurse and anathesiologist for about 30 years."

Horace and Genevieve spent many years in Key West where he served in the Coast Guard during World War II. They were destined to return to their home town after living many years along the Rio Grande River in McAllen, Texas.

Brother Harold, also a Stanford alumnus, joined one of the family enterprises and ended up as sales manager for the Monroe Calculating Machine Co. in the Hawaiian Islands. It was tough duty, but somebody had to do it. Actually, it was. "In those days in 1952, it wasn't everybody who wanted to go out to the islands and build up a sales organization from scratch. Despite the miles separating the Connable brothers, we were always very close."

Back at Kindleberger's Parchment digs for a second go-round, the oldest of the three Connables worked in the unit that produced "fine" papers, did some accounting, went on the road for sales, and performed what amounted to public relations guiding visitors and prospects through the operations.

"That was very enlightening for me and came in handy in my future business career. The half-hour tour began in the rag room, which is where Uncle Jake started in the business back in Ohio. We covered it all, from the beater room to the machines where the finished product rolled off. I enjoyed that training program.

"My boss was Ben Morris Sr., who was vice president for fine papers and had been recruited from the Whitaker Paper Co. in Cincinnati. He was kindly and very helpful. Until recently, his two sons were active and still in the community, Ben Jr. in real estate and Dick in law. Ben Sr. was very instrumental in developing that division. Years later, I met Whitaker's wife when my stepson, Pat, married one of her granddaughters.

"Uncle Jake built up the business in hopes that his only son, Joe, and my old workmate, would follow in his footsteps. After attending Babson Institute in Boston and working for a paper company in Richmond, Va., Joe joined the company in 1925. By 1947, Joe was head of consumer and market research for KVP and was elected president of the Executives Club in town. My brother-in-law, Paul Rood, was active in that group. Uncle Jake had big dreams for his son and rightfully so because Joe had established himself as a community leader. But he died in his home in early 1952. He was only 45 years old. What a shame.

"I knew Joe and his family well. His widow, Helen, later moved to Tucson. They had three daughters. The fellows who filled the leadership void when Uncle Jake died included `Doc' Southon. `Doc' was a tower of strength as the acting president and became a director at the American National Bank. There was also Dwight Stocker, who later served with me on the WMU Board of Trustees, and Ralph Hayward. Ralph was brought in from the University of Michigan where he had been a very well known professor of chemical engineering.

"Hayward was very professional in his approach and was greatly served by 'Doc' Southon, who was there all the time to lend his valuable experience garnered from the early days with Uncle Jake."

The senior Kindleberger died in 1947, taking with him many of the details of his 1931 encounter with "Yellow Kid" Weil, one of America's most flamboyant and slickest con artists. His bunco bravado served as the basis for the Robert Redford-Paul Newman film, "The Sting."

In his autobiography published a year after Uncle Jake's death, Weil, who operated primarily in Chicago, told about his occasional forays in Michigan in the early part of the century. His targets were wealthy Chicagoans who fancied ownership of prime resort land in the Wolverine State. Those suckers dealing with "The Yellow Kid" ended up with worthless sand dunes.

According to Weil, he "stung" the patriarch of Parchment for $15,000 in another kind of scam, one that probably had something to do with the tough times of the Depression in the early 1930s. Uncle Jake wrote the lesson off by paying heed to one of his famous mottos: "Blessed is the man who doesn't bellyache."

While much of the nation suffered a serious economic bellyache during those years, Kalamazoo Vegetable Parchment endured with its greatest periods of growth still ahead in the 1940s and 1950s. Connable would be on the periphery of that, but first he wanted to add another credential to his academic record.

"Maybe I would have been better off to stay with Uncle Jake instead of heading off for graduate school at Harvard. I ended up in Detroit, not a nice place in the Depression years. Kalamazoo Vegetable Parchment came through. Business in Kalamazoo generally came through. Detroit and the auto industry suffered some very difficult times.

"But going to Cambridge and graduate school turned out to be one of the best things I ever did. I majored in finance and investments. There weren't too many business schools at that time and Harvard's hadn't been in existence for too long. After two years at Parchment, I thought I was ready. When I received my master's in business administration in 1929, that wasn't too common a degree.

"I rubbed elbows with some fellows who did quite well later in their careers as heads of national banks and investment firms. At my 55th class reunion in 1984, there were still 40 of us left. They were all retired. I was the only one semi-retired.

"While we were in school there, the way to riches seemed to be channeled through the stock market. So much so that I remember our dean in his commencement address cautioned us not to be attracted to New York City and the excitement of the bull market. He suggested we locate in a secondary city, if we wanted that kind of action at all."

Married to the Motor City daughter of a "canny Scot" and enrolled at a prestigious Ivy League school landed Connable summer work at the Detroit Trust Co. The contacts got him in the door. His talent and skills kept him there. Once his Harvard diploma was in hand, he was invited to join the company on a full-time basis.

Good move. He joined a subsidiary of Detroit Trust, Selected Securities Corp., in June of 1929. If Connable had decided to shop around, the following October would not have been a good time to be scouting for a job. Twelve years later on Dec. 7, 1941, Pearl Harbor would be called "a day that will live in infamy," but "Black Friday" in that October of 1929 ranks right up there for personal toll and tragedy among many Americans. Some lives were lost, thousands others were shattered and millions of hearts were broken.

Connable's business card read "of the Detroit Trust Company" for the next 15 years.

"I started in the bond cage, as an assistant secretary learning yields and how to figure prices. Next came stock analysis and research for trust investments. My first major assignment was to organize and build an analysis department for stocks and bonds. While it's hard to believe these days, that was a relatively new twist in the early 1930s. I was able to attract some really good people, including college chums at both Michigan and Harvard."

As the Depression began to wrap its tentacles around the nation and slowly choke the economy to near death, Connable watched a great city wither.

"Detroit Trust was much more fortunate than commercial banks. It was almost entirely fiduciary. That is, the trust activity was its dominant venture. It didn't accept deposits or make loans. The loan-making function is why so many banks failed and why Roosevelt declared a national bank holiday. Detroit Trust was able to keep going, although about half the staff of 300 was trimmed. I was lucky enough to be able to keep my job.

"One of the problems in Detroit, to my way of thinking, was the enthusiasm of the banks there to get together in holding companies and spread all over. The same is true these days and that kind of worries me. Of course, there's pro and con over this.

"The Detroit Bankers Company was formed to compete with the Detroit Guardian Union Group. Both moved throughout the state to buy other banks. The Guardian group bought the old First National in Kalamazoo, but Charlie Campbell and his investors were able to buy their bank back. Detroit Trust came under the aegis of the other group.

"Well, when the banks were closed, all of the member banks in the holding companies had to go through receivership. The stockholders had to pay double liability, which was the rule in those days. They not only lost the market

The panic that seized investors in the lobby of Detroit's First National Bank on March 24, 1933, was repeated throughout the nation.

value of their stock. They were also liable to pay par value — usually $100 a share — to the receiver.

"We were fortunate that Detroit Trust was able to break away from the holding company during this receivership period and begin to build ourselves up again as a purely fiduciary concern dealing in trusts only."

Meanwhile, back in Kalamazoo, one of the community's prime financial institutions wobbled the day Wall Street played like King Kong taking a header off the Empire State Building. The Bank of Kalamazoo, the largest enterprise of its kind in Southwest Michigan, could trace its roots to the town's first private bank that was opened in 1844 by Theodore Sheldon. Ten years earlier, Sheldon worked as a cashier in the community's first-ever moneyhandler — the state-owned Bank of Michigan that opened a branch in the then village of Bronson in 1834.

The lineage traveled through the Kalamazoo Savings Bank, a merger with Kalamazoo City Bank, and another major consolidation in 1928 with Kalamazoo National Bank. By the end of "Black Friday" on Oct. 29, 1929, 16 million shares of stock had changed hands. By New Year's Eve, the value of stocks had declined by $15 billion. The Bank of Kalamazoo took a hit that was about an eight on the Richter scale.

On Feb. 14, 1933, Gov. William Comstock ordered all of the banks in Michigan closed for eight days. After being allowed to re-open on a restricted basis, they were shuttered again when President Roosevelt followed Comstock's lead and declared the "National Bank Holiday" on March 4, 1933. While many re-opened, the Bank of Kalamazoo was dissolved and placed into the hands of a state-appointed conservator.

From the time of Gov. Comstock's call for a statewide banking holiday, the Bank of Kalamazoo's directors had been crystal-balling their next step. Working with both federal and state officials, they decided in May of 1933 to proceed with forming a new bank using a game plan that had

111

worked in a similar situation in Connable's adopted home town of Detroit.

The Detroit plan was fairly simple. Half of the capital needed for the new bank would be provided by Kalamazoo industrialists and business leaders while the balance would come from the federal government's Reconstruction Finance Corp. Once capitalization was completed, the new bank's board would authorize the purchase of the closed bank's assets. In that manner, depositors would at least get back some of the funds they had entrusted to the liquidated bank.

Who was back of this move to form a new bank? Many of the same people. The majority of the Bank of Kalamazoo's board became the first directors of the new entity, the American National Bank of Kalamazoo — Dorothy Upjohn DeLano (Dalton), Grace G. Upjohn (the widow of Harold Upjohn, the only son of Dr. W. E. Upjohn,

Dunlap Clark led the newly organized American National Bank to fiscal solvency in the 1930s.

who died in the fall of 1928 following what was supposed to be routine surgery), J. Stanley Gilmore Sr., S. Rudolph Light and Stephen B. Monroe. Joining this team were Dwight R. Curtenius, William J. Lawrence, Albert J. Todd, and Alfred B. Connable Sr.

The organizers searched the landscape for a Moses to lead them back to the promised land of fiscal solvency, a Hercules to be a pillar of strength and confidence. That was a tall order and they settled on a tall man for the job — 6 foot 6 Dunlap "Dunnie" Clark, whose legacy in Illinois banking was almost as long as he was. Clark was hired away from Continental Illinois National Bank in Chicago, then the largest bank west of New York.

On the first day of business on Nov. 1, 1933, American National was as fresh as a new-born babe. It had no assets and no deposits because the newly appointed board had decided not to assume the assets of its predecessor.

The new bank was clear of all entanglements and encumbrances. In preparing for the grand opening, expenses were incurred by board members, but all, including Connable's father, paid the bills out of their own pockets so that American National could start free of any debts as Clark began his presidency. The first customer in line to open an account that day was Alfred Connable Sr.

"Certainly, Kalamazoo had its difficulties during those years, but nothing like the conditions in Detroit. The auto industry didn't completely shut down, but production was minimal. It was tough on the streets of Detroit. Poor fellows out of work would trail people to the office, begging for a dime or a quarter. Some took advantage of the generosity, taking their dime or quarter to the nearest watering hole for a beer or two.

"Then, a great idea surfaced. People who could afford to help the down-and-out'ers bought tickets for 10 cents or 25 cents. These could only be exchanged at soup kitchens, not the local saloons. Many Detroiters reached out to help.

"On those weekends I was able to come back to

Kalamazoo, I found conditions quite different. The paper mills were still running as was The Upjohn Co. The economy was more stable and diversified here. The Kalamazoo Gazette supposedly carried other members of the Booth Newspaper chain during those years because the town was on more solid ground than what was happening in Flint, Ann Arbor and the other Booth cities. Detroit and Kalamazoo were two different worlds."

Connable started moving up the ladder at Detroit Trust, advancing from an assistant secretary to assistant vice president to director of the company's investment analysis. He also wasn't the only local man on the staff. Fred Van Zandt, a 1923 Kalamazoo College alumnus, was a member of the corporation trust department. Connable also found time to do some instructing in investments and economics in night courses at the Detroit Institute of Technology for a stretch of 10 years. Building a solid reputation as an authority in business and finance, he preached what he practiced.

In the capacity as a department head, Connable frequently reported directly to Detroit Trust's board of directors. By 1920, John and Horace Dodge, Horace Rackham and all the other minority stockholders had been bought out by Henry Ford. The Dodges formed their own car company that later became Chrysler. He became acquainted with U.S. Sen. Truman Newberry, who was one of the early stockholders in the company that manufactured Packards.

"I worked on their family trusts and investments so I felt pretty close to Detroit's auto scene. I believe that each of the Dodges was worth about $40 million at the time. Quite a bit of money back then. They had so much money their heirs didn't know what to do with it. John Dodge's widow remarried and the couple built a gorgeous English manor house that is now part of Oakland University."

Connable was also somewhat ahead of his times as a commuter, choosing to set up residence in Ann Arbor. "I just couldn't see living in Detroit. It didn't appeal to me even though I really did enjoy my work there. I guess you can take the man out of Kalamazoo, but you can't take the Kalamazoo out of the man. Six days a week, I would catch the Michigan Central train at 7 a.m. and return to Ann Arbor by 5:30.

"We lived near my Delta Kappa Epsilon fraternity house in Ann Arbor and I saw a good deal of the brothers who followed me in that chapter."

Fellow Delta Kappa Epsilon fraternity brother, Gerald R. Ford, starred on the U of M football squad in the mid 1930s.

One of them was born Leslie Lynch King Jr. in Omaha, Neb., in 1913. Young Leslie had a rough time in his infant years. When his divorced mother came to Michigan and remarried, Leslie was adopted by his stepfather. He took the man's name — Gerald Rudolph Ford Jr.

"I was a great admirer when Jerry was at Michigan," Connable says about the man destined to be the 38th president of the United States, "because he worked his way through college."

Ford went back to Grand Rapids to practice law in 1941,

115

but his career, as with hundreds of thousands of other young Americans, was interrupted by World War II. He spent four years in the U.S. Navy before he went home and entered the political arena, which is where his circle would once again intersect with Al Connable's.

The camera captured "mountain man" Al during a trip west in the 1930s.

WHAT PRICE GLORY —
THE WAR YEARS

Too young as a first-year teen to carry the nation's colors in World War I, Al Connable had time on his side — or as his enemy depending on how you want to sail the winds of war — when the nation was again called to arms in 1941.

He was 37 years old and, more important, the father of three when the Japanese decided to launch their naval and aerial forces against the U.S. presence in the Hawaiian Islands.

Daughter Nancy was born two months after his Harvard graduation and their setting up residence in Ann Arbor. Alfred Barnes Connable III arrived the day after Christmas two years later in 1931. John L. Connable made the family a quintet on July 10, 1934.

"I just couldn't sit around and do nothing during the war. I wanted to do something. So I applied for the Office of Price Administration (OPA) and was accepted. I was named the head of price controls for the Michigan OPA and took a leave of absence from Detroit Trust."

The OPA was organized by presidential mandate and nationally headed at the beginning by famed economist John Kenneth Galbraith who would later write highly praised accounts of "The Great Crash" and the presidency of John Kennedy. The agency was charged with forestalling inflation by stabilizing rents and prices, and by preventing speculation, hoarding, profiteering and price manipulation.

As the war escalated, OPA powers in each state were later expanded by congressional action to include the rationing of scarce commodities to consumers and the determination of maximum prices for goods and rents. It was through his OPA duties that Connable got to know attorney Edwin G. Gemrich Sr. of Kalamazoo, who headed the rationing department, and Louis Upton, the co-founder of the Whirlpool Corp., so well.

Connable was sworn in as the OPA's state price administrator for Michigan on May 18, 1942. Based in the Penobscot Building in downtown Detroit, he reported directly to Michigan OPA director Arthur Sarvis. He'd last

The Penobscot Building, where Al worked for the OPA, dominated Detroit's skyline in the 1940s.

just over a year in the job, resigning when what he viewed as a bureaucratic coup robbed the agency of its effectiveness.

Patriotism and anti-Axis fervor generally carried enough clout to gain compliance, but greed can be a powerful force and Connable needed allies in a variety of industries, occupations and businesses to help make pitches.

One of his first recruits was a self-made grocery magnate who thought he and his wife were bound for retirement in Acapulco until the Japanese Navy made a hard right and headed toward Honolulu. Called "God's gift to Michigan housewives" and as a man who "knew his onions," 60-year-old Howard Clay had paid his dues, worked his long hours, and was packed for Mexico.

Then Clay read a newspaper account. The state's newly appointed OPA price administrator (Connable) was looking for experienced retailers, including grocers. Clay rationalized that one can't swap a Detroit Tigers baseball cap for a sombrero, especially when one's country had taken a serious body blow and was reeling. He hung up his poncho, donned a business suit and paid Connable a call. He wanted to know whether there was anything a worn-out, 60-year-old grocer could do for his nation before putting himself out to pasture.

"Sit down," he was told, "because there is plenty you can do for your country. The food situation is the toughest part of price control and we need men like you with your spirit." Clay cashed in his train tickets to Mexico and rolled up his sleeves. Certainly, they were disappointed. But Acapulco could wait. Besides, if the Japanese and Germans had their way, Mexican vacations might be a moot point.

Clay was the right man for the job. As a food broker, manager of both retail and wholesale operations, and an expert in canned foodstuffs, he had the impeccable credentials of being knowledgeable and honest in his field. When Howard Clay spoke about the need to stave off inflation by keeping the prices of food commodities down, his peers listened. He talked their language. He'd been through World

War I, soared through that post-war boom, and then nearly lost it all in the crash.

"Price control," Clay told a reporter from the Detroit News, "protects the businessman just as much as the consumer. Prices got so high in the last war they were bound to topple and we practically gave our food stocks away. This time we won't let them get up there."

The Connable recruit spoke directly to consumers about price complaints, straightened out merchants' price tangles under the OPA regulations, and reported violations to the agency's enforcement lawyers. Clay cut people lots of slack if they were honest and tried to obey the law. But if he came upon willful shenanigans, look out. He was a

OPA ration stamps and tokens became an integral part of life on the home front during WW II.

remorseless prosecutor, burning up the wires all the way to Galbraith in Washington if necessary.

Few peers tried to fool him because it was said Howard Clay could tell a good tomato from a spoiled one simply by looking at the can. Says Connable: "Money couldn't buy what that man brought to our table at the OPA."

Connable came home that September to deliver the same kind of message as he spoke on "What War-Time Price Control Means to You" before the Kalamazoo Professional and Business Women's Club. Here's what he told 100 listeners, one of whom was his father:

"Five million people in Michigan have price-control duty because price control is the best American way to prevent inflation. Set up to put a ceiling on the rising cost of living, price control has a saving effect, allowing more money to be expended for war materials. Four billion dollars already have been spent for war materials and six billion more will be spent in the near future.

"During our Revolutionary War when living conditions faltered and morale fell, the Continental Congress established price controls. It is better to prevent inflation now and avoid the `crash` afterward. A Gallup poll last May showed that 74 percent of the U.S. citizens favored such measures as price control.

"As a job for the OPA, the merchants and the consumers — in order to make sure that price control is effective — there is a list of things each must do. The retailer must file all his prices, post his ceilings, file a list of all his prices with the county ration board, and keep a base price-control book.

"The consumer in turn — if he or she feels the merchant is not complying with price regulations — may talk with the merchants about their prices, see the base price book, ask for a sales slip, and then get in touch with the OPA. The local county boards, in keeping the price lists, act as an information center.

"Manufacturers and wholesalers need not post their

prices, although they must stay under their March (1942) prices. On Sept. 10, the service end of price control became effective on such items as laundry and dry cleaning."

Connable's office later surveyed the state for retailer compliance and Kalamazoo was one of the communities sampled. Non-compliance had been reduced to about 20 percent of the retailers. Those in violation frequently lacked the proper information, a deficiency that was quickly remedied by the OPA. Ignorance was supposedly bliss, but the time was rapidly coming when the "Mr. Nice Guy" approach would be replaced by stiff enforcement.

In a magazine article that lauded the cooperation of the Detroit Retail Druggists Association, Connable issued this caveat: "It is now up to those individual druggists who are out of line to get their houses in order quickly. This is an all-out war effort to beat inflation and it must be done now."

If one thinks that "performance evaluation" is a modern tool for managers of people, think again. Its roots are in the U.S. Civil Service system and Connable was part of that bureaucracy. He passed with flying colors, too, earning a rating of "Excellent" from Sarvis six months into his stint. The rating meant that "the employee has more than met every important job requirement and has not fallen down below satisfactory service in any respect."

"If it ain't broke, don't fix it." The troops in the hinterlands thought the OPA was doing just about as well as it could, given the impossible task. Washington had a different view and adopted not a fix-it mode but a complete overhaul approach as envisioned by the agency's new head, Prentiss M. Brown, who was not a fan of statewide powers when it came to price controls. Later as a U.S. senator from St. Ignace, Brown served as a catalyst for the construction of the Mackinac Bridge in the 1950s.

In March of 1943 while taking a short break in Florida to recharge his batteries, Connable received a letter from Clay that sized up the rumblings.

"Well, it jolts all of us to see the breaking up of a unity

welded together by the severe hardships endured. They speak of the pioneers who worked so hard to develop this country, while we, who really have worked so hard with tools so inadequate, will never be remembered except with possible hatred. . .Mr. Sarvis gave us a real pep talk to hold the line while you were away." The Clays might be diving off the cliffs of Acapulco sooner than expected.

Upon his return, the OPA took a decentralizing step on April 27, 1943, to enlist greater cooperation from the public to control prices. As part of county, district or regional rationing boards, special three-member panels were established on May 8. Their tasks were to keep community retailers informed of the price regulations by providing them with official. up-to-date and accurate information. A quasi-judicial function was to field complaints of violations of retail price ceilings and investigate the charges. The panels would also serve as liaison between the communities and OPA district offices, chronicling compliance, difficulties and shortages in essential foodstuffs.

"The new panels will be composed of outstanding persons living in the area served by each rationing board," Connable told The Associated Press. "Every effort would be made to select community leaders." He sounded convincing, but, unlike his days out west with his dad, he was not a happy camper.

A few days later, a Detroit Free Press political columnist reported this piece of Washington gossip:

"OPA state administrator Arthur Sarvis and OPA price officer Albert (reporter's error) Connable have quietly passed the word along to Prentiss Brown in Washington that any political meddling in the state setup will bring the respectful request that their resignations be accepted."

Then the gossip became "straight" news as reported in the Free Press under a Washington dateline:

"A complete shake-up of officials of the Office of Price Administration throughout the Michigan, Ohio, Indiana and Kentucky district, which has headquarters in Cleveland, became imminent Friday, according to official sources here.

"OPA authorities said they had not yet received the resignations of any officials of the Detroit area, despite persistent rumors that Arthur H. Sarvis, Detroit director, would resign shortly.

"Edwin G. Gemrich, Detroit OPA attorney, has announced that he has sent his resignation to Washington officials and recommendations are already coming in for a successor through the usual political circles.

"The program prepared for OPA administrator Prentiss Brown calls for 10,000 changes in the personnel of the organization, which employs more than 100,000. . .

"This program is one of decentralization and gives to state and local boards additional authority, in addition to more paid employees. The bulk of the resignations will come from the 5,000 workers in Washington and among the 2,700 members of the legal staff scattered throughout the country. The order giving local boards additional assistance was approved today by administrator Brown."

Sarvis' announced departure quickly followed under the guise of the press of private business as the vice president of a bank in Flint and other ventures. Involved in the war effort since December of 1941 as the rationing chief. Sarvis denied emphatically that his withdrawal was the result of any political pressure or because of any disagreement over policies with Brown. "It is unfortunate," he told The Free press, "but many people will interpret my resignation as having something to do with the shake-up in the OPA. That is not the case. It is purely a personal business matter and has no relationship to OPA policy or anything else."

Sarvis claimed that he had first submitted his resignation in February before Brown had announced any intentions to reorganize the agency. "I was asked to continue on the job," he said. "As a matter of fact, I heartily approve of Brown's program of simplification and public cooperation."

Speculation was rampant that Connable would be next, and the rumor mongers hit the bull's-eye. However, the former and future Kalamazooan didn't mince any words in a May 22 statement that his resignation would be effective in nine days.

While he never burned any bridges, Connable cited his unhappiness over the OPA's decision to strip away statewide authority and convert to a district or multi-county system. With such a reconfiguration, he told the press corps, "the present nature and scope of our work has significantly altered the opportunity for individual service. If I have any criticism to make, and I say this in a constructive way, it is that the great importance of Detroit and Michigan in the war effort should put an organization so technically complex as the OPA on the Washington main line and not on the Cleveland side track."

John Fetzer, to the right of Gen. Eisenhower, served as National Radio Censor during WW II.

Connable and Gemrich weren't the only persons with Kalamazoo ties to be handed a major regulatory responsibility that could have significant ramifications on the war effort.

Broadcaster John Fetzer was appointed the national radio censor for a new wrinkle in American society — the U.S. Office of Censorship. Byron Price, a print-journalist colleague of Fetzer's from Indiana, served as agency director. At the time of Price's appointment, he was executive news editor of the Associated Press in New York.

At daily briefings in the agency's Washington office, key staff members were under the influence of a motto viewable near Price's desk: "A censor needs the eye of a hawk, the memory of an elephant, the nose of a bloodhound, the heart of a lion, the vigilance of an owl, the voice of a dove, the sagacity of Solomon, the patience of Job, and the imperturbability of the Sphinx."

The agency was plowing new ground in a freedom-loving society where censorship is supposed to be anathema to the survival of a democracy. There was no such agency during World War I. Radio, as an industry, wasn't even a factor in those days.

Fetzer shepherded more than 900 radio stations and their networks, establishing a system of voluntary, self-regulation guided by the principle that no information should be aired that could be beneficial to those who favored the other side. Even weather reports had to be couched in special terms because alert ears, just like loose lips, can sink ships.

During his four years as a federal censor, Fetzer later reported that broadcast and print journalists stayed the course, not reporting on the movement of troops and ships, intelligence plans, and the development of radar and the atomic bomb when they dug out the information.

His only tough sell was columnist Drew Pearson, who was about to broadcast a scoop that five vintage destroyers that the United States had sold to the Soviet Union were

126

about to sail from Norfolk. A long telephone conversation and some tough words finally convinced Pearson that he might be signing the death warrants for American sailors because German U-boats were off the coast and could pick up his broadcasts. In his own way, Connable had some difficult sales to make, too.

"It was a tough job because everybody wanted the other fellows to keep their prices down while he went along just as before. Then, of course, there were people with no ethics or morals whatever. These were the black-market operators who, by hook or by crook, tried to make a buck at the expense of honest retailers in the sale of meat, poultry or other foods. But on the whole, we received outstanding cooperation from retailers.

"We took those jobs pretty seriously. Nobody likes price controls. I didn't, but it was a necessity. I think we did a pretty decent job, a bunch of practical businessmen with business sense. After the war, the OPA for all practical purposes, dissolved."

So did Fetzer's Office of Censorship as he led the effort before Congress to end this particular level of bureaucracy he considered anathema to what the United States was supposed to represent.

What it all represented to Al Connable was simple — it was time to go home.

COMING HOME: I MUST BE ABOUT MY FATHER'S BUSINESS

On the brink of his 40th birthday, Al Connable had to face one of those forks in life's road in the wake of his resignation from the Office of Price Administration.

Did his future rest with Detroit Trust or, unlike Thomas Wolfe, could he and his growing family "go home again?"

A little bit of commuting goes a long way and 14 years of Ann Arbor-to-Detroit-and-back-again travel time had worn more than a little thin. Even though the network of roads on the eastern side of the state had improved steadily to facilitate the war effort and train rides had given way to car-pooling, Connable did not appreciate using his time that way. His kids were 14, 12 and 9, changing almost daily, and he wanted to be a part of that as much as he could.

The tip-the-scales factor was family-related, though. The senior Connable was in his 70s and if some fresh legs weren't added, the Peck-Connable enterprise would never move into a third generation.

"He was handling the business as a private trustee and investment counselor all alone with only a bookkeeper. He kept wanting me to come back. During the war years, he handled it pretty much himself, although I did come to Kalamazoo to help make some decisions and we advised each other over the telephone.

"But he really needed more than that because the days of the one-person or limited-person shop in his business were coming to an end. The war had killed 55 million people across the world and it also killed the good old days in his kind of business. The web of regulations was growing. One tax form a year had been about it.

"Today, there is a tremendous amount of reporting that is required, which is a good thing, I believe. Regulatory bodies like the Securities & Exchange Commission and the Internal Revenue Service require a constant stream of reports. So did our clients. This trend was just starting to

Alfred Connable, Sr.

happen after the war ended, and that's why computers are so invaluable today.

"So all of that was weighing on my mind. Besides, Kalamazoo is a pretty nice place to come back to. I had never lost my love for the community. And, after my disappointment about what was happening with the OPA and controlling prices didn't make me the most popular guy at the country club in the first place, the old home town was looking better all of the time. Let me say that I still believed in the OPA mission. I even took a temporary position at its Lansing district office before returning to Kalamazoo for good in the fall of 1943."

The face and fabric of Kalamazoo had changed in the 16 years his mailing addresses had read Cambridge, Detroit and Ann Arbor. The Upjohn Co. had undergone a tremendous spurt in sales growth and facilities expansion. The community's cultural and educational resources, always rich and flowery for a town its size, had blossomed into a Garden of Eden.

Kalamazoo's first skyscraper, the Kalamazoo National Bank Building, shown under construction in 1907.

Connable was 3 years old when Kalamazoo's first sky-scraper, the eight-floor Kalamazoo National Bank Building, arrived in the fall of 1907 at the southwest corner of Michigan and Burdick. Viewed as a social, economic and geographic event, the project prompted one proud citizen to write a letter to the editor to the national magazine, "Collier's Weekly."

The "reach-for-the-sky" structure watched the Hanselman Building go up in 1912 and, as the Kalamazoo Building, witnessed its destruction six decades later as a controlled demolition prepared the way for the Kalamazoo Center.

Connable was heading out for Harvard when the State Theater was built three blocks to the south the year that Babe Ruth hit 60 home runs in 1927. Two years later, the Dewing Building came out of the ground kitty-corner to the first skyscraper.

In 1929, to mark the merger of two of the city's major banks — Kalamazoo City Savings and Kalamazoo National (the one based in the town's skyscraper) — the resulting Bank of Kalamazoo broke ground on what would be the community's "Empire State Building" and the future home of "The Connable Office."

While its building began to dominate the downtown's skyline, the new bank would not be a part of Kalamazoo's financial landscape very long, failing to survive the federal government's remedies for a knocked-out economy. Like a phoenix rising from ashes, the American National Bank of Kalamazoo, housed in the structure by 1933, sprung from the skeletal remains of the depression-closed financial insti-tution.

The 15-story building, which carried a $1.25 million price tag when blueprinted, was quite a marvel in its own right when completed in 1929. Designed by a Chicago architectural firm, the general contractor was the forerunner of the Miller-Davis Co. All of the 378 windows were man-ufactured in Kalamazoo.

The 15 story Bank of Kalamazoo Building was completed in 1929.

The slate floors and walls came from Travertine stone, which is an Austrian first cousin to onyx and is formed in caves by drops of water that build up decorative patterns of deposits over eons. The elevator doors were cast in bronze as were the drinking fountain and the mailbox with its 15-floor chute. The ceiling of the banking area rose 32 feet above the floor. Otto Stauffenberg, a native of Hamburg, Germany, was brought to Kalamazoo from Chicago to paint the ceiling a la Michelangelo. The herculean task took him 600 hours as he reclined on his back on scaffolding and applied two coats of muted-color paints. The teller windows were made of boubinga wood, imported from the Belgian Congo. The wood is so dense that carpenters blunted two sets of saws working with the material.

Connable's father was part of all this as a charter director of the fledgling bank. Al Jr. almost was, which would have brought him back to Kalamazoo in 1933 instead of a decade later.

"The new bank's board formed a search committee to find a man to serve as the chief operating officer. The committee asked me to come over from Detroit for an interview. The members' thinking was that here was a Kalamazoo man who had financial experience and they offered me the job.

"But I really didn't have any practical knowledge in commercial banking. It is entirely different from trusts and investments. I expressed my appreciation of their confidence in my ability, but I frankly told them I didn't think I had the qualifications to do the job they were looking for. They found the right man for the job in Dunlap Clark. He was there for 14 years and was there when I came home.

"Like me at Detroit Trust, 'Dunnie' took a leave of absence during the war. He accepted a commission as a lieutenant colonel in the U.S. War Department's fiscal section at the Pentagon. Dr. Rudolph Light, Dick's father, took on the presidency for those two years. 'Dunnie' left Kalamazoo in 1947 to become president of a bank in

Oakland, Calif."

By then, Connable had replaced his father on the American board. Other directors of that vintage included Dr. Charles Boys, Clinton Buell, J. Stanley Gilmore Sr., Light, Allan Milham, Henry Shakespeare, Dwight Stocker, Louis Sutherland, Albert Todd, Dr. E. Gifford Upjohn, and L. R. Verdon. Of the 1933 organizers, only Gilmore, Todd and Light remained.

The 6-foot-6 Clark had cast a long shadow and the roots of growth were deeply entrenched. The organizers needed an extrovert like Clark to get the bank off of the ground. A different kind of leader was needed to move to the next level. They chose Garret Van Haaften, known as "The Quiet Man."

"That was truly the right choice. Van was the son of a plumber. Both his parents died when he was still young. He didn't drop out of Kalamazoo Central High School. He was forced out as a teen-ager to support a younger brother and sister."

Van Haaften's career began with a job as a bank messenger at the old Kalamazoo National Bank in 1921. He took to the world of finance like celery seeds took to the mucklands of Kalamazoo. Van Haaften became a self-taught banker, performing every job from the ground up and taking every course he could. Light, Connable and the rest of the board liked his common sense, his savvy and his impeccable integrity.

"When Van moved up to chairman of the board in 1964, Harold Jacobson was elevated from the No. 2 post to the presidency. Jake also came up from the ranks at American National and had a great sense of humor. That was evident from the fun we had with the Barge on Gull Lake in the summers. It was Van and Jake who sold Charles Chase, president of Home Savings Bank, on joining American National, which also brought Glen Smith into the fold in 1963. That was a red-letter day."

That fall day in 1943 when Al Jr. came home for good

was also a red-letter day for Alfred Sr.

While Detroit Trust didn't prep him to step into the No. 1 slot at American National, the investment exposure in the Motor City made him more than the senior Connable's right-hand man back in Kalamazoo. He'd learn the ins and outs of accounting, taxation, bonds, securities and common sense.

"Our type of business is unique, especially in this community. You see plenty of corporate trustees these days, but not private trustees like our office. We found in a survey that most private fiduciaries comparable to our office are located in Boston, Philadelphia, New York and other older cities. They date back a number of generations, like ours. For us, it has worked out very well. Our clients seem to be

Affable Glen Smith accepts the first "de-paws-it" from Al's poodle Fauvette during the opening of the Crosstown Branch of the American National Bank.

135

very pleased and we are able to provide them with all the services that a trust company would in an environment that is a little more private and confidential.

"By 1960, The Connable Office had decided not to take on any new clients unless they were family-related to our existing accounts. We thought we could do a better job by staying small, and not following the growth patterns of trust departments at banks or trust companies. Our growth has been pretty much internal from the expansion of trusts already handled by our office and by the creation of new trusts by our old clients.

"Trusts aren't easy to understand. Under current law, one can plan for this generation and then several more generations ahead. The tax law permits that. You can place your property in a living trust and it can pass through the next generation, leaving the asset to whomever you choose as an income beneficiary. But at some point into the third generation, it must be distributed out of the trust.

"Many of the trusts we handle in the office have gone through this phase because of new levels of families from the original donors. As they come into their inherited property, they in turn create new trusts, naming our office as principals and trustees and starting a whole new series. This is what I mean by internal growth.

"Although we have remained small and private in nature, the staff had to grow to meet the increasing reporting and accounting regulations. We've been able to keep up and deliver even faster service. When I came back from Detroit Trust, I became only the third person in the office.

"I immediately went to work, sorted things out and began to establish new systems. For instance, securities were physically separated, with a safe-deposit box assigned for each trust. In the old days, one large box containing everybody's certificates was adequate. Accounting procedures were updated to be ready for surprise visits by federal auditors. That kept you on your toes and, as I said, I never had any problems with that."

The son also hit the rubber-chicken circuit, speaking before local banquets and groups much like he had done in his year with the OPA and as a Michigan regent. He explained the workings of the New York Stock Exchange and why its health was a barometer of the nation's economic vitality.

He stressed that investing was as American as college football on an autumn day, turkey on Thanksgiving, and voting for a president every four years. "Ownership of securities is open to everyone. The production worker on the automobile assembly line owning a few shares of General Motors or the farmer who has put some of his savings into Sears Roebuck stock is just as much a capitalist as the original founders of American industries."

Speculating in stocks and bonds, he told an audience of 250 in the Civic Auditorium in 1950, should never be a leap-before-you-look proposition. Such basic needs as home ownership, adequate insurance, government bonds and a savings account in a bank should be secured before one takes a plunge into the stock market. In advising a well-rounded investment portfolio, he told his listeners, "I am an investment counselor, not a tipster."

At another speaking engagement, he said: "The importance of being a conservative investor in handling one's own investments cannot be emphasized too strongly. It is the wise and safe way to proceed and reduces the possibilities of getting hurt when prices soar or dive."

Those who "play the market" keep track of such hedges, trends and shifts. It's a form of gambling and they get a rush out of the challenge, much like playing the horses. The rules are the same. If you can't afford to lose, then you can't afford to play. Others don't have the time, the talent, nor the interest in tracking the securities, yet they don't want their financial resources sitting idle. Connable frequently recommended the mutual-fund approach where the investments of thousands of people are pooled, thus spreading the risk. The funds are placed in the hands of trained money managers at a nominal cost to each shareholder. In some respects, that's how the Connable office functioned. "A client provides us with money to invest. In most cases, we are given a free hand to invest in the stock market, buy bonds, capitalize a new business, or purchase property. However, investment authority can be limited by request. For instance, if anybody is wedded to a particular stock, say Upjohn, he or she can specify in the trust instrument that the trustees must hold that stock. Or, on the buying side, he or she can specify that only government bonds can be purchased.

"A big part of our job is to analyze and plan the best type of portfolio for individuals, depending on such questions as whether they need more income, more capital gains or other factors. We decide on what percentage should be in stocks or in bonds, the kinds of stocks and bonds, and whether real-estate investments are producing ample yield. We also help clients decide how their income should be returned to them. Our fee system depends on the type of services we provide our clients, from clerical to the closing of an estate.

"Whether a trustee is given full or limited authority, the trust is a great convenience to the donor and the beneficiaries. It relieves them of many responsibilities — deciding what investments to make, filing complicated tax returns, bookkeeping, and auditing reviews.

"We are trust officers and some of us, as my father was, are attorneys, although we do not practice law. Our office also engages lawyers for drafting trust instruments, for appearing in probate court, and for representing our clients.

"From the days of the Peck brothers and my father, we have held these to be very personal matters, much like an attorney-client relationship. It may include making a judgment on buying a new car, or what steps to take to help a client's child who has a problem. We give a more complete service than you get from a corporate trustee.

"After four generations of contact with families, we are something of a staple, like an old and trusted piece of furniture. Children, because of their parents' experience, just expect us to be there when needed. An out-of-town client once told me that he thought the office was a money machine. He'd call up and out came the money.

"There are people in Kalamazoo who, because of family trusts and finances, have literally never worked a day in their lives because of self-generating income. In that way, the money hasn't helped them because they don't know what they are missing. Everything is too easy for them. At the other end of the spectrum, we have a client who doesn't want to appear wealthy. He is a hard worker who wants people to think he's poor. We are trying to get this fellow to enjoy his riches a little more. We don't have a psychiatrist on our staff. Maybe we should.

"One of our most important functions is to teach our clients to live within the limits of their budget, especially the younger ones who seem to need all kinds of help. In times of downturns in the economy, the office really gets into high gear. Yet it's the younger clients who seem to adapt better to recessions. Trusts supplement a person's earned income and earn honored status in a young person's family. Of course, they've never experienced anything like the early 1930s. Still existing are accounts that date to the Peck brothers, but some of the companies they helped start no longer exist.

"Our office has been quite conservative in the best sense of the word, which is in keeping with the general tone of the community. I'm pleased our office has been able to maintain a stream of steady growth, and that's been a great thing for Kalamazoo. Many good things have been done for the community through public service and through financial contributions by our office personnel and many of our clients. With younger clients, especially those whose parents were brought up here, the importance of getting involved in community activities is encouraged. In adding people to our staff, we have recruited those who expressed great interest in being active in civic, cultural, educational and corporate affairs.

"My father was very anxious to have my brother, Harold, return to Kalamazoo and join the office. But that was the last thing that Hal wanted to do. Hal told me, 'If Dad makes it tough, I don't know what I'm going to do. I really love what I'm doing.' At the time, he was working in production for the Monroe Calculating Machine Co. in Orange, N. J., with the intention of going into sales. I finally convinced my father that Hal would be miserable if he came home and that would impact negatively on the family business.

"That stance helped our recruiting. If Hal had come, despite his wishes, I could have never recruited a man of the quality of Mike Hindert to a relatively small office in Kalamazoo where the boss and two sons were already ahead of him. It was Mike who conducted that national sur-

Mike Hindert joined the Connable team in 1948.

140

vey to find similar situations to ours so that we might exchange ideas and procedures. He only found a few old-time firms that could be called private fiduciaries like ourselves."

As the first non-family member in a leadership position, Hindert joined the Connable investment house in June of 1948, fresh from his graduation from Michigan's law school. The credentials of Hindert, who was born and raised in Holland, Mich., included a 1941 engineering degree from Michigan. After three years in the U.S. Navy's submarine service from 1942 to 1945, he returned to Ann Arbor to study law.

A decade after Hindert joined the Kalamazoo office,

James Hilboldt joined the firm in 1958 following graduation from the U of M Law School.

James Hilboldt came from the same resource, followed by still another U of M Law School clone, James Westin. The Ann Arbor link was broken with the arrival of Richard Shumar and David Kruis, certified public accountant graduates from Western Michigan University, which was acceptable because by that time Connable had served on the WMU Board of Trustees. A third C.P.A., Jerry Love, came from Notre Dame, which makes the office an interesting place during the football season. The U of M connection was later restored with the addition of Jamie Melvin, who brought three degrees — in law, engineering and business — from the Ann Arbor campus. Now that's what you really call a triple-threat man.

Another U of M graduate, James Westin, became a partner in the Connable office.

Connable remembered the valuable lessons he'd learned during his days at Detroit Trust. As he recruited the future of "The Connable Office," he suggested the prospects experience working with investment houses in Detroit and, while in law school, branch out to take courses in estate planning and business administration. Hindert and Hilboldt followed that advice.

The pages of American business history are full of sad sagas where successful fathers forced their sons to follow in their entrepreneurial footsteps, leading to the emotional demise of the progeny and a flood of red ink for the venture. However, there have been significant exceptions.

"Neither of my sons took to finance, nor did my daugh-

**Partner Jerry Love, a graduate of Notre Dame,
defends the fighting Irish during football season.**

ter for that matter. Like their mother, they leaned toward the fine arts — theater, music and writing. What I had advised my father about regarding my younger brother was the advice I also had to follow with my family. But The Upjohn Co. is an example where what I guess you can call nepotism worked. Much of that success is due to Donald Gilmore. He was almost uncanny in his selection of members of the Upjohn and Gilmore families for the right positions.

"In that same regard, I'm not worried about the office curling up its heels and disappearing when I do. It is well-structured and operating on all cylinders. I'm semi-retired and only a consultant, but the office is moving along in fine shape. I have the utmost confidence in the people in charge.

"I was the third generation. I think the fourth and the fifth are locks."

WHERE THERE'S A WILLKIE, THERE'S A WAY INTO POLITICS

Al Connable's first leap into political waters ended in a drowning when he failed to win a 1939 bid to become one of the Republican Party's two candidates for the University of Michigan Board of Regents.

But that foray built a strong base of support for the member of the board of governors of the Michigan Club of Detroit, and he'd swim the next time to victory.

There was a political gene or two in Al's DNA. His father served two terms as mayor of Kalamazoo and a great uncle on his mother's side of the family, Julius Caesar Burrows, had been sent to Washington as a congressman from 1889 to 1895 and then as a U.S. senator from Michigan from 1895 to 1911.

"I was a guinea-pig prospect in 1939. The Republican Party in the late 1930s had a political-boss, old-guard system that — there's no other way to say it — was corrupt as hell. That's what happens when the public doesn't pay attention to voting and lets things kind of drift off."

A reform group organized and one of its Grand Rapids leaders was Gerald Ford's stepfather, which is how Connable's fraternity brother later got involved in politics after World War II. Another supporter of the Young Guard was State Sen. James Milliken, whose son, William, was destined to serve as governor of Michigan.

"Alumni in Detroit and Ann Arbor asked if I would be willing to throw my hat in the ring at the party's convention in early 1939. I was still at the Detroit Trust and commuting daily from our home in Ann Arbor so I had contact with both camps — Michigan alumni in Detroit and friends of the university on the home campus. The group's feeling was that the current board of regents seemed rather aloof and remote, out of touch, so to speak. Nothing wrong with age because I'm there myself, but the consensus was that it was time to turn the controls over to some younger blood. I

145

Al's Great Uncle Julius Caesar Burrows served as a powerful Republican U.S. Senator at the turn of the century.

was asked to run and, after thinking it over carefully, agreed.

"At the time, reformists in the Republican Party were challenging the well-entrenched establishment. For years, it had been practically impossible for anyone outside the machine to run for state office because the bosses had strong control over the more-populated counties. Delegations from Wayne, Oakland, Genesee and Kent counties always controlled the nomination of candidates and swung the Republican state conventions. On the east side of the state, reform leaders like Fred Alger (later

Michigan secretary of state) and Wilbur Brucker (governor of Michigan from 1930 to 1932 and Secretary of Army under President Dwight Eisenhower) were among those who wanted me as a sacrificial lamb.

"What made me willing was that in Grand Rapids, the home base of the reigning bossman, Frank D. McKay, some prominent Republicans surfaced to oppose this kind of tight, strangling control. Joining Jerry Ford's stepfather were Paul Goebel (later mayor of Grand Rapids and a U of M regent himself), (insurance executive) Jack Hibbard, (industrialist and Michigan classmate) Fred Vogt, (industrialist) Dave Hunting, and Dorothy Judd (a highly respected community activist)."

Included in Connable's "young lions" camp were two prominent Ann Arborites, Eugene and Sadye Power, who he got to know during his undergraduate days. Their support crossed party lines and helped build Connable's base. "When Gene later ran for the board of regents as a Democrat, I supported him. Because our terms overlapped, we had the chance to work together on many important projects and issues."

The state convention that year was held in Flint and, according to the ways of boss politics, McKay summoned me as one of the young turks who had the audacity to oppose the mainline slate.

"I was escorted to his hotel room and he said to me, `Young man, you look like a nice fellow. We'll remember you next time.' Well, my supporters had been lobbying the convention and advised me that `next time' was right now. A student-based `Connable for Regent' committee had been extremely active. Clark MacKenzie, chairman of the Kalamazoo County delegation, placed my name in nomination and Ralph Heikkinen, an All-American football player at Michigan, seconded it.

"Although we didn't win that time — the vote at the January convention was something like 300 to 800 against me — the spirited opposition was a jolt to the machine. The show of strength encouraged the anti-boss faction to con-

147

tinue building its organization across the state for another run at it in two years."

The second time was a winning plunge, as illustrated by this campaign rhetoric: "Elect a vigorous young man (he was 37) to the Board of Regents, whose loyalty to his state and university has never been challenged. Elect a militant, liberal young Republican, who believes in the sound principle of American self-government, in the doctrine of higher education for those who seek it in our great university — opportunity for all, special favors for none."

This time, he was easily nominated by fellow Republicans at the party convention and in statewide balloting that spring, Connable was elected to the university's board of regents. In those days, Michigan's educational and judicial elections were held in the spring and the legislative races were staged in November as they are now. His Republican runningmate, Earl L. Burhams, a state legislator

Al and his running mate, Earl L. Burhams from Paw Paw, won election to the Board of Regents in 1941.

from Paw Paw, also was elected to the Michigan governing board.

When he was sworn into office in January of 1942, there really wasn't all that much to celebrate because the sting of Pearl Harbor was still burning in the psyche of every American.

"One of the first items of business was to determine how the university could convert its resources to the war effort. A regents war committee was formed and I was one of the three members, later serving as chair. The first step was a comprehensive study of the ways each of our colleges could best assist with the war effort. Our administration seemed a little slow at first to respond, but later in 1942, things moved faster. Two of the measures included the medical school's overseas unit and the law school's judge-advocate program.

"Our board had both Republican and Democratic members. Two Democrats were Jack Lynch, a Detroit attorney, and Ed Shields, a lawyer from Lansing who also served on the Democratic National Committee. In war time, one couldn't tell the difference between a Democrat and a Republican. But that was the case most of the time during my two terms and 16 years as a regent. All the members were interested in the welfare of the university, not partisan politics."

One of the idiosyncrasies of University of Michigan governance is that the president of the university serves as the board chair and is an ex-officio member. No other college or university in the state operates under that proviso. Connable saw no problems or conflicts with that modus operandi during his regency.

With successful status as a university regent came a degree of clout in the Michigan Republican Party, which is how he struck up a friendship with Wendell Lewis Willkie.

Willkie, he of the unkempt hair and constantly hoarse speaking voice, was an Indiana-born lawyer whose affiliation with privately held utilities elevated him to a leadership

149

Al served as a regent with U of M President Alexander Ruthven. (ca. 1945)

role in the opposition to President Roosevelt's Tennessee Valley Authority, a federal power project.

Born in Elwood, Ind., in 1892, Willkie launched a law career in 1916 with a diploma from Indiana University hanging on his wall. Like the Burdick boys, he was swept up in American patriotism and served overseas during World War I, attaining the rank of captain in the U.S. Army. After more than a decade as an attorney in Akron, Ohio, and with a law firm in New York City where Connable first met him on business trips, Willkie became president of the Commonwealth and Southern Corp, a utility holding company. He was on a collision course with FDR's New Deal.

Willkie, then 48, captured the Republicans' 1940 presidential nomination to challenge Roosevelt's bid for a third

Wendell Willkie campaigned in Kalamazoo in 1939 prior to his GOP nomination.

151

term. While he was avalanched in electoral votes (449-82), Willkie did capture 22.3 million votes compared to FDR's 27.2 million. With America's entrance into the war, Willkie, too, threw down his party's colors and picked up the red, white and blue, declaring total support for Roosevelt.

"Wendell did a good enough job that many Republicans wanted him to take another shot in 1944. I became interested in his candidacy. He still seemed like a refreshing choice to a war-weary Roosevelt. I asked if I could help out, and was named chairman of the Willkie for President Campaign in Michigan in early 1943. Although I was still in Ann Arbor at the time, having taken a leave of absence from Detroit Trust to work for the U.S. Office of Price Administration, I managed to line up some good people locally — Mark Putney, Charles Monroe, and others We had good people, including many of my supporters, all over the state, including my brother, H. P., and his wife, who were living in Detroit at the time.

"In that capacity, I saw quite a bit of Wendell. FDR was enough of a formidable challenge without obstacles inside the Republican Party. Wendell in effect had to run outside the fold and build his own organization because he didn't have the solid support of mainline Republicans.

"Wendell finally pulled out of the 1944 campaign, which disappointed a lot of good, hard-working people in Michigan because we had him set up for all kinds of speeches and appearances. He called me with the news from Omaha. He cited non-support of his candidacy. I challenged his decision. After all, we had youth and fire and determination. We could win this thing. He stuck to his guns in spite of our disappointment."

In effect, Willkie had become a member of the "if-you-can't-beat-`em-join-`em" camp as an influential spokesman for Roosevelt's war policies, which offended Republican hard-liners. Some shunned him as he traveled as Roosevelt's semi-official envoy to China, the Soviet Union and other allied nations. Willkie described his experiences and his opinions about global peace in a highly acclaimed book, "One World," published in 1943.

"It's always enlightening to touch elbows with an ideal. Wendell lifted all of us with his idealism. I doubted that any of us regretted for a minute the hard work we put in supporting his cause. Idealists are threatening to the status quo."

That conversion to internationalization did him no good with staunchly isolationist Republicans. Willkie dropped out of presidential contention possibly because of a premonition. He died in 1944. The GOP's standard bearer in the attempt to prevent FDR's fourth term was Connable's old choir mate, Tom Dewey, who managed to poll 20 million votes, less than Willkie's total four years earlier.

Connable had moved back home to Kalamazoo by the time he sought renomination to a second term on the Michigan board in early 1949. He agreed with the remarks delivered at the Kalamazoo County Republican Party's pre-primary convention by MacKenzie, who had been a party activist for nearly a half century and had placed Connable's name in nomination a decade earlier. MacKenzie's message was basically the same — that the caliber of the party's leaders was not keeping pace with the quality of Republican principles.

"The principal things we need are a revitalization of the party and new leaders," MacKenzie said. "When we have state leaders under whom the party loses 500,000 votes in two years, something is wrong. We have been lulled to sleep. It is time we assumed our own responsibility. With revitalization and new leadership, we can win back the state in 1950 and we can win back the nation in 1952."

Much of MacKenzie's hoped-for metamorphosis came about as Michigan Republicans convened in Grand Rapids in February of 1949. While Connable had been in office for eight years, he was still regarded as new blood and was again selected as a party standard bearer.

"By then Jerry Ford had graduated from the Yale Law School, served in the Navy and was home in Grand Rapids with Phil Buchen as a law partner. Phil had supported my first candidacy while he was at Michigan's law school. Jerry and I belonged to the same fraternity and honorary societies. The 1949 convention was much different than the

Vote April 1st

REGENT UNIVERSITY OF MICHIGAN
Al's campaign poster from the mid 1950s.

1941 affair. Jerry's stepfather was chairman of the Kent County delegation and anti-boss groups were in control. Jerry had announced his candidacy for a first term in Congress and won a solid endorsement. He was on his way to the White House."

Connable had built some prestigious credentials to again warrant statewide support from voters. With the dawning of the 1950s, the university's assets had crested $100 million and enrollment stood at 22,000, according to newspaper reports. Al also had a friendly face on the governing board — Ralph Hayward, president of the KVP Co. in Parchment.

Connable's peers across the nation had elected him president of the Association of Governing Boards of State Universities and Allied Institutions, an organization that drew membership from regents and trustees of more than 100 publicly supported universities and colleges in the United States. The association could trace its conception to Ann Arbor and the 1920 inauguration of Marion Burton as Michigan's president. Regent Julius Beal suggested the confederation when trustees from across the country gathered for the ceremony.

"I served from Pearl Harbor to Sputnik. I served when our country converted to war for a fight to the death, during the conversion back to peace, and the arrival of a different kind of a struggle — the Cold War. I saw faculty and staff leave for battle and I saw the advent of all kinds of specialized programs. Many who answered their country's call never came back to campus, but those who did returned highly motivated. Their eyes had been opened to new opportunities. They had a better idea of what the world was all about. It was the university's job to help them grasp those opportunities."

The prime resource that helped the University of Michigan and other colleges meet the veterans' needs was the G.I. Bill of Rights. Along with heavy corporate investment and high rates of unionism, the G. I. Bill of Rights was in the package of generous federal assistance (public-works projects, student loans and housing subsidies) that gave young families a jumpstart, created predictable paths out of poverty, and led to unprecedented increases in real wages.

All of these factors, acting together, is what made the 1950s "the good old days." They should also be known as "the good old unique days" because it is doubtful whether all of those forces will ever simultaneously reach critical mass again. They hadn't before in the two-century history of the United States and likely will never again.

"The G. I. Bill was probably the most effective piece of legislation ever enacted by the federal government. When the G. I. Bill was adopted, people at universities wondered what kind of students military men would be. They were conscientious, they knew exactly what they were doing, and they excelled.

"Professors never had to work so hard before in their lives. These weren't 18-year-old kids fresh out of high school they were facing. They were battle-scarred veterans who couldn't be buffaloed. They'd been shot at and faced death. These people had something to say in their essays, they knew how to communicate, and they weren't afraid to say it. They pushed the professors, and most of the instructors liked the challenge."

Those prognosticators who predicted that the sirens of battle had also tolled the death of American higher education turned out to be the ones who were dead wrong. The influx was unparalleled. From this flood of talent and broad experience would come Michael Hindert, destined to be the first non-family member of The Connable Office.

"At Michigan, we underestimated the flood of students who enrolled after World War II. We got thousands more than we planned for, including those who were married, had families and required special housing. There weren't enough chairs in the classrooms and beds in the dorms. Some bivouacked in gymnasiums. They slept wherever they could find a place. We embarked on a massive expan-

U of M President Harlan Hatcher (seated on left) and his Board of Regents in the late 1940s.

sion of the physical plant and of the faculty because enrollment was in the process of doubling.

"When Roscoe Bonisteel, one of the regents who lived in Ann Arbor, suggested that we extend the campus to the north, we all agreed to that wisdom, as did President Harlan Hatcher. That move brought in several hundred acres across the Huron River and gave the university ample room for growth because trend studies predicted college enrollment around the state would double by 1970. It was similar to the two-campus approach at Western that required coordinated transportation and classroom scheduling.

"The Ann Arbor Trust Co. had pioneered a self-liquidating financing plan that was copied by other financial institutions and colleges throughout the country. It sold bonds that were secured by the revenue from student fees. The system had been used at Michigan in the 1930s prior to the war, but came into practice big time after the war. When I served on the Western board years later, Ann Arbor Trust was recognized as a leader in the field and we used it for our campus projects."

In addition to bonding, Michigan depended heavily on the generosity of alumni to support building projects. Connable's early mentor, Horace Rackham, stepped forward as a philanthropist to build a new home for graduate studies. The student union, the library, and the law school had strong alumni support. But these were not organized fund drives per se as private colleges had been staging. One of Michigan's first came during Connable's first term. The Phoenix Project was launched to find peaceful uses for atomic energy.

The Connable years also saw the establishment of the School of Social Work and a commitment to explaining the function of organized labor. "Professors traveled to communities such as Kalamazoo and taught courses for union members. Right-wingers thought we were encouraging unionism, but that wasn't the purpose. I was also on a committee charged with evaluating whether beer should be sold in the Michigan Union to students of age. I visited the University of Wisconsin where the practice was well-entrenched on campus. To me, there were as many pop bottles on the tables in the student union as there were beer bottles. I favored it, but the majority didn't want to fight that battle in the 1950s."

Connable's direct connection with the governing board overlapped the heralded era of Fritz Crisler, Michigan's legendary coach and athletic director. "Because the athletic fund is separate from the general fund, we had little official contact with Fritz, except that he always came before the board with plans to expand the football stadium and to improve the other athletic facilities. He wanted general approval.

"I'll say one thing about Crisler. He never saw a hand that he didn't want to shake. That's why he was always so successful in finding support for Michigan athletics. He was an athletic statesman."

During the second term, the regents were charged with finding a successor for the retiring president, Alexander Ruthven. Instead of hiring a head-hunting firm as is the practice today, the regents assumed the responsibility.

"The board acted as the selection committee because the regents had the final responsibility. We did all of the work. We invited suggestions from alumni, faculty, students and friends of the university. All were welcome to pass on ideas. There was a limited expense budget and the whole process took well over one year. Interviews were conducted with candidates in conjunction with business trips that regents made in their private lives. Each regent would then report back to the full board.

"We narrowed the field to three or four candidates and selected Harlan Hatcher, who got the most votes among the finalists. Sure, he was an Ohio State man, but Michigan has found some of its best football coaches down there. Why not a president? My first choice was our provost, Jim Adams. Even though I didn't vote for Harlan on the first ballot, when he was selected I went to him and pledged my total fealty, which I unfailingly gave whenever we were in agreement.

"The biggest job of a regent or any policymaker is to stay out of the administration's hair. It took me a little time to realize that. The primary function is to set policy. Prior to that, the No. 1 task is to pick the best president you can find and let him run the school. If he's no good, fire him and find somebody else.

"Harlan had some problems. Everybody does. One of them was getting along with John Hannah, the president of Michigan State. They got together too infrequently to my way of thinking. Paul Sangren, president of Western, was responsible for one of the exchanges when the Council of State College Presidents met in Kalamazoo. Good for Paul.

"Some of the antagonism was rooted when Michigan State staged a campaign to change its name from college to university. I can understand why Paul took it upon himself to bring them together. Personally, I never regarded the name change as such a big problem nor something to worry about as my colleagues did. They thought the world was going to change. Ridiculous and preposterous scenarios were posed. The universities would get each other's mail. Hogwash. I thought a little competition between the universities would be a good thing, and it has been.

"The Michigan Legislature sometimes enters arenas where it doesn't belong. For instance, the University of Michigan has an excellent pharmaceutical program while Ferris State has the largest. But each is very different from the other. Ferris' program appeals to those who want to work as pharmacists in drug stores. Michigan appeals more to the researchers, people that companies such as Upjohn pursue. Lawmakers couldn't figure that out when it came to state appropriations and other regulations."

Often a lone wolf in addressing issues, Connable had nothing but a fortress of support in opposition to a change in the requirements for certifying K-12 classroom teachers that was being heralded in Lansing in early 1956. What sounded like a good idea — the beefing up of training in teacher-education courses — was being piggybacked with something that didn't enthrall universities and those interested in quality teaching. The boost could only be accomplished by the corresponding decrease of studies in a teacher's particular field or major. Could better teachers be produced by increasing professional training at the expense of subject matter? Or was the foundation of effective teaching rooted in sound knowledge of subject matter?

Connable, representing his university, was joined by Kalamazoo College president Weimer Hicks, WMU representatives and the head of the local chapter of the American Chemical Society in soundly trashing the proposed revisions.

Also making a statement was his old "west-end gang" cohort, Dr. Richard U. Light, who had grown up to become a world traveler, brain surgeon and college administrator. He was skeptical about whether the ability to teach can be cultivated in a lecture hall. "Skills in the medical profession are achieved to best advantage by practical experience in the operating room," he said. "You simply can't acquire skills by talking about them. You do them."

Light's son, Timothy, took time out from his studies as a senior at University High School in Kalamazoo for some podium duty during the public hearing sponsored by the State Board of Education. "Good teachers are very well versed in their subject matter," he testified. "Students have little respect for teachers who do not know their subject matter."

Lansing calling the policy-making shots for all public colleges and universities in the state was and still is anathema for the man who served 16 years as a regent.

"What our state must keep away from is a super governing board that regulates all colleges and universities and from which everything is allocated from on high down to the individual campuses. Many states have such a super-board system. They often look in admiration at how the state of Michigan does it. My attitude and perspective on this issue was formed during my presidency on that national association of governing boards. We benefitted from each's backgrounds and experiences.

"Our state's system of individual governing boards has become a national model. Prior to the adoption of Michigan's new state constitution, Western Michigan, Eastern Michigan, Central Michigan and Northern Michigan universities were all operated under one board that had only three members. Now each has its own board of trustees that can concentrate on one university.

"The super-board idea sounds great, but it doesn't serve the individual institutions well. They all depend on the legislature for financial support. In return, the lawmakers want to know that their appropriations are being judiciously spent. They can be reassured that in the vast majority of cases, university and college presidents do that under the policy-making power of these individual, diverse governing boards."

As a Republican activist, Connable was always preaching about the need for new vitality, new attitudes and new perspectives. In his keynote address as chairman of the Kalamazoo County Republican Party Convention in 1957, he said:

"There are certain facts about our party that give me concern. . . In this day and age, voters easily recognize cheap political tricks. They will get us nowhere. We will profit in the long run by forgetting immediate advantage won by demagoguery, by not playing up to sensationalism, and by not doing those things that will get us a few votes at the expense of the welfare of the people of this nation.

"Let us ask ourselves, `What is good for Michigan?' and `What is good for our nation?' and even `What is good for mankind?' And then set our sights in those directions. If we do that, people will respect us and will give us their support. But if we simply seek partisan advantage, we will lose out in the long run."

162

More than a few local, state and national elections might have been salvaged by Republicans over the years if the Connable way had been the platform's main plank. Be that as it may, Michigan voters didn't buy his message this time and the senior member of the Michigan Board of Regents was defeated for re-election in April of 1957. So was the other Republican candidate in an avalanche show of public support for Democratic Gov. G. Mennen Williams and his party.

At his final meeting in December of 1957, fellow regents cited Connable's service: "He had great admiration for the autonomy of the board as a constitutional corporation and took pride in explaining this concept to others, particularly to such groups as the Association of Governing Boards of State Universities and Allied Institutions."

The Kalamazooan responded in spades:

"It is never easy to say goodbye to old friends, or to terminate a labor of love of 16 years to one's alma mater. . .My term of office has been a thrilling experience for which I shall always be grateful. I was a freshman regent when President Ruthven and our board successfully converted the university to the defense of our country. As I leave the 1957 board, our learned scientists, mobilized by the timely call of President Hatcher, are giving us glimpses of the universe.

"The speed and initiative with which President Hatcher and the regents have acted to probe the educational implications of this epochal breakthrough (Sputnik), augur well for the future leadership of our university. . .I have visited many campuses and met educational administrators from most parts of the country. I have also visited a number of universities abroad. At the risk of complacency, I feel that Michigan's administration in ability, imagination, character and understanding has few peers. . .

"It takes time to realize, and I am still learning, what makes a university really great — the students, the faculty, the administration, the governing board, the environmental traditions? I have learned that true distinction can stem from one or all of these components of university life.

"But the solid base that permits such distinction at Michigan is the constitutional corporation — its mandate that gives complete responsibility for the affairs of the university to the board of regents, and the protection it has afforded the university, over the years, from political interference.

"As a result. Michigan has gradually evolved those intangible values essential to true educational greatness — a liberal tradition of faculty and student expression, a stimulating environment for scholarly exploration, and a responsiveness to the needs of the people. As I see them, those are the all-important values to be preserved and nourished in the years ahead."

Carl Brablec, one of the Democrats who unseated Connable, had mixed emotions about the outcome of the election, expressing a non-partisanship that the Kalamazoo regent had mentioned early in his first tenure.

"Displacing a man like Al Connable weighs you down," said Brablec, the 48-year-old superintendent of schools in the Detroit suburb of Roseville and a political unknown who was placed on the ballot as part of the slate of Gov. G. Mennen Williams. It was Brablec's first venture into state politics since an unsuccessful bid for the Michigan House of Representatives in Lenawee County in 1936.

Calling Connable an "outstanding regent," Brablec said, "he has established himself, has a rich background of experience, is very capable, and has a liberal record. You just wish a person like that didn't have to leave the scene of the action, but it presents a challenge to us."

When Gov. Williams scheduled a meeting in July of 1957 of members of the governing boards of colleges and universities in the state, Connable and the other "lame duck" Republican regent were not on the invitation list even though they still had about six months to serve before leaving office.

Possibly at issue was a reported breach between the

board of regents and the governor in union with key Democratic lawmakers over the control and amount of funds to operate the university. Was it politics as usual or an unintentional error in the governor's office in Lansing? Gov. Williams issued a statement hoping that the error would be rectified.

Commented Connable: "I am very appreciative of the governor's statement. I fully understand that such an over-

Al (center front row) is shown at his 1925 graduation from the U of M.

sight would be very easy to make in the press of business in Lansing." If the invitation was forthcoming, he'd determine at that time whether his schedule allowed him to make the July meeting in Gaylord. The invitation came and Connable, ever the affable warrior who didn't hold grudges, attended and offered his best services.

Besides, Connable would never be "done" with the University of Michigan. Beginning with his father's graduation in 1894, his own in 1925, and having 20 family members part of the Ann Arbor scene, it would be impossible to sever the maize-and-blue umbilical cord.

Granted emeritus status in 1960, he often represented the institution that was flexing its muscles even more with extended doctoral programs and research initiatives. The steady drumbeat to those making state appropriations, to alumni and to funding agencies was that for every dollar it took for freshman-sophomore instructions, it took two at the next two levels. The dollar had to be multiplied four times for graduate and professional work.

There was a high cost for Michigan's academic reputation at the master's and doctorate levels — advanced study called for smaller classes, closer personal supervision, elaborate equipment, extensive libraries, and experienced teachers. Connable and fellow Michigan classmate E. Gifford Upjohn, then chairman of the board of The Upjohn Co., were appointed to a national executive committee charged with raising $55 million as part of "The Phoenix Project." At that time, the target was the largest ever undertaken by a tax-assisted university and its culmination was timed to coincide with the university's 150th anniversary in 1967.

So Connable was not exactly echoing Gen. Douglas MacArthur's self-intoned "swan song" about old soldiers slowly fading away. He was hanging around and would live to serve again, this time at a university in his home town.

TANGLING WITH TAILGUNNER JOE

Allegiance to the Republican Party has always been a source of pride to Al Connable.

A true believer? Definitely! A blind follower? Never! He tangled with U.S. Sen. Joseph McCarthy when the Wisconsin Republican went on a witch hunt to eradicate the influence of the Communist Party in American higher education.

From his base as a University of Michigan regent, Connable had been elected president of the Association of Governing Boards of State Universities and Allied Institutions. In that capacity, he told an audience in 1949: "There is no more loyal group of people in America than the students and faculty on university campuses. Of course, there are some pinkos, but then there are lots of reactionaries, too."

He observed McCarthy attracting national attention in early 1950 with charges that the U.S. State Department had been infiltrated by members of the Communist Party. McCarthy later leveled broadsides at the secretary of the army, accusing all his targets of subversive activities, none of which was ever substantiated.

Known as "Tailgunner Joe" during his World War II service in the Marine Corps, McCarthy had returned to his home state, practiced law and was elected a circuit judge. From that political and super-patriotic base, he was elected to the Senate in 1946 and gained a second six-year term in 1952.

As chairman of the Senate subcommittee on investigations, McCarthy adopted a "They're everywhere, they're everywhere" mentality during his second term. He claimed that the Red Plague had pandemically infected the U.S. military and college campuses.

One of his blistering broadsides was delivered at Connable's beloved University of Michigan. As George C.

Scott said in his Oscar-winning performance as Gen. George Patton after a German fighter plane strafed his headquarters: "By God, that's enough!"

"McCarthy was a pretty vicious fellow. He was attacking people I knew at the university. They weren't communists, for goodness sakes. He was persecuting, often by innuendo, some of our top professors in the press and he subpoenaed them for hearings in Detroit.

"Three were targeted to be communists. They were all examined thoroughly by a special committee of the University Senate. Its members included law professors and some of the most prestigious members of the faculty as

**Sen Joseph McCarthy had need to mop his brow
after tangling with Al Connable.**

well as administrative appointees. The committee spent an entire summer reviewing McCarthy's findings and reached different conclusions in two of the cases. The committee suggested that one be dropped, another be put on probation, and that charges against the third were groundless.

"McCarthy always painted with a broad brush. What about a faculty member who might have dabbled in communism as a youth but who changed his mind with the passage of time and thus became an even better instructor?

"Political pressure was put on the regents to fire all three. I took exception to that. I spent a long time reading those detailed reports and agreed with the committee's recommendations.

"I thought the least I could do was to register my objections and I did. Many of my fellow regents didn't feel all that strongly opposed to McCarthy's tactics and would have preferred that I not go public. I felt good about it. I had the strength to do it because I knew those faculty members. I certainly knew them better than he did. On principle, I wanted to stand with the faculty whether our other regents did or not. In the end, I think my stand had a blunting effect on some of McCarthy's unfair attacks."

In the wake of his testimony at McCarthy's hearings, Connable later presented a speech to the Association of Governing Boards at its 31st annual meeting in Florida. He warned that academic freedom on college campuses was being threatened by the tactics of the Wisconsin Republican and called for his peers to take a stand. In a country that supposedly stood for freedom of speech, there have been chapters of ugly repression, he noted, including incidents of university presidents and college professors being fired for their stand on "free silver."

"The freedom of opinion that we treasure so greatly," Connable said in his remarks in December of 1953, "includes freedom of inquiry — freedom to teach and freedom to learn, freedom to question, to disagree, to challenge. It's in the schools (at all levels) that the habits of thought must be learned and the practice acquired that can enable our people to live and work together in a free society. And it is our institutions of education that would be the first to be seized and controlled by those who would impose conformity on our people and dictate their opinions."

He discussed the tight rope that a university must walk, making certain that it does not destroy the fabric of a democracy's defense against treason and overthrow, while protecting the treasured rights of freedoms so that citizens can express their opinions without fear of punishment or sanctions. That's a fine balancing act. He delivered some strong words that McCarthy, if he had heard them, would have painted Connable in a reddish hue.

"The federal government has no business defining the subject matter that shall be taught, the students who shall be taught, or the teachers who shall do the teaching in our colleges and universities," he said, specifying that his caveat stretched across the executive and legislative branches. He acknowledged that such questions and issues are complex, requiring mature and expert judgment. . ."all the more reason why the federal government should not make those decisions or dictate the answers."

While Connable said he firmly believed there was no more loyal group of citizens in America than college professors, he recognized that even the House Un-American Activities Committee was duly authorized and constituted. When it targeted the University of Michigan as one of its targets for investigation, it behooved the administration, the board of regents, and the faculty to cooperate as best they could.

Circling the wagons, they also bonded together in a united front so as to retain as much control over the process as possible. He told his listeners that the only other time there is such unity on campus is on football Saturdays when the Wolverines take the field.

While there were no "rifts in the official family," Connable admitted to his Florida audience that "we slipped badly in one respect. We forgot the students and that, I think, was a mistake. They wanted to know what it was all about. The president intended to give them a full explanation, but in the rush of things just never got around to it. I think we are all to blame in that respect. So they blew off a little bit in the Michigan Daily and we got a few headlines around the state. If they had understood it I think they would have taken quite a different attitude. Steps are being taken to correct that situation and to have better communications with them"

Whether his colleagues on governing boards heeded his message or not, broadcast journalist Edward R. Murrow finally did, sprinkling enough water on the wicked witch hunter of the North to have him melt from the national spotlight.

The tables were eventually turned on McCarthy by his fellow politicos, who started using some of his own tactics on "Tailgunner Joe." He was cleared of charges brought against him but was censured by the Senate for the methods he had used in his investigations and for his abuse of certain senators and the Senate-committee system. Although he remained in the U.S. Senate until his death in 1957 at the age of 48, his clout on the political scene had the strength of well-done spaghetti.

In the year of McCarthy's death, Connable was asked to speak before the Kalamazoo County Republican Party. He said:

". . .We must stop baiting important elements in the electorate. We aren't going to win elections by conducting a crusade against organized labor, for example. We want the labor vote. We need it. And we must stand for the things that will merit our support by labor. That doesn't mean we must kow-tow to everything the labor leaders want. But we must listen to them, and we must at least try not to drive them into the other party."

That rather liberal perspective often put him at loggerheads with the party and university establishment.

"What used to bother me was the business about hon-

Al suggested Walter Reuther for a U of M honorary doctorate.

orary degrees," he says. "At Michigan, they always gave them to captains of industry or to some great intellectual thinker. They always ignored the leaders of organized labor."

To Connable, Walter Reuther, as president of the United Auto Workers and a leader in the merger of the AFL-CIO, had the credentials for receiving an honorary doctorate from the University of Michigan. That was not a popular suggestion, it turned out.

"According to Joe McCarthy, Reuther was also a communist. That's because he had been to Russia, working in an auto factory for two years. To Joe, if you went to Russia, you were a commie. My father visited Russia and he wasn't a communist.

"I asked the university administration for a list of the people who had received honorary degrees over the previous years. They were all captains of industry, with a few professors spread around. I made the suggestion that we recognize a labor leader who had made a real dent in the relations with industry."

His motion did not receive a ringing endorsement from fellow regents. But the next time he offered Reuther's name, an election had been held and the board had some new blood. "Walter was approved very easily and now the university is very proud of its actions."

Another of his prospects for an honorary was also initially discouraged. This one was intended for a 1936 graduate of the University of Michigan, playwright Arthur Miller who had won top awards for his work even while still a student on the Ann Arbor campus.

"In both instances, I received solid support from across party lines. My good friend and fellow regent, Gene Power, who was a Democrat, helped me instigate these honoraries. Gene served with distinction, and so has his son, Phil, who took Gene's place on the board. Phil brought the knowledge of a career in newspapers with him and that's wonderful, broad-minded experience."

At the time, Miller was in the national spotlight, not for his 1949 Pulitzer Prize-winning play, "Death of a Salesman," nor for an equally acclaimed 1953 drama, "The Crucible." Headlines were linking him romantically with Marilyn Monroe.

"The university wasn't interested in that kind of publicity. Plus, Miller had been to Russia, too, which made him a communist, right? Miller's plays are intensely concerned with the moral responsibility of every man to his fellowmen. They are written in a simple colloquial style, and have provided influential commentary on the moral and political problems of the 20th century. My gosh, why shouldn't we honor such achievement? But I pushed it through and, again, the university today is very proud of the fact Miller was given an honorary and is a distinguished alumnus of Michigan.

"When we contacted him about the degree, he was on

his way from the West Coast to meet Marilyn in New York City. For whatever reason, I never saw a guy who was so serious instead of being happy. Most fellows envied the heck out of him."

Al at about the time he tangled with Joe McCarthy.

A CALCULATED MOVE

The likes of Samuel Morse and Marcese Guglielmo Marconi were at the root of it. The wizards who helped break the German and Japanese codes during World War II propelled it, and the Information Age is the result of it.

Electronic computing — be it compiling, warehousing or providing words, numbers or bits of information quickly and accurately — is making "It a Small, Small, Small, Small World" as Hollywood once proclaimed in one of its more madcap comedies.

When these hybrids of electronic and mechanical ingenuity began to make their presence felt in the 1940s and early 1950s, one of the contraptions could just about fit in a two-car garage. Today, as society races pell-mell toward a new millennium, computers the size of a new-born babe's fingernail are routine, and they are getting smaller.

Yet, a half century ago, the smirks on the faces of those who ran businesses such as the Monroe Calculating Machine Co. would be understandable and condoned. After all, one of their mechanical marvels was small enough to fit in a shoebox. Who'd want a computerized calculator that needed to be hauled in by the truckloads?

While Al Connable has anecdotes about many of the companies he served, his connection with Monroe remains special for a couple of reasons — the founders were all University of Michigan graduates while his granduncle Charlie Peck and his dad were major investors in the fledgling years around 1912.

The Monroe story goes back even further, all the way to Theodore Sheldon's establishment of Kalamazoo's first privately held bank in 1844. For a dozen years, Sheldon's was the town's only bank. By the 1880s, five had set up shop.

In 1884, Kalamazoo lost its distinction of being the nation's largest village as voters approved cityhood. That was also the year that Sheldon's private venture was reorganized as the Kalamazoo Savings Bank with Charles J.

Monroe as its president. Monroe had been instrumental in the passage of new state banking laws. His institution was the first in Michigan to receive a charter as a state bank under the legislation.

In 1910, Kalamazoo Savings merged with Kalamazoo City Bank, which had opened its doors in 1870 as the town's fourth bank. The consolidation yielded the Kalamazoo City Savings Bank, which set up headquarters in a still-new building where Portage Street emptied into the downtown's main thoroughfare. The first president was Stephen B. Monroe, Charles' son. In 1931, three years after the formation of what evolved into the Industrial State Bank and then Comerica, Charles S., Stephen's son, took his position as the head of that bank.

The origins of the calculating company are traced to J. R. Monroe, who was from South Haven and who was a cousin of Kalamazoo banker Stephen B. Monroe. Connable picks up the story:

"When J.R. was working for Western Electric in Orange, N. J., he came in contact with a man who had a patent on a rotary-type calculator. Thinking that this hand-operated technology held great promise for the future, J.R., still a relatively recent Michigan grad, resigned from his job and came to Kalamazoo to raise some capital. That's how his cousin (Stephen B. Monroe), Charles Peck, my father, and some of J. R.'s friends in South Haven got involved around 1912 as stock subscribers. S. B. Monroe and my father were close friends and business associates as co-investors in ventures. That was a pretty active time for the office because the KVP thing was taking shape as well. S. B.'s sons, George and Charles S., joined in later.

"The total original capitalization was around $100,000. J. R. Monroe took control of 51 percent of the stock because of his organizational efforts. He was the entrepreneur who put the project together. Our office took about 35 percent and S. B.'s family around 12 percent.

"Based in Orange, N. J., the company grew slowly at

first and I was told that stockholders were called upon to ante up some more capital to keep it going. After World War I, the action increased and more machines were sold. Prosperity arrived in the 1920s and 1930s. When I came back to Kalamazoo in 1943, my father asked me to take his place on the board and I was elected by shareholders to do so in April of 1944. So was my brother, Horace."

Something the brothers Monroe, the Peck family nor the clan Connable never calculated was the corporate infighting brewing that would require some classic and clandestine wheeling and dealing. J. R.'s death led to the appointment of E. F. Britten Jr. as Monroe's president in 1937. Britten brought with him a production background, which led to a clash of philosophies with the head of the sales division, William "Zang" Zaenglein, and a penchant for nepotism,

S.B. Monroe

placing his son as the head of the manufacturing unit and a brother as company secretary.

"Other than the fact that productivity was down, deliveries were behind schedule and employee morale snail-low, everything was just great. J. R.'s widow and his son, Malcolm, became very suspicious of Britten, who was also co-executor of the family estate. The family members sensed that he was conspiring to gain control of their stock, and Britten did manage to delay the closing of the estate to prevent them voting their shares. My father began to have some doubts about Britten's veracity so when I replaced him on the board, I was asked to keep an eye on the situation. Chuck Monroe was on the board, too, at the time."

While younger brother, Harold, who was working in production in the Orange plant in New Jersey, certainly didn't play the role of a "Deep Throat" a la Watergate, he did confirm low morale, gremlins in the assembly line, and other suspicions shared by the Monroe family.

"Bill Zaenglein, as vice president of sales, was highly capable and well-liked, but he, too, was being affected by the rift in the company. This was in 1948. The strategy was to select me the chairman of a meeting of shareholders. Our faction acted in extreme confidentiality, we mustered our forces, and gathered up enough proxy votes in a closely held company to install Zaenglein as president.

"Everyone kept their mouths shut. There were no leaks. At the meeting, which we rehearsed for several times in advance at my brother's house in Orange, we simply voted Britten out. He couldn't believe it. I was voted chairman of the meeting that brought about this management reorganization and then was elected chairman of the Monroe board of directors.

"You know, I doubt if a company these days, even one as closely held as Monroe was, could pull that off. With modern, press-of-the-finger communications, stuff is public knowledge even before it happens. In later years, when we all got together, we marveled that we were able to keep the lid on so effectively. It was fascinating to see how quickly the business recovered under new management."

By May of 1952, Monroe was taking the wraps off of a $1 million addition to its manufacturing plant in Bristol, a community with the distinction of having territory in both the states of Virginia and Tennessee. Connable presided over a major shindig that attracted Gov. John Battle of Virginia, U.S. Sen. Harry Byrd (a States Rights Democrat who despised President Truman), and Bristol's two mayors — the one who lived on the Virginia side and his counterpart on the Tennessee Bristol.

Broadcast over a statewide radio network, the dedication soiree packed the local civic center with politicos, corporate bigwigs, and an unbelievably huge corps of journalists. From the list of editors and reporters printed in the local newspaper, it seemed like there were more journalists gathered in Bristol than on the beaches of Normandy for the D-Day invasion. Of course, it was a lot safer that day in the two-state city listening to Sen. Byrd rail the White House occupant and hear the governor talk about Virginia's potential as a mecca for industry.

Also sharing billing as a featured speaker that May was James Kilpatrick, destined to become a syndicated political columnist but then editor of the Richmond News Ledger and the youngest journalist in the country in such a prestigious position. Kilpatrick gave his more polished version of "Save Your Confederate Money, Boys, the South's Gonna Rise Again." His proof was the $1 million Monroe project.

The Bristol daily was effusive in its coverage, arranging for the top newspaper cartoonists of the day to do special strips signifying the event. "Flash Gordon," "Ozark Ike," "Barney Google and Snuffy Smith," "Rip Kirby." "Buz Sawyer," "Maggie and Jiggs in Bringing Up Father," and "Blondie" all had some nice comments.

The Bristolians and their newspaper didn't realize it, but a Kalamazoo methodology had come to their town, as cited in this editorial comment:

"People of Bristol are proud of Monroe, too, for the part the company has played in community activities, for the good citizens they have brought to Bristol, and for their progressive and enlightened employee-relations program."

Al Connable was right in the middle of the excitement, exchanging political commentary with a U.S. senator and swapping stories with one of American journalism's rising stars. He was also in the middle of Monroe's heeding the call of European countries courting U.S. enterprises to establish international branches after World War II.

"Already well under way was the European Recovery Program, known as 'The Marshall Plan,' that was launched in 1947 after President Truman had appointed retired Army general George Marshall as secretary of state. I was keeping track of that because one of the plan's first appropriations was designated for Greece in its battle against communism. The top administrator there was Jack Dawson, whom I knew as one of the best law professors on the Ann Arbor campus.

"We sent some of our people to Europe to scout out Great Britain, The Netherlands, and other potential locations. Holland was the place to go for us because the welcome mat was really spread. The Nazis had just about flattened The Netherlands and Dutch leaders realized the way to quicker recovery was through American business locating there. Everybody, including Prince Bernhard, was out selling the viability of the country. The Dutch in effect came to us and made a pitch, not the other way around."

From its sales office in England, Monroe sent out two of its own scouts to, as Paul Harvey would say years later, "get the rest of the story" about Holland, which turned out to be just as rosy as Prince Bernhard's version.

One was the founder's son. Malcolm Monroe, a Williams College graduate in history, aspired for a career in academics. But when his father died, he felt an obligation to continue the family business. His academic leanings were a nice fit with his duties — vice president in charge of foreign operations. Joining him on the exploratory trip was accountant Fred Sullivan, destined for a bright future in the company. Reporting back from The Netherlands, the duo knew what Brigham Young meant when he said, "This is the place."

"Holland and the Dutch people were just great. They froze wages in an understanding between labor and management. The Dutch government provided tax incentives that made it attractive for outside interests to rebuild its war-torn economy at top speed. I have a warm spot in my heart for that country because of how the people in all walks of life, from workers to royalty, rallied to return to normal life.

"We started in May of 1954 with a small plant near the airport at Amsterdam and a staff of about 17 skilled Dutch precision workers. The payroll grew to 300-plus. They did

Willard Wichers, of Holland, Michigan, expedited the Monroe Company's Netherlands venture.

181

a terrific job producing and assembling Monroe business machines. We needed their research to develop new types of machines to adapt to British and European markets.

"We were greatly helped in those early days by Willard Wichers, who was director of The Netherlands Information Bureau in Mike Hindert's home town of Holland. Bill was chairman of the board of trustees at Hope College. Many times he'd make a call to the Dutch ambassador in Washington or telephone The Hague direct to expedite matters and ease the project through.

"Monroe was probably one of the first American companies to commit to The Netherlands after the war and we never regretted it. Later, while attending a University of Michigan Board of Regents meeting, a fellow regent, Leland Doan, then head of Dow Chemical Co., asked me about Holland. I told him it was a first-class experience. Dow later located one of its large subsidiaries there and I'd like to think I played a role in that decision.

"I made a number of trips there as board chairman to cultivate our overseas market. There were many formal dinners at the famous Amstel Hotel in Amsterdam. Leading bankers, government officials and even the prince himself attended those affairs. I gave Prince Bernhard a Monroe calculator with a Dutch keyboard. Supposedly, it became the favorite toy of his daughter, Beatrix, who became queen of The Netherlands.

"I got the idea from an earlier marketing gimmick. I was a Michigan regent and Prince Mahmoud Reza Pahlavi, brother of the Shah of Iran, was a senior in the School of Business Administration. I thought it would be a great gimmick for the university and for Monroe so we gave him a calculating machine with a Persian keyboard.

"When we had extensive business to prepare for, Malcolm and I would travel by boat. Most of the time, though, it was a flight from New York to England and then to the Schipol Airport in Amsterdam, with a quick stopover for fuel at Goose Bay, Labrador. That was long before jet

Al engages in repartee with Prince Bernhard of the Netherlands at the Armstel Hotel.

and supersonic carriers. Overnight prop-powered flights took about 16 hours. The planes were equipped with curtains for the windows and the seats could be converted to beds, much like Pullman cars in the heyday of the railroads. There were even some upper berths for sleeping. It's no more than an eight-hour trip these days.

"Of all the business with which I was affiliated, I guess I spent the most time on Monroe affairs. I went to New Jersey for a week each month, plus handling Monroe matters in our Kalamazoo office. I was chairman and 'Zang' was president. We didn't have a chief executive officer. We worked very well together. I think the results showed that. We, along with Malcolm and his mother, constituted the board's executive committee, which gave the organization a strong sense of direction.

"I was proud of Monroe's achievements. Under the Britten management, there was never a feeling of cooperation among the company and its stockholders. Nor was there any kind of reporting to them. We learned that minority stockholders in South Haven only heard from the company when a dividend was issued. With no reports, they often wondered what was happening within the company. "One of the first actions of the new management team was to publish an annual report. We even held regional stockholders meetings in South Haven even though only 10 or 12 lived there. Zang, Mac and I updated them on the company, earnings, prospects, dividend policy, anything they wanted to know. It was their company, too.

"We attended divisional sales meetings for our 175 offices around the country where we announced a long-overdue retirement plan. Monroe had never offered such a benefit. We weren't forced to do it. Just like W. E. Upjohn with his people, we thought it was the right thing to do. That generated a lot of appreciative letters across the country, even before the checks started arriving in the mail during retirements."

Sales personnel who treated the company well by

adding to profits were in turn treated well. Monroe officialdom responded by staging thank-you-good-and-faithful-servant excursions. The first was a skiing junket to Sun Valley, Idaho. "I had just had an operation for hemorrhoids and sat on a pillow for the entire train trip out there. I scheduled a doctor's appointment and when I told the fellow I was from Kalamazoo, he told me he had just set a broken leg on a Kalamazoo woman. Turned out to be Sally Kirkpatrick, one of the first in this town to be a very active skier. The second outing was a week in Bermuda. Monroe commissioned a small ship for meetings and parties. About 300 salesmen qualified for that one."

During Connable's reign as chairman of the Monroe board, another director he invited to join was Whirlpool Corp.'s Louis Upton, whom Connable assisted when he established the Economics Club of Southwestern Michigan in 1954. The club routinely attracts some of the most prominent world figures of the times to Benton Harbor for speaking engagements.

Bulging profits, sweet dividends and market successes don't escape the notice of American corporations that want to practice their own form of "Manifest Destiny." It was take-over time and the giant advancing from the rear was Litton Industries.

"I think Litton was the first of the conglomerates that we see proliferate in American industry today. It was started by Charles B. `Tex' Thornton, who was one of the famous `Whiz Kids,' a group of men who served the federal government during World War II. Tex was in the Air Force. Another `Whiz Kid' was Robert McNamara, who went on to become president of Ford Motor Co. and then U.S. Secretary of Defense.

"The Litton people were pretty smart. They looked at Monroe's financial statements with annual sales of about $40 million, our organization that included more than 350-company owned outlets in the U.S., the quality of our factories, and our overseas operations. Malcolm Monroe was then approached with an offer to join Litton.

"The Connable Office thought the price was too low. They were tough bargainers, but so were we. The two negotiating teams gathered at the Biltmore Hotel in New York City for three hard days of talks. Monroe was represented by me, Mike Hindert and George Monroe, a director and S. B.'s son. While George and I were in one room, puffing on our pipes and listening to Litton's pitches, Mike was in another suite going through figures and charts, all of which was to prove Litton's offer was not in the ball park.

"We knew we had a great company and we weren't going to sell it at the first price. You've heard of `The Battle of the Bulge.' Well, this was `The Battle of the Biltmore' and it went on for three days. When Tex Thornton heard we weren't budging, he took one of those red-eye overnight flights from California.

"George was beautiful at throwing them off balance in their presentations. They'd explain the great things that Litton could do for Monroe, wonderful stuff, and George would lean back, take a puff, and say, `Let's talk about college football for awhile.' That exasperated them and is what really wore them down. They ended up giving us a much better price, about half again more than the original offer."

The merger between Monroe and the Los Angeles-based enterprise was announced in mid-October of 1957. Litton was regarded as a major player in electronics, operating labs and manufacturing plants at a dozen locations in five states. Its breakthrough developments in electronic digital computers and controls were highly praised by those involved with the nation's defense and most of those innovations had ramifications in industry, commerce and business.

"Litton had done much advance work in navigational systems for missile and aircraft guidance, radar and other countermeasure technology, magnetrons and microwave power tubes. They were well into the Space Age. We were only getting into that phase prior to the Litton merger.

Brother H. P. had become acquainted with an electronics researcher, Jay Quinby, during his World War II days in Key West. The guy had 300 or more researchers under his command working on sonar. As a Monroe board member, H. P. convinced Quinby to head our new electronics research department, so we were on our way.

"I served on the Litton board of directors for about three years, leaving in 1961. Fred Sullivan, who at the time of the merger was our president, stayed as chief executive of Litton's Monroe division. He was a bright guy. Litton recognized that and kept moving him up the ladder."

Still given a place of honor in Connable's office is one of the original Monroe calculators. It may be a candidate for a museum, a dinosaur from another era.

But not Al Connable. He'll never be a dinosaur in action, thought or deed. He has the wrong genes for that.

FIERY ENCOUNTER

Because he was once a few seconds from becoming a human blow torch, Al Connable's optimistic outlook on life stems from the reality that your next breath could be your last one.

On a warm Florida day during the Korean War years, Connable narrowly escaped a fiery final breath when a ride on a jet trainer turned into a brush with death.

He had been chosen by the U.S. Defense Department to take part in a 1951 tour of military installations so that business and civic leaders could get a close look at how their tax dollars were being spent by Uncle Sam. Connable at the time was the chairman of the board of directors of the Monroe Calculating Machine Co.

"They staged these promotional tours about every three months. There were about 100 of us on my tour and we were hauled around on four DC-3's. After a two-day briefing by Gen. George Marshall and other Pentagon brass in Washington, we saw the Marines in action at Quantico in Virginia as they staged a mock battle and showed the budding capabilities of helicopters in warfare. We went out on an aircraft carrier from Norfolk and witnessed some anti-sub maneuvers."

Forty years later, he would remain equally impressed with how the Marines handle themselves, and one member of "The Corps" in particular. Thanks to CNN, Connable watched his grandson, a Marine corporal, carry the flag of the Soviet Union when President George Bush hosted Mikhail Gorbachev at Camp David in June of 1990. Cpl. Ben Connable was used to that kind of duty, having served earlier that year as a member of a Marine honor guard that welcomed West German Chancellor Helmut Kohl to the presidential vacation spot.

One of the stops in 1951 took Connable to Eglin Air Force Base east of Pensacola in Florida's Panhandle. Connable jumped at the invitation to go up with a pilot in a

**Al's grandsons, Marine Officer Al Benjamin Connable (left)
and Joel Connable in 1995.**

jet trainer.

Something didn't seem right at the start, especially when he heard the pilot say, "Don't be alarmed. We're running out of power but I'll get this plane up someway."

"We had a heck of a time getting airborne and just missed a wall at the end of the field. Then I could smell exhaust fumes. Smoke poured into the cockpit."

Soon came the words that he dreaded to hear: "We're in trouble, Mr. Connable. But hang on. You're going to be all right."

The pilot explained their options — splash in the Gulf of Mexico, eject and ride parachutes down, land on the beach, or try to make it back to the base. "I don't know why he asked my opinion because it was his decision to make. I believe he was only thinking out loud in order to keep me as calm as possible, and he did a pretty good job of that. I told him I was OK, even as the black smoke got thicker."

The pilot chose the fourth option — returning to Eglin for an emergency landing. Like comedian George Carlin, Connable preferred the sound of those words to the alternative — "crash landing."

"You could see all of the emergency equipment mustering for the landing. They were moving the other planes out of the way. The foam-shooting fire engines were already racing down the landing strip. I thought we were on fire and would need that ambulance speeding down the runway."

Preparing for the landing, the pilot had given Connable some simple instructions. "When we come to a stop, pull the hatch, get out and run like hell!"

As the jet made contact with the runway, the rescue rigs were racing alongside it. The plane jackknifed off the surface into the grass. As it came to a halt, the pilot followed his own advice. He disengaged the cockpit, unbuckled his seat belt, and jumped out, looking over his shoulder as he ran. Where was his passenger?

"I couldn't get out. I was so nervous I couldn't unstrap myself. The pilot came racing back, unhooked my seat belt, and hauled me out of there. You could see the look in his face. He thought it was going to explode any second."

Thanks to the quick action of the rescue rigs, the foam smothered any chance for an explosion that the two thought was imminent. Later that evening, at the base's watering hole, the happy ending was toasted and the 47-year-old Kalamazoo businessman was christened "Tailfeathers Connable."

"The commandant asked me if I was OK, which I was. He said I was a lucky fellow because that plane was within a few seconds of blowing up. Somehow, something got bent and fuel was being sprayed on the engine.

"The investigating officer interviewed me and the pilot

as the mechanics tore the plane apart to find the trouble. I asked how I could help my pilot, who had done such a superb job and saved both our lives in my opinion with his instinctive response to what was happening. I was instructed to write a letter stating the facts. The letter would be presented at a hearing. I did that. The pilot wrote me a letter afterward. He said he thought he was up for a demotion because of the incident, but because of my letter, he was up for a promotion."

The explosion would have made headlines back in Kalamazoo, but Connable, the wanna-be journalist, preferred the ending that wasn't very newsy.

Gen. Marshall had wanted to make good impressions on American industrialists with his Defense Department initiative. Thanks to one pilot's guts that avoided an inferno, he made a hell of an impression on one who lived in a place called Kalamazoo.

PAPER EMPIRES
AND PULP "FIXIN'S"

"Rock, Paper and Scissors" is the "everybody-wins-everybody-loses" game that kids can always fall back on when there is absolutely nothing else to do.

On the count of three, each player shows a fist for rock, two outstretched fingers for scissors, or a flat hand for paper. Paper covers rock. Rock smashes scissors. Scissors cuts paper.

If you "won," you whacked your opponent on the fleshy side of the wrist with your outstretched fore- and middle fingers. If you "lost," you got slapped on the soft side of the wrist. Generally there was a two-edged sword in each round. Everybody went home with wrists the color of ripe tomatoes.

While the gurus of Kalamazoo's industry over the years didn't go around slapping each other on the wrist other than to compete for skilled workers in the same labor pool, there is something of a metaphor in the child's game.

"Scissors" could represent the metallic-based industries that have called Kalamazoo home over the years — the Kalamazoo Stove Co., Durametallic Corp., Checker Motors and other metal fabricators.

"Rock" could be the granite-solid Upjohn company that ironically started to make a mark in the pharmaceutical world when its physician founder devised a way to make medications "friable" — meaning one dose could be crushed by the power of a thumb instead of remaining a rock-hard pill that sometimes went through the body intact without liberating its miracle potions.

And then there is "Paper," which by 1885 was "king" in Kalamazoo, sharing marquee status with celery and later Kalamazoo stoves before the community became a powerhouse for pills. The Connable Office had its hand in paper more than just buying envelopes and letterheads.

"The paper industry was a dominant force in Kalamazoo

for 75 years. At one time, there were 10 mills in operation. There were more mills inside the city of Kalamazoo than any community its size in any other part of the world. We were known as being a leading manufacturing center for paper around the country."

Back in the early days when folks thought the word "ecology" was a poor speller's attempt at "economy," nobody voiced environmental concerns. Raw sewage was channeled into streams and creeks. The Kalamazoo River paid the price for the town's reputation as a paper producer. As the 1950s inched toward a new decade, the river often looked like a white milkshake meandering northwesterly through Allegan County on its way to Lake Michigan. With economic and workforce changes, Kalamazoo's proliferation of smaller mills began to stumble over each other. Large, integrated mills with faster and updated equipment ate into local profits.

"More and more mills were located near the source of raw materials, plus companies in the South entered the picture. Southern pine grows so much faster, making pulp cheaper. The water-pollution measures down there were minimal and manufacturers basically had a free hand.

"I think another factor, too, was that many of our mills were started by local entrepreneurs. Their second and third generations were not interested in carrying on. Local control passed to boards based elsewhere. Profits were never large enough to warrant the latest machinery that technology was developing. It was a self-defeating downward spiral.

"The local companies didn't have access to the capital markets that the larger firms did. Upjohn, while still private, was able to finance its own rapid growth because of higher profits. If a paper mill was bringing in a 5-percent profit, praise the Lord! Ten percent was euphoria. At Upjohn, a 20-percent return was a routine year.

"If Kalamazoo's paper industry tended to allow manufacturing machinery to age and not be periodically replaced after depreciation, it wasn't because of overpaying divi-

193

PLANT OF THE BRYANT PAPER CO.
KALAMAZOO, MICH.

One of Kalamazoo's largest mills, The Bryant Paper Company, sprawled over many acres.

dends, I can tell you that. Most of the mills were conservative in dividend payouts. There just wasn't a sufficient profit margin because of the spiraling costs of operations, especially with raw materials.

"Yet, this has to be said. For many, many years, it was the paper industry that gave Kalamazoo such a stable economy. The wage scale was lower when compared to the auto industry, but employment was steady and not cyclical. Unions were few and far between in those days. Unionization later brought higher wages and other employee benefits, but I don't think that was a major factor in the shrinkage of Kalamazoo's paper industry.

"Upjohn again picked up the slack. Its workforce steadily grew and the company followed the lead of the founder, paying employees top dollar, from the bottom up to the hierarchy. The more money in the paycheck, the more money that was returned to the local economy. Upjohn made good money, and it paid good money."

Even before papermaking and The Connable Office were joined at the hip by capitalizing Uncle Jake Kindleberger's mill north of town, it had linked with the industry through George Wigginton. Wigginton, a transplanted easterner, had prospered after taking over the Kalamazoo Loose Leaf Binder Co. in 1906 and marketing its leather-covered ledgers and bookkeeping systems globally.

In 1912, the Bond Supply Co. was formed through Wigginton's alliance with Fred Bond, Connable and some of his investment cohorts. Its niche was supplying the equipment and machinery parts required to make paper. Before Bond Supply arrived on the scene, a breakdown at a Kalamazoo paper mill meant a costly shutdown in production that could be extended because repair parts had to be shipped from elsewhere. Bond Supply provided quick delivery and short shutdowns.

About the same time that Al's father helped seed the origins of the Kalamazoo Vegetable Parchment Co. and the christening of Bond Supply, some fresh ideas rode into town in the form of William Joseph Lawrence Sr. He'd play a major role in the shifting and drifting sands of Kalamazoo's paper future.

Lawrence was not born with a silver harpoon in his mouth. He was a self-made man, an achiever who had to pull himself up by his whaling boots. Born Jan. 2, 1891, in Nova Scotia, he experienced what the sages meant about "going down to the sea in ships." His father, grandfather and great-grandfather were sea captains who carried cargos to ports around the world. When his great-grandfather rescued the crew of a U.S. brig, the Nova Scotian was presented with an engraved gold watch by President Abraham Lincoln. Captain James Lawrence wasn't as lucky when he was washed overboard in a severe storm a few years later and was lost at sea.

Nova Scotia became family history when Lawrence's father died in 1903. His Arcadian-French mother relocated with her 12-year-old son to Providence, R. I. To earn money for the widowed household, he ran the town's ice-skating rink and worked in a trunk factory. As he finished his schooling, Lawrence dabbled in chemicals and established the "W. J. Lawrence Co.," marketer of a typewriter that sold for $5 and came equipped with the capacity to print both small and capital letters.

Before birthday No. 20, Lawrence joined Providence Drysalters Co. where he nurtured his interest in chemistry, especially the science's links to the paper, soap and textile industries. The next step was to the Paper Makers Chemical Co. in Easton, Pa., where he was offered the chance to build a new plant and serve as its first superintendent. Lawrence moved from Rhode Island in 1910, not knowing he was ticketed for a place called Kalamazoo, which he had probably never heard of in his short life.

With the blessings of the leadership in Easton, Lawrence shifted his base in 1913 to southwest Michigan where he spearheaded the construction of a satellite plant in a place called Parchment — the Western Paper Makers Chemical Co. Three years later, he and a local woman, Borgia Wheeler, were man and wife.

Lawrence's enterprise of producing alum and waterproofing chemicals for paper flourished with production outlets in Milwaukee, two in Florida, one in Georgia and in the Pacific Northwest. Consolidating with eastern operations in 1926, Lawrence headed a global business. As with his seagoing ancestors, he was seeing the world but not at the wheel of a ship. In 1931, Hercules Powder absorbed the business with Lawrence staying on for another six years as division president in Kalamazoo until he severed connections when the name of his old business was dropped from the letterhead.

Lawrence could have retired at age 47, staying active through his memberships on the boards of several local

The Hercules Powder Company in Parchment, ca. 1938.

paper companies — Michigan Paper, Bryant Paper, Sutherland Paper, Hawthorne Paper, and KVP. He and Alfred Connable Sr. were more than just passing friends on Burdick Street. Among other shared ventures, they sat on the KVP governing board and were charter organizers of the new American National Bank.

Lawrence, however, decided to launch a new career. He'd been on the periphery of the papermaking business, but this time he accepted the challenge of day-to-day management as the chief operating officer of Bryant Paper in 1938. That might have led to his death from a heart attack at the age of 50 a week before the attack on Pearl Harbor.

"Bill Lawrence Sr. was really the one who set the stage for the merger of KVP and Sutherland Paper. It was his contention that the two were too similar in operations and should combine. Nobody listened for a long time, until things began breaking badly for Sutherland and suddenly the consolidation made sense.

"I first got to know Bill Sr. when I was fresh out of college and working for Uncle Jake at KVP. His plant, the Western Paper Makers Chemical Co., was right next door. That was so long ago, people still regarded Michigan as being somewhere out west. He was a hard-working and wise man and I'd often go talk to him.

"It was actually his son, Bill Jr., who replaced his father on many boards as I did my dad, who moved the merger forward. As a KVP director, I watch Bill Jr. in action because he served on both KVP's and Sutherland's boards. He started the discussions, put in a lot of time, made it look attractive, and then helped smooth the transition. He's been another of those special people who has given Kalamazoo its unique definition of citizenship."

Connable Jr. took his seat on the KVP board in 1946, beginning a 20-year affiliation with papermaking that extended to the Allied Paper Co.

"To take the sting out of the growing costs of raw materials and compete better with the South, KVP took owner-

Al and other KVP directors enjoyed a good day's fishing during a trip to Espanola in the early 1950s.

ship of a plant and a sulphite pulp mill in Ontario. A group from Kalamazoo would make quarterly, sometimes monthly, trips to Espanola for board meetings and inspect the wood-pulp operations."

Espanola is in upper Ontario, due north of Manitoulin Island — 900 miles by car, 500 by wings. With the ice gone, the Kalamazoo contingent would take a side trip for fishing Lake Panache southwest of Sudbury. The travelers included Connable Sr. and Jr., C. Hubbard Kleinstuck, William Lawrence Jr., Alfred "Doc" Southon, Charles "Chuck" Monroe, Frank Mossteller, and Ralph Hayward. They'd be joined by their Canadian counterparts.

"Ralph had the good sense to buy the mill at a favorable price. He sold the directors on the approach and convinced them that modernizing the facility would be a wise investment. The company had logging rights on several hundred square miles of land belonging to the Canadian government. A producer of pulp only at first, it added papermaking later, shipping the end product to Hamilton. KVP became an integrated operation. When it combined with Sutherland, the result was a diversified paper company.

"Ralph had a lot of good foresight. He saw the advantages of entering the Canadian market with finished paper products. That's why he forged ahead to buy Appleford Paper Co. in Hamilton, which made parchment rolls and paper napkins.

"Kalamazoo capital also started Interlake Tissue Mills Ltd. near Niagara Falls in Canada. A Scotsman named George Carruthers came to Kalamazoo to raise the money. That's an indication of the reputation Kalamazoo had in the paper industry. Our office invested in the project, so did S. B. Monroe and his family, and the Curtenius family from the Kalamazoo Paper Co.

"If I do have to say so myself, my experience working for Uncle Jake in the cutting room and later handling plant tours was a real asset in later years. I could walk through a mill and understand pretty well what was going on. I could speak intelligently with fellows working in the beater rooms and the machine rooms. When the paper broke on the rolls, I knew the skills these men needed to feed it back through and start production again. You don't make any money when the machines aren't threaded.

"When I first got acquainted with Kalamazoo Paper Co., it was headed by Alfred Curtenius. He was a most capable man with a delightful sense of humor. His wife, Amy, was very active in music circles around here and much beloved in the community. The first love of their son, Fritz, was cars, not paper. After his 1930 graduation from the University of Michigan, Fritz landed a job testing the vehicles that came off the Packard Motor Co. assembly line. It wasn't until the mid-1930s that he heeded the advice of his father and joined Kalamazoo Paper."

The junior Curtenius was something of an inventor, too, designing and building a precision, quick-working, paper-

Alfred E. Curtenius headed the Kalamazoo Paper Company in the 1920s and 1930s.

piling machine that became a staple in the industry across the country. Kalamazoo's version of Thomas Edison held 12 patents on other labor-saving and safety-oriented gadgets and gizmos.

"Founded in 1867, Kalamazoo Paper became part of Georgia-Pacific a few years before its centennial. The company attracted some quality people. Burt Cooper was one — a lifer. He was later elected to the Kalamazoo City Commission. Our office was represented by my father on the Kalamazoo Paper board of directors for years. When he retired, Mike Hindert took his place.

"Alfred Curtenius turned the company's reins over to one of my childhood friends, Jim Wise. The son of a dentist, Jim studied chemical engineering and papermaking at Yale. When he returned here, he joined Kalamazoo Paper and moved up to the presidency. His technical skills and reputation were such that he was brought on to the KVP and Sutherland board.

"It was after Jim retired that Georgia-Pacific bought control. I think the most important thing a person can do is groom a replacement that will keep the ship on course. Too many of the old guard didn't do that. That proved to be a problem and a reason why we experienced merger-mania. An organization runs dry in leadership.

"Dwight Curtenius, who was an associate of my father, was Alfred's brother. Dwight started out in the foundry business but shifted gears and ended up a very successful manufacturer at the Allied Paper Co. Dwight recruited good people, too, bringing Fred Fischer, a Massachusetts Institute of Technology alumnus, to Allied in the 1920s."

It was supposed to be a temporary assignment. Like a consultant today, Fischer came as an efficiency engineer to blueprint ways to improve productivity. He sampled the lotus blossom of what life is like in Kalamazoo, lost that big-city ambition and stayed. He wasn't the first and he wouldn't be the last.

"Fred was in a sound enough financial situation during

the depression that he was able to buy sizable chunks of Allied stock, which had become greatly undervalued. General Motors' stock was even down to single digits back then, I think as low as $4 a share. Those were almost give-away prices. As a company manager and stockholder, he had access to the financial statements. He gambled and won. Not just Allied stock. He invested in many kinds of stock when no one else would touch the shares because of the risk.

"Fred married Wildie Statler, who also grew up in my neighborhood and became one of the town's lovable characters. Her dad was a prominent physician. Her mother's side of the family was one of the pioneer Dutch families, which is why her given name was Wilhelmina. Wildie's mother was the sister of Alfred and Dwight Curtenius."

Yet, conservative Dutch ways were as foreign to her as holes in the dikes back in the mother country. Shades of Caroline Bartlett Crane, Wildie's mother was active in the suffragette movement and ran for Congress, which in those days women just didn't do. She was a progressive thinker, much ahead of her time.

"Wildie inherited many of her mother's independent traits. Together, she and Fred contributed much to the community, particularly in support of Kalamazoo College's tennis program as well as that offered at the YMCA.

"I took my father's seat on the Allied board a few years before it was sold to SCM Paper. Much of the Kalamazoo operation has been dismantled. There have been so many mergers and sales over the years that I've lost track. What happened to Allied is similar to the fate of many of Kalamazoo's paper mills. It's no longer the community's main industry. What strings there are, are being yanked in some other city.

"I also replaced my father as a Bond Supply director. The business had really done well while diversifying from mill supplies to heating supplies, and hardware for builders and plumbers. By 1940, it was based in a large three-story plant in the 200-block of North Rose Street, right across from the old Michigan Central Railroad station that is now Kalamazoo's transportation center. The city knocked the old Bond Supply building down to make way for its Metro Transit System garage and headquarters in 1977.

"When I was on the board, we elected (H. Frederick) Fred Mehaffie Sr. as company president. He had married Wigginton's daughter, Lucille, who was also a very close friend and traveling companion of Genevieve Gilmore and my sister, Josephine. Hugh Jr. replaced his father when he died in 1967 from hepatitis he contracted after undergoing heart surgery.

"Lucille was a regular globetrotter. She and one of our office's close associates, George Monroe, who was secretary of Bond Supply, went on a tiger hunt in India and they each got one. The Mehaffie family had a majority interest in the company and we eventually encouraged them to buy us out.

"In the 1920s throughout Kalamazoo's papermaking industry, there seemed to be an abundance of younger managers who were in line ready to move up, people like Jim Wise, Fred Fischer and Dwight Stocker. They were well-trained professionals waiting their turn.

"Dwight was a methodical manager, who planned well and carefully. He came to this part of the state to join the Plainwell Paper Co., which during World War II was owned by Booth Newspaper Inc. That plant no longer produces newsprint and has changed ownership and product lines many times in my lifetime. That's pretty typical for Michigan's paper industry in the second half of the 20th century.

"When Ralph Hayward died, I was chosen by my fellow KVP board members to serve on a selection committee to find a successor. We had some top-caliber finalists, but selected Dwight Stocker because he had great experience and was well regarded in the community. He ran KVP conservatively and thus built up its assets and surplus capital.

Jim Wise's addition to the KVP board was tremendously helpful, especially when we moved ahead with expansion plans into Ontario. Jim and Dwight worked well with the Canadian team Ralph had assembled prior to his death to run the pulp-mill and wood operation.

"Few people realize how radical a departure that was some 50 years ago. It wasn't routine to go out and buy a mill to furnish the pulp that was needed. Ralph's creativity and ingenuity envisioned the potential of a single corporate entity going from woods to making its own pulp to shipping the raw materials to a plant for paper-product manufacturing. He was way ahead of his time in that kind of boldness.

"The plant in Espanola had been dormant since the depression. Ralph inspected the premises. Everything was in good condition. The machinery had been well-greased and packed away by the bankrupt owner. We bought the pulp mill and 3.4 million acres of forests in May of 1946. It was a bold investment and paid great dividends from the early 1950s, especially after we opened a parchment plant there in 1952, until KVP-Sutherland was purchased and merged with the Brown Co. in May of 1966. That's when I severed my connection as a board member. I think the place is still functioning."

So is Kalamazoo's paper industry although there is no longer a connection these days with the Connable Office that lasted more than a half century.

What does remain, though, is the Kalamazoo River, still curving its way toward "The Big Lake," and looking much healthier than it did in Kalamazoo's papermaking heyday.

DOWN IN LOUISIANA AND OTHER INTERESTING PLACES WITH ALLIGATOR AL

Acting as private trustees, individuals in The Connable Office have represented clients on the boards of companies in which those clients have had substantial interests and investments.

Connable's father had reached an age when he wished to retire from these directorships. "Junior" took his place and became firmly entrenched, often taking leadership positions in what amounted to a virtual "Who's Who of Kalamazoo's Business Climate" as well as in other enterprises around the state.

"People might think that gee, Connable was so involved with the affairs of so many companies that he was neglecting his own business. Well, representing clients at these board meetings was our business. We were protecting their interests. I'd estimate that 50 percent of my time was spent on corporate boards and management issues."

The line-up and years of service included:
* Monroe Calculating Machine Co. (1944-58) and later its parent company, Litton Industries Inc. (1958-61)
* Kalamazoo Sled & Toys Inc. (1944-68)
* Kalamazoo Ice & Fuel Co. (1945-72)
* American National Bank and Trust Co. of Michigan (1946-76)
* Kalamazoo Vegetable Parchment Co. and its connection to the Sutherland Paper Co. (1946-66), plus subsidiary operations in Espanola, Ontario, and the Appleford Paper Co. in Hamilton, Ontario
* Hayes Industries Inc. of Jackson and the Hayes Albion Company created from its merger with Albion Malleable Iron Co. (1945-67)
* Lafourche Realty Co. of Kalamazoo
* Allied Paper Co. (1951-55)
* Kilgore & Hurd Co. Inc. in Detroit (1947-67)

* Detroit Fire and Marine Insurance Co. (1950-58)
* Interlake Tissue Mills Co. Ltd. in Toronto (1946-64)
* The Kalamazoo Building Corp., the holding company that owned the Kalamazoo skyscraper that housed American National and Connable's office, (1947-67)

He also provided counsel and advice to Kalamazoo Manufacturing Co., three other Kalamazoo-based enterprises — Star Brass Works, Park-American Hotel Co. and Bond Supply Co. — and the Ampco Twist Drill Co. in Jackson.

By the time the third generation joined "The Connable Office" in 1943, it was firmly ensconced on the 12th floor of the American National Bank Building. The office with its staff of 27 has since spread to space on the 13th floor in what is now known as the Old Kent Bank Building in downtown Kalamazoo.

The Kalamazoo Sled connection dates back to the Peck brothers who helped capitalize the venture in 1894. Horace B. Peck was company vice president and William Kidder served as secretary-treasurer in those early years. As a kid, Al could have cared less. He was more interested in streaking down Prospect Hill aboard the company's finest product, "The Champion," that vied with the "Flexible Flier" as the nation's best sled.

"After Mr. Kidder died, the presidency shifted to Burnell Weirick. By 1911, my father was vice president. The product line concentrated on sleds and toboggans, but eventually moved into plastic saucers, garden furniture and folding aluminum chairs. During World War II, it produced a special type of toboggan that the Army could use in winter operations. I later served on the board with Kent Kidder, son of the organizer. The company was eventually bought by a New York concern.

"I was on both boards at Hayes Industries in Jackson and Albion Malleable Iron when the companies merged. Albion Malleable had one of the most efficient foundries in the country and strong contacts with Western Michigan University's instructional program. That's why I could see the advantages of consolidation. It did very well.

"When I reached the board retirement age of 70, Jim Hilboldt took my place. I had been involved since World War II when I was asked by one of Albion's officers to represent his interests on the board while he served in the U.S. Navy. I brought Dwight Curtenius, president of Allied Paper, with me to be a director because he was an excellent manager and competent foundryman.

"Some of the companies, like Star Brass, never adjusted to a changing market and faded away. When streetcars and trolleys that needed energy from overhead wire became obsolete, so did Star Brass. The development of plastics didn't help products made from brass, either. The Kalamazoo Railway Supply Co. lived up to its name for years, then adjusted to a broader range of products and became Kalamazoo Manufacturing."

Diversification was part of his portfolio, too. While at The Detroit Trust, Connable organized Kilgore & Hurd, a quality retail outlet for men's clothing. When Connable returned to Kalamazoo, he was asked to serve as an outstate board member for an insurance company. The office had no interest in the company. Connable saw it as an opportunity to better learn the workings of the insurance business. A side benefit was the chance to get better acquainted with fellow director Prentiss Brown, the president of Detroit Edison and chair of the Mackinac Bridge Authority.

Because of his connections to the University of Michigan and its governing board, Connable moved into a different circle of media.

"Gene Power, a fellow regent, had an inventive mind. One of his great interests was microfilming. He was one of the pioneers in this revolutionary technology. In its early stages, Gene was asked to come to London while the Battle of Britain was raging to microfilm precious books and documents stored at the British Museum in the event that revered institution took a direct hit.

"His company was University Microfilm Inc. and my partner, Mike Hindert, and I served on the board of directors. It was really a expansive growth situation and within a few years a space crunch necessitated a much larger plant. University Microfilm later became a division of the Xerox Corp. and Gene served on that board. One of his family's tremendous gifts to the university is the Power Center for the Performing Arts."

Falling in the category of "you win some and you lose some," the Peck-Connable office had no connection — other than friendship — with the Kalamazoo Stove Co. whose slogan, "A Kalamazoo Direct To You" put the town's name on the global map, along with a crunchy variety of celery, long before Glenn Miller and even before The Upjohn Co.

Founded in 1901 by men who had been involved in the heating industry earlier in Detroit, the Kalamazoo Stove Co. chose to market its steel ranges and cook stoves directly to consumers. Two years later, the famous motto was coined and sales soared around the world.

There wasn't even a blip during the Depression as operations spanned to a 20-acre tract and provided work for more than 2,000 employees who manufactured 200 styles of stoves, ranges and furnaces. More than 300 factory outlets across the country swelled the ranks of the payroll. One of the first mistakes in the 1930s was naming a new line of furnaces the "Dictator."

As the allies tried to stem the tide of battle against more than a few real-life dictators, the Kalamazoo Stove Co. turned to making it hot for the enemy by fashioning parachute flares, armored plating for tanks and landing gears for warplanes. Reconversion to peace-time products required costly retooling and Kalamazoo Stove couldn't recover, disappearing in the 1950s.

"My father knew the company's president, Arthur Blakeslee, who was quite a salesman. Our office didn't happen to have any interest in the business. He and Art were friends and they shared membership in an elite fraternity — they both served as mayor of Kalamazoo. I think the company started having problems when wood-burning

The massive Kalamazoo Stove Company was one of Kalamazoo's biggest employers in the late 1930s.

stoves started to become passe, plus they never got back on track after World War II.

"We missed out on the stove company in Dowagiac, too. Sid Tremble, who became its president, and I were fraternity brothers at Michigan. His mother and my mother, Frances Peck, were neighbors in Allegan. When Sid became president, he saw the future and converted from the production of stoves to air-conditioning units. Many companies in Kalamazoo were not that visionary. The community has been fortunate that The Upjohn Co. and its steady growth took up the slack over the years.

"When I replaced my father on American National's board in 1946, the bank was only in its 13th year. It grew strong for a couple of reasons — great leadership and quality of competition from First National. Charles Campbell was the grand old man of First National. Matching Charlie's caliber as an individual was his son-in-law, Merrill Taylor, a contemporary of mine who joined the bank after college and became head of the trust department. They established the bank's solid foundation, along with another of its presidents, Mark Putney. James Duncan, who was a genius when it came to understanding the anatomy of a merger, and his associates, took the bank to the next level — First of America. That's quite an accomplishment and a feather in Kalamazoo's cap.

"American National had to match that kind of leadership and we thought we did with the likes of Garret Van Haaften and Harold 'Jake' Jacobson. Van was a great example of developing leaders from within. He knew the banking business from top to bottom. Van was much respected for his sound judgment in banking and in community affairs.

"As a personality, Jake was much more aggressive. He hailed from the Upper Peninsula, attended Western just like Jim Duncan did, and worked his way up like Van. I think he started working at the bank when he was a college freshman.

"As a bank president, Jake was versatile, creative and expansion-minded. The zest he possessed for his work and life was contagious. He was fun to work with. He frequently burned the midnight oil at his Gull Lake home, writing down ideas and concepts to flash before officers and my fellow directors the next day. He was once hospitalized because of overwork. Instead of taking a rest, he arranged a telephone connection from his bedside to the board room so he could conduct the meeting and not miss a thing.

"One of Jake's first expansionist moves as president was bringing in Home Savings Bank, the epitome of a small-town bank. Often on the way to work, I'd walk down the alley connecting Rose and Burdick streets in the years before the Kalamazoo Mall. The bank faced the alley. There would be the president, Chuck Chase, or Glen Smith, the vice president, literally sweeping the floor getting ready for the day's business. Now there's a class act. Smitty's been a treasure not only for the bank but for the entire community.

"When Jake relinquished the presidency and eventually retired as chairman of the board, I was on the executive committee that brought Harold Holland to the bank. When he became chairman, Ted McCarty moved up. Now American National is a part of the Old Kent family."

That name is history in Connable's lexicon of business endeavors. Surviving, though, from an investment venture that dates to his father is the nickname of "Alligator Al."

The story dates back to the first two decades of this century when a group of investors from the Midwest plowed $300,000 into a fruit-growing and cattle-raising venture in Cajun country about 75 miles southwest of New Orleans. The 18,000-acre swampland property had been fed for eons by silt from a branch of the Mississippi River. The midwesterners reasoned that they were investing in topsoil that had once been part of their own neighboring environs.

Investors in the banking firm's 1912 bond issue took the name of Golden Meadow Farms because that was the name

**Al first served on the American National Bank's
Board of Trustees in 1946.**

of the town closest to the property in Lafourche Parish. The Connable Office bought some of those bonds. The fruit-raising business turned out to be the pits and the assets rotted away. Golden Meadow Farms went bankrupt. There

213

wasn't enough money to pay the taxes.

"With title to the land about to be lost, my father and two other men — Alan Dusenbury of New Orleans and Carl Wisner of Chicago — stepped in with a few thousand dollars in 1920 and formed what is called a bondholders' protective committee. They re-organized the venture. Bond owners in Golden Meadow Farms became stockholders in the Lafourche Realty Co. Inc. that had ownership of 18,000 acres on Bayou Lafourche."

After the peaches became history, the main business of the company was trapping muskrats, a function supervised by a man named "Papa John" Plaisance, whose family had inhabited that part of Louisiana for generations. Shrimp and fishing boats also went in and out of the bayou. Enough was made off the land to keep the tax collector away.

"Most of the muskrat trappers were Cajuns, who could trace their ancestries back to days of the French colony of Arcadia in Nova Scotia. The investment was an interesting situation and nobody knew whether it would ever pay off. My father and his two fellow investors met once or twice a year in Chicago for a board of directors meeting. Wisner was an attorney who kept the books. Dusenbury was an engineer, a transplanted Michigander who had settled in New Orleans. They hoped the muskrat population held out until something else developed."

Like oil and natural gas.

In the 1930s, oil companies started leasing the swampland in search of crude. The drillers had their share of success. "I first went down there in 1951. It is an intriguing piece of property — fishing camps on stilts. I love the Cajun people. They are intelligent, friendly and witty. They love to play tricks."

Which is where Connable picked up the moniker of "Alligator Al." He had gone to bed for the evening, with visions of shrimp Creole dancing in his head. One of the sons of "Papa John" slipped a baby alligator into Connable's room and scared the bejeebers out of him.

Connable's response was to head for the tallest chair and reach for the ceiling.

"The oil business is highly difficult to predict. Sometimes, you put more money into the ground than you take out. Some of the wells are 13,000 feet deep and more. But we were able to make money for our stockholders. It was a happy day when we finally reached the point where the company paid back in cumulative dividends all of the original amount of the bonds that was almost lost. The muskrats have pretty much disappeared, but Lafourche Realty survives as an investment entity and as a protector of the environment.

"One of the biggest problems with the Louisiana property is the erosion caused by hurricanes, tides and boat traffic. The soil is spilling over the so-called Continental Shelf and disappearing into the Gulf of Mexico. All that oil-drilling activity has contributed to the erosion. Lafourche hired experts from Louisiana State University to devise a long-range protection plan.

"We went ahead with their recommendations in hopes of setting a good example for other landowners, oil companies, and those in the fishing industry. It's a major operation, one that is jointly financed to install a system of dikes, dams and other water controls."

After the natural gas and oil declined in the early 1980s, the company, which Connable then chaired, increased its real-estate investment back in Michigan. That's partly how a company with a French name ended up headquartered in Kalamazoo.

In the fall of 1958 as plans for the Kalamazoo Mall inched from blueprint toward ripping up a street, Lafourche engineered the $206,200 purchase of land at the corner of Burdick and Lovell streets from the city of Kalamazoo. Lafourche and Miller-Davis Co. were co-purchasers of the public land.

What had been for a half century the cornerstone of Kalamazoo's community fire protection would be torn

Central Fire Station, Kalamazoo, Mich.

The old Central Fire Station was demolished to make way for the new Jacobson's store on the Mall in the late 1950s.

down to make way for a building block to the future — an anchor store (leased to Jacobson's Stores Inc.) at the south end of the first pedestrian shopping mall in the heart of a city in the United States. As the new 36,000-square-foot, $600,000, multi-level store came out of the ground, so did a new central station for the Kalamazoo Fire Department on Cedar Street about a block away.

Another of its local ventures was the Mall Plaza property in the downtown. Trustee Jim Westin tells the story:

"After we acquired the old Woolworth building on the mall for potential redevelopment, we decided to see whether we could duplicate what was happening at suburban shopping centers by having something like an internal mall.

"The Woolworth building had Gilmore Brothers on one side and Jacobson's Store for the Home on the other. What happened was a first in downtown Kalamazoo, and possibly a first in any downtown in the country. Because Al knew Irving Gilmore and the chairman of the board of Jacobson's very well, he asked the two men to meet him in the central courtyard of what we were calling the Mall Plaza. He explained what Lafourche wanted to do and they liked the idea of flow-through entrances to their businesses. It became reality."

"Big Al" strikes again.

HOW THE WESTERN WAS WON AND PROSPERED

Give or take a day, Alfred Barnes Connable Jr. and Western Michigan University could have been conceived about the same time. Be that as it may, their fortunes were joined 60 years later when Connable granted Gov. George Romney's wish for him to accept an appointment to Western's first board of trustees.

So were their formative years linked somewhat. Both were "Hilltoppers" — the nickname of early Western athletic squads because of the campus' vantage point overlooking the city while much of Connable's youth was spent in the white-pillared house up on Prospect Drive hill.

On paper at least, Western came into existence on May 27, 1903, when Gov. Aaron Bliss signed Public Act 196 that ended a lot of politicking and created the "Western State Normal School" to take its place alongside Michigan's other rather innovative institutions for the training of teachers — Michigan State Normal School in Ypsilanti (1853), Central State Normal School at Mount Pleasant (1895) and Northern State Normal School at Marquette (1899).

Advancing the calendar exactly nine months brings the date of Feb. 27, 1904. Alfred Barnes Connable Jr. was born in a home on South Street, the family's temporary quarters, on Feb. 20, 1904.

Because Kalamazoo had to outmaneuver such towns as Grand Rapids, Muskegon, Hastings and Allegan to land the plum of hosting a normal school for the western side of the state, local citizens acted quickly to cement Lansing's decision in perpetuity. Taking the lead was the core of what later became the first chamber of commerce, a group that probably included Connable's father and the Peck brothers.

Within a week, options were secured on 24 tracts of land that could serve as a prospective site. Kalamazoo agreed to donate the chosen parcel plus contribute $40,000 in private funds to develop the campus. The city pledged to donate the cost of extending public utilities, for providing temporary quarters for the school, and for paying half of the salaries of the instructors — voters willing.

The State Board of Education was impressed then and again on Oct. 19 when Kalamazoo voters, by a 9-1 margin, approved a $70,000 bond for the campus project. Not bad for a place that would advertise itself as a "debt-free city" during the Great Depression. The decision took 15 ballots before Kalamazoo surfaced as the winning town among members of the state board.

The preferred site, as recommended by the same landscape planners who created New York City's Central Park, was a 20-acre parcel that was flanked by Davis Street on the east and irregularly on the west by what was then known as Asylum Avenue (Oakland Drive). Like young Mr. Connable's future neighborhood, it, too, was called Prospect Hill because steep sides rose to a crowned plateau.

Warranty deeds were presented to the state board on March 24, about a month after Connable's birth. Already hired as the normal's first "principal" (later changed to "president"), Dwight Waldo faced a Sept. 1 deadline that the new school "be ready for occupancy." Waldo convened

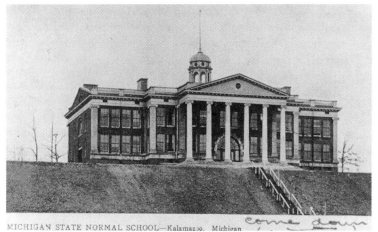

MICHIGAN STATE NORMAL SCHOOL—Kalamazoo. Michigan

Western State Normal School's entire campus in 1906 consisted of this structure.

the first series of summer classes on June 27 for 117 students in temporary quarters in the old Kalamazoo High School on Vine Street. A dozen instructors including himself offered 78 courses. Male students organized "club" football and basketball squads, spurred to great athletic accomplishments by this spirited cheer:
"Hy-lo-zoo
Hy-lo-zoo
Western Normal
Kalamazoo."

Meanwhile, Western's "East Campus," later called by beloved cowboy philosopher Will Rogers as "The Acropolis of Kalamazoo County," was on its way and so was Western Michigan University as Waldo successfully lobbied the state legislature for building funds in 1905 and succeeding years. In June of 1908, local and state dignitaries gathered to dedicate two new structures on the hill, one of which was a gymnasium that featured such avant-garde luxuries as showers, a swimming pool and a baseball cage.

As the decades passed, other buildings and property acquisitions swelled the size and complexity of the original campus. Waldo served as president of Western until 1936 when he was succeeded by Paul Sangren. As Western metamorphosized from a normal to a college (Western State Teachers College in 1927) and then to a university, enrollment would grow to more than 25,000.

Following World War II, a modern campus sprang up across Stadium Drive and the original locations shifted to housing the WMU College of Business. The carefully conceived landscape, for many years only visible in old postcards, would revert to a tangled thicket obscuring the majestic facades of Kalamazoo's "Acropolis." Under the presidency of Diether Haenicke, Western's roots have been reenergized to once again become a focal point of the university.

Beaten for a third eight-year term as a Michigan regent, Connable thought his days as a university decision-maker were over with the dawning of the 1960s. He was content

Left to right, Prof. Jousef Alevi, Gov. William G. Milliken, President James Miller and Al posed in the early 1970s.

with the status of regent emeritus from his alma mater.

Connable had watched Western evolve and helped when asked, such as serving on an advisory committee for the WMU Department of Industrial Technology because of his Monroe connection. In 1962, Connable received from Western an honorary doctor-of-humanities degree "for his distinguished service to higher education in the state of Michigan and for his generous leadership and support of the musical and cultural life of Kalamazoo."

What had caught his eye was the reign of James W. Miller as Western's third president. He liked Miller's savvy, his political gamesmanship and his sense of humor. One of Miller's favorite ways to warm up a crowd was to tell listeners he was the only man to tag a defeat on Rocky Marciano, the only heavyweight boxing champion to retire without a blemish on his record.

Miller and Marciano both hailed from Brockton, Mass. "I pushed him all over the park one day," Miller would say. "He wasn't so tough." Then came the punch line. "Of course, I was a 15-year-old ballplayer and Rocky was only 4 years old. Even then, it was a split decision."

Miller approached the Western job as an academic, a sportsman, an educator, a public servant, a statesman and as a patron of the arts. From the beginning of his tenure on Jan. 1, 1961, through his retirement on the last day of 1973, Miller guided Western from its emphasis as a "normal school" for training teachers into the forefront as a cosmopolitan and diversified university, a feat that warranted naming Western's new auditorium in his honor. The Miller regime saw enrollment spurt from 12,000 to 20,000.

What Miller accomplished required money and lots of it from the state. He knew his way around Lansing and the Michigan Capitol. He had been a full professor of political science at Michigan State University and the head of teacher education when Gov. G. Mennen "Soapy" Williams named him state controller in 1955. After five years, he was appointed secretary of the MSU Board of Trustees, which

222

was his post when he was tapped to be Paul Sangren's successor at Western.

A little item known in headline talk as the "Michigan Con-Con" changed Connable's status from "regent emeritus" to "active trustee" at the university in his hometown. The 1962-63 updating of the Michigan Constitution, as approved by voters, restructured the governance of some of the state's colleges and universities, shifting from the jurisdiction of the State Board of Education to each's independent and separate board.

Gov. George Romney scanned the ranks of Michigan citizens for people who had experience in such matters and "who would represent the state in the way it should be represented." His spotlight fell on Connable's 16 years at Michigan. The fact that Connable lived in Kalamazoo made the perfect match for one of the eight Western Michigan University appointments.

"Jim Miller liked to say that my 16 years of experience as a Michigan regent qualified me to serve on his board at Western. I think Gov. Romney and Jim consulted on possible choices. My name surfaced and I got a call from the Kalamazoo County Republican Party to check how my winds were blowing. I said I would be proud to serve and the governor called me. Party politics wasn't the defining guideline. John Dykema, an attorney from Detroit, was a Democrat and Dorothy Dalton wasn't associated with any party."

Joining them on that pioneer Western board were fellow Kalamazooan Dwight Stocker (his papermaking colleague), auto executive Fred Adams (formerly of Kalamazoo), Mildred Johnson of Muskegon, Phil Watterson (a Western alum and president of a steel company in Plainwell) and Julius Franks of Grand Rapids. The latter was a University of Michigan All-American football player and a highly successful dentist. The appointments were announced in February of 1964.

"It was an outstanding board, probably the finest of its

Western Michigan University's first independent Board of Trustees in 1964.

kind in the state at that time. They were all dedicated public servants who volunteered their time. That doesn't mean I believe an appointment system for governing boards at universities is better than an election method. So much depends on who the governor is. George Romney was determined to have an outstanding board at Western and he wasn't afraid to cross party lines.

"An election system isn't all that ideal either because it is very difficult to get quality candidates. It takes time and money to run a campaign and too often the races are lost amidst all of the other things on the November ballot. I did prefer spring elections for judicial and educational positions, the way we used to do it.

"I know that Jim Miller relied on me heavily during the organizational period because the new constitution contained few details. One was that the new governing board should be patterned after Michigan's, which is why Romney wanted me. In Ann Arbor, the reigning president chairs the board of regents. The board opted to do that at Western, too. That has since changed. The members now choose a chair and vice chair from their own ranks. Other than that, the two entities are very similar.

"The appointed boards could call themselves whatever they wanted — regents, governors, trustees. The Western board chose the term 'trustee.' We also had to decide how to organize as a board, who the officers would be, adopt bylaws, and determine how many times we would meet each year. In all of these issues, I think my experience at Michigan came in handy, as did the offices I held with the Association of Governing Boards of State Universities and Colleges.

"While the association has changed and grown since I was president in 1948, the quality of learning that regents and trustees receive attending national conventions and workshops remains outstanding. Board members have to be educated in what are and what are not their responsibilities — the making of policy versus administering that policy.

225

That's a valuable lesson also for faculty members and administrators. We each have our function, and should stay out of the other's territory. Times may be changing, but not that consummate principle of separation of powers and responsibilities.

"I urged my peers on the Western board to attend association seminars. That's how I first crossed paths with David Breneman, who spoke at the one of the conventions as a staff member of the Brookings Institute prior to his appointment as president of Kalamazoo College. I am very proud that the association was conceived at my alma mater at the 1921 inauguration of a University of Michigan president."

Connable's trusteeship wasn't 100 percent "Roberts' Rules of Order" as the board's vice chair. He made his only trip to Africa while representing the brown-and-gold colors of the Broncos. Instigated by Russell Seibert, one of Miller's most trusted administrators, the university put out a feeler to the U.S. Agency for International Development in 1960 saying it was ready, willing and able to undertake an overseas project. How about Nigeria, which is located on the west coast of Africa where, if the continent was an ice cream cone, the chilly, tasty stuff would be overflowing and sliding down the outside.

Nigeria wanted some assistance in establishing a technical college in Ibadan, the largest city between the south shore of the Mediterranean and South Africa. Western jumped at the invitation, sending teams of faculty and administrators to explore the project. For the next eight years, six to eight faculty members spent two-year hitches in Nigeria. Seibert made the journey a couple of times himself, as did Miller and his wife, Jane. On one occasion they were accompanied by Connable.

"Jim Miller wanted someone from the new board to check out what Western was doing in Nigeria. He was the chairman. Me being vice chairman made me the obvious candidate. Not too tough a decision to make. It was only a

10-day trip in November of 1964 and we were never idle for a second. My admiration for Jim as an administrator and a scholar grew daily as he handled the multiple problems and challenges we encountered. If you travel with Jim Miller, you move fast."

Connable "got some ink" as the Associated Press filed a dispatch datelined Lagos, Nigeria:

"'Nigeria has great resources — material and human,' the chairman (Oops) of the board of trustees of Western Michigan University said Monday.

"Alfred Connable made the comment after a week-long inspection of Western's project to establish Ibadan Technical College in Nigeria's western regional capital.

"The Kalamazoo (Mich.) institution has a contract with the U.S. Agency for International Development (AID) to organize the school to train middle-level technicians for industry in Africa's most populous nation. Connable said he was heartened by the country's potential.

"'Nigeria should be a real force in the future,' he said. 'They seem to have everything going for them, including great enthusiasm. Our purpose in coming here is to find out what is needed and then do what we can when we return to Michigan to back them up.'

"Western has six instructors at the two-year college in Ibadan, which is turning out technicians in mechanical, electrical and civil engineering. Ibadan Technical College was established in 1960 and Western Michigan hopes to phase out its staff in the next couple of years.

"'It will be a sign that our job is successfully completed when we are able to replace Americans with Nigerian teachers,' said Western president James Miller who accompanied Connable on the fact-finding mission."

Connable and Miller were invited to the home of the Timi of Ede, a member of the Nigerian royal family.

"The royal palace was a nice farmhouse with some chickens in the front yard. The Timi was a great fellow and was held in high esteem as a maker of miracles.

"Radio and television practically didn't exist in Nigeria and cellular phones were pie-in-the-sky gadgets that Chester Gould drew in his Dick Tracy comic strip. The Timi's people did their talking by drums. Each beat had a meaning. It was fabulous.

"I can remember sitting on the Timi's porch, which in effect was his throne. He asked Jim what the president of an American university would like to say to his people. Jim said something like, `Tell them that we like Nigerians.' Out went the message by drums and back came the response. It was the African version of smoke signals, except that nobody got choked up nor had to cut a lot of wood to keep the lines of communications open.

"Whatever we did as a Western board, it all worked out well. Jim Miller was a strong university president. He had strong ideas and was able to get things done. I don't know if anybody else could have pulled it off as well. With that well of experience in state government, he was very skillful at presenting Western's case to the Michigan Legislature. Because of Jim, my loyalties are as strongly tied to Western as they are to Ann Arbor."

Michigan Attorney General Frank Kelley saw to it that those loyalties were prematurely affected before the terms of Connable and Stocker were due to expire at the end of 1968.

In a conflict-of-interest opinion released in September of 1967, Kelley ruled that an officer or governing-board member of a state institution of higher learning is a state officer and, as such, is prohibited by the Michigan Constitution from serving as an officer or director of a bank doing business with his/her college.

Connable at the time was a director of the American National Bank & Trust Co. of Kalamazoo while Stocker served on that board as well as the board overseeing the National Bank of Detroit. Both trustees always abstained from voting on issues when the WMU board considered financial matters involving those banks. Both immediately

228

submitted their resignations to Gov. Romney, although both disagreed that "a conflict of interest exists."

"These years at Western," Connable wrote, "have been significant years of policy determination, appropriate to a growing and dynamic university that is exceedingly alert to its educational responsibilities. In my opinion, the future of Western looks extremely bright." He told fellow trustees: "Our board has set a high standard of unselfish dedication to the task of building a great university."

Privately, James Miller was seething. Publicly, he was as polished as ever, stating to the press:

"Western will always be grateful for the unselfish, dedicated and effective leadership that trustees Connable and Stocker have exerted as members of our board. Few men can claim a more distinguished record of sensitive, ethical and responsive service to education in general and Western in particular.

"It is regrettable that laws meant to protect the public interest must be applied so broadly as to deprive public institutions such as Western some of their most effective leadership."

Across the state, the presidents of Michigan colleges and universities had to choose between career and public service on bank boards. Those such as John Hannah of Michigan State and Michigan's Harlan Hatcher resigned their positions as bank directors to stay in academia. The cream of the state's industrial hierarchy made the same decision going the other way, leaving public service so as to not sacrifice their business careers. Miller believed that state universities would be paying an unfair price for lost leadership because of overzealous pursuit of the letter of the law.

Within a month, some of Miller's fears were proven groundless when Connable's spot on the board was filled by Charles "Chuck" Ludlow, an Upjohn Co. vice president and treasurer.

"I believe that ruling was ultimately reversed, but it was

229

WMU President Diether Haenicke led the applause for Al at the dedication of the Alfred B. Connable Board of Trustees Room in 1996.

in effect long enough so that throughout Michigan about 12 Romney appointees had a tough decision to make. It was a tough one for me, I know.

"Being on these governing boards was never a figurehead position. There was always a lot of reading to do to background yourself. And the pay was terrible. Nothing. They pick up the tab for travel and expenses these days, but when I was at Michigan and was on university business, I paid my own expenses. There's probably still a lot of that going on because the people who serve on these bodies are a dedicated lot.

"Plus, the Open Meetings Act has come into play. It must be hard to figure out when you are doing the public's business and when you are breaking a law while having a chat with a board colleague or two. Heck, if you speak under a street light or have a cocktail in a bar, you may be holding an illegal public meeting.

"But I truly enjoyed my service at both universities. I appreciated what Diether Haenicke said at his inauguration as Western's president. He pointed to the trustees and to the emeriti gathered and said, `These ladies and gentlemen do this as a labor of love. They receive no compensation of any kind.' When I was campaigning for a seat on the board of regents, people couldn't understand why I was doing it. What was in it for me, they wanted to know. Public service. It was a labor of love."

Some of that love came back in spades when, on Connable's 92nd birthday, the room in the Bernhard Center on Western's campus where the trustees go about their business was named in his honor — The Alfred B. Connable Board of Trustees Room.

It's the same room where he sat when Gov. Romney appointed him to Western's first independent governing board in 1964. He's been a stallion of steadfast support in the Land of the Broncos ever since.

231

ON MY HONOR
I WILL DO MY BEST
TO SERVE MY COMMUNITY

Alfred Barnes Connable Sr. arrived in Kalamazoo in 1896, fired by the ideals that any 25 year old has to make his mark in the world.

He had first heard of Kalamazoo as a prospective mecca while in college and pledged to apply what he had learned in life and on the campuses of Michigan and Northwestern in a place whose name sounded like a college cheer gone haywire.

Alfred B. Connable, Sr. and daughters Virginia (top) and Josephine, ca. 1900.

The community's esprit de corps that has marked the 20th century was still in its formative stages, adding credence to the claim that Alfred Sr. helped shape it during the first two decades.

When he unpacked his baggage for good, stored inside his personality was the essence of community service. Alfred Sr. had watched his father in action as the postmaster of Petoskey. For a boy of 8, it's pretty powerful stuff to have dad receive a presidential commission, especially when it came from a Civil War hero, Rutherford B. Hayes. Four years later in 1884, a second commission came to Ralph Connable from President Chester Arthur. After less than a year in the practice of law, Connable joined the Peck brothers' enterprises, specializing in liens, investments and trusts with his legal background. His firm belief in public service was a trait he passed on to his namesake son.

There was no better fellow practitioner of that philosophy than Dr. William E. Upjohn who subscribed to the theory that productive, contented and fairly paid employees equated to community-active employees. He practiced during the work week what he preached during informal Sunday-afternoon colloquia Upjohn hosted in his South Street house, some of which attracted the Pecks and new son-in-law Alfred Connable Sr.

Upjohn so wanted his employees committed to public service for the good of the community that he led the way, serving as an alderman on Kalamazoo's city council in the 1890s. By the second decade of the next century Alfred Sr. was part of the established power structure but he didn't particularly cotton to the local political system. He was serving as mayor under the city's old aldermanic method in 1917 when he joined forces with Upjohn, then serving as president of the Kalamazoo Chamber of Commerce, to structure some reform.

"Dad and Dr. Upjohn shared the belief that the aldermanic ward-like system was very inefficient. Too much partisan politics came into play. It was `The War of Wards,' with one ward being played off against the other, and the

233

general public be damned.

"They instigated a review of Kalamazoo's system, brought in outside consultants from across the nation to explain other forms of municipal government, and championed a switch to the commission-manager method. They organized a campaign to elect a charter commission to draft a new municipal magna carta for the city of Kalamazoo. Dr. Upjohn was elected as its chairman. Dad was chosen by voters to be a charter commissioner, too."

To nobody's surprise, the charter commission recommended the adoption of the commission-manager form of government. To the surprise of those who liked the status quo, city voters by a large majority endorsed the new charter. In the 1918 municipal election, the first under Kalamazoo's new charter, Upjohn, then in his mid-60s, led the field of candidates to become the city's first mayor

Dr. Wiliam E. Upjohn, Kalamazoo's first mayor under the commission/ manager government in 1918.

under the commission-manager system. Joining him on that first Kalamazoo City Commission was Alfred Sr.

"The at-large system, in which the first seven finishers are elected to the commission and the most popular candidate is mayor, is unique in the United States. When my father died in 1951, he still believed that it was the best form of city government in the country."

A case can be made for that first Kalamazoo City Commission leading the way toward the establishment of Veterans Day as a national observation. Reacting to the surrender of Germany, the freshly empowered mayor and his fellow commissioners decreed on Nov. 11, 1918:

"Conceived in the spirit of power and a desire for world domination, a `day' was promised when the world should kneel at the feet of the Kaiser. Today is the world's answer to that autocratic ambition. . .I therefore, as mayor of the city of Kalamazoo, pronounce this Nov. 11 and all succeeding anniversaries of this day, `Liberty Day for Kalamazoo,' and ask that all people observe this as a holiday in which there shall be no work. I ask all factories, stores and schools to close and join with one accord in the celebration of this great day."

The Kalamazoo Gazette reported the action this way:

"Kalamazoo, keeping its feet on the ground while other communities were rejoicing over false rumors, was the first to designate Nov. 11 as a legal holiday for all time to come. . .The petition asking that this day be set aside, with the Fourth of July in commemoration of the victories of democracy, will be sent from this city to Washington at once."

President Woodrow Wilson apparently didn't get the message until much later because his proclamation establishing the new Armistice Day national holiday wasn't issued until Nov. 11, 1919 — one year later. In 1954, the doughboys of 1918 started to share the podium with the fallen of World War II and Korea when Nov. 11 officially became known as Veterans Day.

An effective, non-partisan city government and a possible role in establishing a national holiday weren't the only major Upjohn-Connable collaborations. Upjohn's vision of some kind of an umbrella entity that could serve as the community's conscience and "cookie jar" crystallized in the formation of the Kalamazoo Foundation in August of 1925. The following April, Connable was appointed to its first "distributing committee," a trusteeship he would retain until 1934.

Possibly with tongue in cheek, his brother Ralph's family genealogy chronicled Alfred Barnes Connable Sr. this way: "Among his accomplishments as mayor, he closed up the gambling and sporting houses, and abolished every form of slot machines. He also stopped a vicious run on the largest bank by taking the presidency for one month."

With "junior" on his own working for Detroit Trust Co. and earning a few extra bucks teaching at the Detroit

South Burdick Street about the time when Kalamazoo adopted its new civic government.

Institute of Technology, a father received an unsolicited letter in 1929 that tends to make one's day. The letter writer told his wife during dinner that "Alfred Connable was one of the finest young men that I have had the pleasure of knowing. You will be glad to know that he is doing splendidly in his teaching work with us. It is quite remarkable

Alfred Connable, Sr. and wife Frances, ca. 1925.

that he can be so successful in spite of his comparative youth. Most of our instructors are very much older because we have more mature students than the ordinary college. In fact, it is an 'Adult School.'"

Responded the senior Connable: "If your letter is based on fact, I see where my job is set for life. I was brought up with the idea that I should try to be as good a man as my dad. Now you hand it to me to be as good a man as my dad's grandson. Am I never to arrive?"

He did enough of his share of arriving. Upon his death in 1951 at the age of 80. the Gazette's editorial was more forthright and celebratory of a man's contributions to his community:

"When death took Alfred B. Connable, this community lost a singularly distinguished figure. His distinction came, on the one hand, from his public spirit and public service, and, on the other, from the rare quality of his mind and character.

"Trained in the law, he gave much of his time and talents to business and industry, helping to found and to guide a number of the city's major enterprises. But he was also called upon for leadership and counsel in a variety of governmental, civic and educational undertakings.

"He served Kalamazoo as mayor, member of the city commission, and member of the board of education, as well as member of the board of health and of the zoning commission. He associated himself helpfully with several civic and social organizations. A member of the First Presbyterian Church, he served for a time as one of its trustees.

"As a public figure, he was indeed noteworthy. But it is as a man that he will be held longest in the affectionate remembrance of those who knew him.

"Honors came to him easily, but he did not seek them. Wealth and great influence left him unspoiled. He remained, from the beginning to the end of his life, a kindly, simple, modest, unassuming man, a man of character, a

238

man of truth and integrity, one who might well serve as an example to our troubled era of what an American citizen ought to be and how he ought to live and act.

"This community will cherish long and gratefully the memory of Alfred B. Connable Sr."

For a son, those were major shoes to fill and powerful words to live up to, which Alfred Jr. began trying to do when he returned to Kalamazoo shortly after World War II. While the son's public service was confined to university trusteeships, his shadow of community and civic affairs was just as long and broad. In many cases, they were carbon copies of each other, as with the Kalamazoo Symphony and the Chamber of Commerce.

"Dad believed in becoming involved in civic affairs as insurance for a progressive community. We shared a genius for being appointed to boards that paid with pats on the back, thank-you's and certificates. Those were the best boards on which to serve."

Connable's local roster included the Community Chest, the Douglass Community Association, the Senior Citizens Fund, the First Presbyterian Church, the Rotary Club, and the Park Club. One of his first assignments upon returning to his home town was as the chair of the advance-gifts division in a 1946 campaign to expand Bronson Hospital. While a Michigan regent, he hosted the annual Brotherhood Banquet of the Kalamazoo chapter of the National Association for the Advancement of Colored People.

On a state and national level, the affiliations were equally varied: the Michigan Committee of the United Negro College Fund, the American Symphony Orchestra League, the Michigan Crime and Delinquency Council, the Association of Governing Boards of State Colleges and Universities, the International Music Camp at Interlochen, the American Hearing Society, the University of Michigan Club chapters in Kalamazoo and Detroit, and the Harvard Club in New York City,

In 1956, Connable's statewide reputation was recognized when he was named to a 16-member citizens committee to map strategies to reduce crime and juvenile delinquency. Michigan's action was the second statewide initiative of its kind in the nation. A five-year, $600,000 grant was awarded by the Ford Foundation to finance the project.

Joining Connable on the blue-ribbon panel were the president of Central Michigan University, an Episcopal bishop, a high-ranking officer in the Michigan Farm Bureau, the dean of the University of Michigan School of Social Work, Dan Gerber of Fremont's Gerber Products Co., top executives from the auto industry, the editor of Jackson's daily newspaper, the president of the Michigan CIO Council, a United Auto Workers regional director, a member of the Detroit Board of Education, and former state officials. Connable was a representative of Michigan's industrial sector as chairman of the Monroe Calculating Co.

Among the committee's prime findings was that in too many court jurisdictions punishment was meted out to fit the crime and not the perpetrator. People, especially youthful, first-time offenders, were unilaterally and indiscriminately sent to prison because probation opportunities were either minimal or non-existent.

Punishment, which probably rarely worked, was preferred to attempts at rehabilitation, which had a better track record. In the mid-1950s, the cost to keep a person in any kind of detention was $2,500 a year, compared to a probation type of service that carried a price tag of $300 annually. That ratio is still in effect in the 1990s.

In February of 1961, Connable was ready, willing and able to answer the call of his community in the wake of a 6-1 Kalamazoo City Commission vote approving a new housing ordinance. That action by a commission headed by Mayor James Gilmore Jr. created a five-member citizens panel to begin studying needs and identifying ways to provide low-cost housing for the city's financially stressed families.

Among Connable's fellow appointees was Lee

Gemrich, wife of attorney Edwin Gemrich with whom Connable had served in Detroit and Washington during their war-time duties. Reminiscent of the public-versus-private-ownership debate about electrical power a few years earlier, this issue packed the Kalamazoo City Commission chambers on many a Monday night and was translated by opponents less altruistically as "public housing."

The six supporting commissioners and the five appointees went into a wait-and-see mode because opponents, strong both in voice and numbers, had two weeks to collect the signatures of 1,000 voters to petition for a referendum. The foes were successful, the ordinance was rejected at the polls, and Connable's housing commission was never empowered. A second attempt at establishing a housing commission in the early 1970s also was the victim of a referendum, losing by the same 3-2 ratio among city voters.

Connable and those of his philosophical leanings had better success in another project. His old friend at American National Bank, Garrett Van Haaften, named him

Fraternity brothers Al, Congressman Gerald R. Ford and Mark Duffield enjoy a laugh ca. 1965.

to a Community Activities Center Coordinating Committee in January of 1968. There would be plenty of friendly faces around that table — Irving Gilmore, C. H. Mullen, "Buzz" Ham, Bill Lawrence, Jud Knapper, Richard Chormann, Robert Kittredge, Elwood "Woody" Schneider, and Western's Jim Miller. From these origins grew the Kalamazoo Center, which, when rescued years later by The Upjohn Co., served as the cornerstone of Arcadia Commons and the community's vanguard into the 21st century.

Two of Connable's longtime business associates, James Hilboldt and James Westin, have closely followed (and tried to emulate) the impacts that their senior partner and colleague has had on higher education and his home community.

"In higher education," says Hilboldt, "Al has been so superb in ways not apparent to those on the outside. It may be behind the scenes through the president or through a particular faculty member. He's always encouraging people to go on, to try to achieve what may be impossible. Many of those impossible dreams have come true.

"In these times when there is so much criticism of what's going on in the world of education," Hilboldt says, "it's wonderful to see somebody like Al Connable, who's been doing it for something like 70 years, still avidly supporting higher education."

"His dedication to the growth and vitality of downtown Kalamazoo has been a paramount interest all his life," Westin says. "There's barely been a project or activity in the downtown that he hasn't touched in some way directly or by encouraging other people to come involved."

"When I first came into his office," Hilboldt recalls, "Al was a U of M regent. That brought home to me the importance of education in our country and the community. So early on, I became interested in the local school system and we constantly shared our ideas about education. That continued as he served as a Western trustee.

"To this day, Al writes letters to political leaders in the

state and around the nation to egg them on to do something better," Hilboldt says about his mentor. "I remember seeing one that he wrote to U.S. Sen. Arthur Vandenberg in the mid-1940s. He was encouraging the Michigan senator to do something in connection with world affairs. I also saw the personally written response. It's that kind of hands-on contact that he was doing long before I came into the office and he's still doing it today. It's amazing."

Equally amazing to Hilboldt and Westin is Connable's perspective about city government as it's been practiced in Kalamazoo since 1918. Striving for one that is fair, honest and forward-thinking instilled in them the confidence that the community had political, social and economic stability for their business future.

Weather willing, Connable in his 90s continued to walk from his residence in the Hinman Skyrise to his office on the 12th floor of the Old Kent Bank Building. Along the mall, he greets all the people he sees, whether he knows them or not. "He's cheerful, optimistic and has an attitude that always looks to the future," Hilboldt says. "That's his most remarkable characteristic."

That's what community service will do for a person.

KALAMAZOO'S
GUARDIAN ANGELS

Near the end of the 19th century and the start of the 20th, a community's social and financial elite throughout the Midwest could be found sipping tea in gazebos on fine summer afternoons, engaging in mini-Chautauquas on the issues of the moment while puffing on Cuban cigars, and exchanging invitations to fund-raising charity balls. That wasn't exactly the style of the Peck Connable coterie as its members traveled in the stratosphere of Kalamazoo's community hierarchy. Yet, they were part of that circle.

Rising to the outer limits of Kalamazoo's version of nobility were the Upjohn and the Gilmore families whose status locally became almost intergalactic when they were linked through marriage.

In how much esteem were Alfred and Frances Connable held by Dr. William E. Upjohn and his second wife, the former Carrie Sherwood Gilmore? When the Connables' first son married Dorothy Malcomson from Detroit, they attended the 1927 ceremony held in California.

After "Dr. Will" donated $1,000 in seed money to germinate the concept of the Kalamazoo Foundation in 1925, one of the men selected to guide its fortunes as a charter board member was Alfred Connable Sr. Another pioneer member was William Lawrence Sr. "W. E. was a good friend of my father. Their ideals were the same for the future of Kalamazoo, its economy, and structure of local government. Of course, they also had the University of Michigan in common. I think our families have stayed pretty close through the years, from traveling together out west and playing together as kids, to jointly supporting community projects, to having a lot of laughs together, as Irving Gilmore and I did for years."

Via two British-born and New York-trained brother physicians, the name Upjohn started appearing on public documents in this part of the state in the mid-1830s about the same time that the Barneses began staking out the Gull Plains.

William Erastus Upjohn was born on the family farm on June 5, 1853, one of 11 siblings. His father, Uriah, was a saddlebag doctor who rode the medical circuit along traditional Potawotami trails dispensing hope and health to patients in Kalamazoo, Allegan, Barry, Calhoun and St. Joseph counties. He eventually based his practice in the village of Richland.

Like many of the Upjohn sons, W. E. attended Michigan to study medicine and, upon his graduation in 1875, the young doctor known as "Rastus" in boyhood joined his doctor uncle, William, who was practicing in Hastings. Over the next decade, he proved he had a knack for knitting broken femurs and for productive tinkering.

Dr. Uriah Upjohn, saddlebag doctor from Richland.

Like an oyster working on a single grain of sand, Dr. W. E. Upjohn was polishing a pearl of an invention to make prepared medications more effective, accurate, reliable, and convenient.

He was also working on a family, having married the former Rachel Babcock, the daughter of a Kalamazoo pharmacist, in 1878. They had met when the doctor-to-be clerked in her father's downtown store.

This turn-of-the-century Upjohn Company letterhead emphasized the company's original product, friable pills.

Working in the attic of his Hastings home, "Dr. Will," probably accompanied by frustrating trial and error, designed his process. Instead of forming pills from gooey paste that dried as hard as lead shot, which was the technology of the day, he built them up from "starter" particles in a revolving pan. He alternately sprayed these particles with moistening agents and sifted powdered drugs on them. The procedure yielded a pill whose medicinal ingredients could be precisely controlled and that needed no gums or adhesives to hold together. Because of the pill's "friable" (easily crumbled qualities), the workings of the inner body could easily dissolve — or pulverize — the dosages and distribute the appropriate medical charge.

Armed with a patented process by January of 1885, the inventive doctor was running out of space, ample power, and capital at his Hastings base. He thought he had something, but wasn't certain exactly what. In search of greener pastures and capital, he wrote to his oldest brother, Dr. Henry Uriah Upjohn, who practiced medicine, had done well in real estate in Kalamazoo, and was one of the area's first celery growers.

Henry was just as well known around the community for his own brand of farm-bred inventive tinkering. The holder of several patents himself, he sold his rights to a hay-binding machine that tied knots to Cyrus McCormick, credited with inventing the reaper, although that has been highly disputed in this part of Michigan by those who support the case of Climax's Hiram Moore.

Dr. William E. Upjohn owned one of Kalamazoo's first automobiles.

"I have got to make my choice," he wrote to Henry, "between making pills in quantities much larger than I have been doing (and to do this I shall have to use someone else's money) or stop making pills entirely as it is too much trouble to carry it on. I am on top of the fence and don't know which way to jump."

He jumped toward Kalamazoo, then in its second year of cityhood, with a population of 16,500 and growing, and, buoyed by rail service, with a reputation as something of a small-town industrial Hercules. The rest is pharmaceutical history, as they say.

Already there were the Gilmores. The brother merchants John and James were born on a farm at Killyleagh, Ireland, in County Down near Belfast in the 1840s. John, the older, was apprenticed to a dry goods house in Belfast for five years before, at the age of 20, he sailed for the United States. He learned the American breed of merchandizing working at stores in Pittsburgh, Cleveland and Chicago.

At the latter stop, he somehow encountered the former Mary Downey of Portage and dropped anchor in Southwest Michigan. Shortly after their marriage, John and Mary Gilmore on Aug. 20, 1881, opened a small store on the west side of Burdick Street in the heart of "The Celery City," directly across the street from the current site of Gilmores on the Kalamazoo Mall.

The "Brothers" part of the store's name arrived when James, who had learned his mercantilism at shops in Belfast and New York City, formed a partnership in Kalamazoo with John on Jan. 15, 1883. A year later, the Gilmores' store had moved to the east side of Burdick. In 1886, as sales continued to boom, the brothers connected to a small building that had served as the first address of what a special trade edition of The Kalamazoo Telegraph termed "a peculiar manufacture" — The Upjohn Pill and Granule Co. It would not be the last connection between the two families.

Three years after choosing to settle in Kalamazoo,

J. Stanley, Donald S. and Irving S. Gilmore, ca. 1925.

James married Carrie Sherwood, a Galesburg lass. When brother John died in June of 1895 at the age of 43 from pneumonia, full responsibility for the emporium fell on James and his wife.

Although John's heirs were still involved financially and would be bought out in 1916 for $150,000, full control and ownership of what became Kalamazoo's finest department store transferred to Carrie when her husband died in September of 1908. He was only 51 years old.

The Gilmores were the parents of three sons, J. Stanley, Donald and Irving. When Rachel Upjohn, the pillmaker's first wife, died in 1905, four children were left without a mother — Winifred, Dorothy, Genevieve and Harold. By then, the two families, because of their ventures' economic successes — as illustrated by the fact that "Dr. Will" bought

249

the second car that ever chugged its way across town — had bubbled to the top crust of Kalamazoo's elite citizenry.

In 1913, the two dynasties synergized when the widow and the widower married. It would happen again three years later when the youngest Upjohn daughter, Genevieve, wed Carrie's middle son, Donald. The marriage of step-brother and stepsister lasted almost exactly 63 years. Entrusted to their progeny, the enterprises that the pillmaker and the dressmaker wrought are still around, too.

"I grew up with members of both families. Dick Light was the son of Winifred Upjohn, the oldest daughter. We had fun and got into lots of trouble together as kids. My cousin, Dorothy Peck, was Genevieve Upjohn's neighbor and closest friend. They both went out to Colorado with us on family vacations."

After studying at Yale, Donald Gilmore went to work in his mother's store in 1916 when he was 21. By 1930, though, his stepfather had recruited him for The Upjohn Co., launching a long and distinguished career in pharmaceuticals. "Dr. Will" liked his ability as an organizer and his track record "for getting things done."

In a way, Donald was replacing another son-in-law — S. Rudolph Light, Winifred's husband since 1908. The son of a Dayton, Ohio, minister, Rudolph was another Michigan alumnus, having earned his medical degree there. He came to Kalamazoo for an internship in psychiatry at the "State Asylum." Light actually joined Upjohn the year prior to his marriage in 1907. As he moved up the ranks as a vice president, retiring in 1930, Rudolph's community stature also ascended.

Because of the death of his only son, "Dr. Will" had to look elsewhere for a successor and set his sights on Lawrence Northcote Upjohn, the son of his entrepreneurial brother who capitalized "friable" pills. Lawrence arrived from New York in 1930, the same year that Donald shifted family businesses. Lawrence would serve as company president until 1944 when he was elevated to chairman of the board and Donald took the presidential reins in his hands. In turn, Lawrence's son, E. Gifford, took his place in line to become Donald's successor.

"Before Upjohn moved from being a family-held company to one that issued stock publicly in 1958, one of our trusts had a few shares. I thought those shares should be represented at an Upjohn annual meeting, which in those days was like a family reunion. So I called Donald and said, "I don't want to surprise you by appearing at your shareholders' meeting, but we do have a few shares here and I'd like to be able to report to our owners of the trust about what's going on. Do you mind if I come over?'

"It was like the guy on that TV give-away show, `The Price is Right' — Al Connable, come on down.' So I did. I was the only one there outside of the family, but there were a lot of friends. Donald just read some figures. What was interesting to me was comparing the kinds of returns Upjohn talked about to the paper companies and their products. It was like a different world. Donald read those figures, looked at me and winked. And it wasn't because I had gone camping with his wife as a kid.

"Irving Gilmore and I were neighbors in what is now the South Street Historic District. As you can imagine, he was a very large stockholder in Upjohn so it was important to gain his approval for going public. Problem was that Irving wasn't convinced that would be a good move. He was worried the company would lose its community orientation with Kalamazoo. Widely held stock might shift concentration elsewhere.

"Irving wasn't quite agreeable at first to see control go outside the family because the company and the town were very precious to him. We were close enough friends that we had many conversations about going public. The midnight oil burned in his home and Donald and other family members finally convinced Irving that Kalamazoo would gain, rather than lose, if Upjohn went public, which it did after a 25-for-1 split.

"Another factor was that the federal government through the Internal Revenue Service was taking a closer look at stockholders in privately held companies. It would be better for Upjohn to go public on its own terms. Relatively few shares of the old stock were traded, which made it difficult to determine worth, leaving the holder open for an argument with the IRS.

"Thirty years later, though, companies were going back to private ownership. But the Upjohn offering was a good thing from many standpoints. For once, the stockholders got a true reading of the value of their stock when it went public and was listed. After the split, the new stock leveled at more than $40 a share. That set the old, closely held, unlisted stock at about $1,000 per share, which exponentially boosted the corpus of the Kalamazoo Foundation, for example.

"In making the public offering, the Securities and Exchange Commission required `Investment Banker' to publish a roster of the large Upjohn stockholders. That gave the public an indication of how many millionaires lived in Kalamazoo. Another advantage of going public was that it enabled some of the so-called `Crown Princes,' who really wanted no part of the pharmaceutical business, to draw out their money and pursue what they enjoyed more. It was an opportunity for them to get away and advance their own interests. Nothing wrong with that.

"Irving, for one, never wanted to be part of Upjohn management. After Upjohn went public, he was able to increase his many philanthropic and charitable gifts to the community. The foundation he created and the international keyboard festival that it sponsors has become one of the community's crown jewels. Irving certainly was one of its gems in his lifetime."

He and older brother J. Stanley remained as merchants, each retiring as the president of the department store that Carrie continued with in her years of widowhood. Whether she brought her own brand of ingenuity to the table or picked it up during table talk with her second husband, Carrie plowed planning and foresight into the family department store that enjoyed its greatest expansion under her stewardship.

Carrie was the one who pushed for the purchase of adjacent property — referred to as the "Farmers Shed" in the horse-and-buggy days — because her Henry Ford-like vision was that most Americans would be driving cars and Gilmore's needed parking spaces for shoppers. She set the store's philosophy about "changing with the times;" hence, departments were added while others fell by the wayside. The store is still in family hands, guided by Martha Parfet, the daughter of the Gilmore brother who made his mark at The Upjohn Co. Like "The Connable Office," Gilmore's is into its fourth generation.

J. Stanley Gilmore started working for his mother in 1909. He was 19 and had done an apprenticeship of sorts at

Donald Gilmore, Carrie Gilmore (front seat) and Irving Gilmore (running board) posed in the family's 1909 Cadillac.

the Marshall Field store in Chicago, earning $10 a week. After a variety of assignments and positions, he replaced his mother as company president in 1931. J. Stanley retired as chairman of the board in 1959, completing a half century of service.

While cardigans were on his shelves at Gilmore's, cars were in his blood. Ten years after his stepfather had scared every horse in town belching along in a tiller-steered, kerosene-fueled "Locomobile," J. Stanley was racing one of these "horseless carriages."

"Dr. Will" became a major investor in Kalamazoo's thriving automobile industry, which featured as many as 14 manufacturers in the first quarter of the 20th century. The pill doctor was president of the Michigan Automobile Co. that in 1905 produced a topless, buggy-like vehicle called "The Michigan." A car-loving stepson and his family would learn that lesson well, too.

As an adventurous 20-year-old, J. Stanley and a partner entered the 1910 "Dealers' Endurance Run," which was intended to be an 80-mile jaunt from Kalamazoo to South Haven and back again. One of the first auto races in Michigan, it so far has been the last one staged in the city of Kalamazoo, other than the unsanctioned drags by teen hot-rodders in the 1950s.

J. Stanley's 1909 Cadillac was one of 25 entries in the field that included wooden-spoked Buicks, Maxwells, Hupmobiles, Stanley Steamers and Ford Runabouts. A June overnight rain had slicked the streets as the cars were dispatched at one-minute intervals in a race against the clock. The "Caddy," with a top speed of 50 mph, was the 20th to be flagged off the starting line.

Behind them, a "Michigan" got the green flag and sped west along Main Street. It veered to pass a wagon, swerved back to avoid an oncoming car, and spun out of control, ramming a telephone pole. The driver was tossed from the car and killed. End of race. Gilmore and his partner were declared the unofficial winners because they reached South

Al and his long time friend Irving Gilmore ca. 1958.

Haven first.   Decades later, J. Stanley and his son, James Gilmore Jr., would be deeply involved in the automobile business, with the junior Gilmore taking the family's racing interests to the highest level by sponsoring such drivers as A. J. Foyt and Gordon Johncock at the Indianapolis 500. His only daughter, Gail, married Glen Smith.

"I knew Stanley, but not as well as Irving. When I'd walk down Burdick Street on the way to the office, there at 7 in the morning would be Stanley, ready to open the store for the day, not too much unlike his father did in the 1880s. I guess he felt that it was his job to open the front door each day. That's the kind of fellow he was. And, after checking this and that all over the place during the day, he was the guy who probably locked up at night. I know his employees really felt close to him."

As a child, Irving played with spinets instead of spark ignitors. He was more in tune with a machine that had 88 keys than a contraption that could muster 88 horsepower. From his days as a Kalamazoo high school student through a prep-school encounter in New Jersey, Irving saw himself on stage as a concert pianist. Although his 1923 degree from Yale identified him as an English major, he gave his musical talents a year to blossom in New York City studying under one of the renowned pianists of the era. He reached the harsh but honest decision that competition was keen and his skills might not be of star magnitude.

Irving scuttled his dreams, returned in 1924 to join the family store, never regretted the path he chose, and lived a full, piano-playing life. Like his two older brothers, Irving was assigned by his mother to learn the business from the dirt-floor basement up. He started in the receiving department, handled his share of broom details, and advanced to positions that allowed him to make some buying decisions. When Donald left for Upjohn, Irving was appointed secretary. With J. Stanley's retirement, Irving moved up to president, retiring from that position in 1971.

"Irving was a dear friend to people in all walks of life. Much of his philanthropy during his lifetime was always behind the scenes. The best way to get Irving to not rally to someone's assistance or to some cause was to let the word out that he was going to do something. In his own quiet way, Irving helped hundreds and hundreds of people in this town. Heck, many times they didn't even know it was Irving who was helping them.

"We worked on a lot of community projects together — the Kalamazoo Symphony and its series of `Starlight' concerts, the Kalamazoo Chamber Music Society, and all kinds of others. Music was very important in his life. He studied it constantly. You felt privileged being there when Irving decided it was time to play the piano.

"Irving loved to laugh and pull surprises on people. For years, Gilmore's had an outdoor cafe on the mall. His directors thought it was a waste of money. They said it was `just a place where Al Connable and Irving Gilmore can sit, talk to each other, and watch people watching them.' Donald Gilmore was a close friend of Walt Disney. He brought

Little Irving can be seen on the far left in this early 1960s view of the mall.

257

Walt to the outdoor cafe and had great fun in seeing if people recognized the man behind Mickey Mouse and, if they did, their reactions.

"Irving, Garrett Van Haaften, and Al Heilman had a wonderful friendship that reached `can-you-top-this' proportions in celebrating each other's birthdays. Irving once took them to Chicago and bought each a new suit. But I think they collaborated to top him the best. They rented the entire main ballroom of the Kalamazoo Center for a birthday luncheon. This little table in the middle of a huge ballroom. And only three people. It was classic."

And then there is the legend of "Little Irving."

The rites of spring are celebrated in different strokes by different folks. For those locked in winter's doldrums up north, there's spring-training baseball in Florida and Arizona. For the home gardener, the promise of summer's vivid colors begins with tender green strings shooting out of small flower pots scattered around the house. For the lakesiders, there are the smells of paint and analgesic for aching muscles from the annual as-soon-as-the-ice-is-gone installation of the dock.

From the mid-1960s to the early 1970s, there was a spring ritual on the Kalamazoo Mall that attracted some of the community's shakers and do'ers, no matter how busy they were with their jobs. The only requirements were a sense of humor, the need for a dose of hearty laughter, and the pretense that winter was truly on its way out.

The focal point of the celebration was a granite statue of a Cupid-like boychild who, as best stated in the famous tale, was "in the altogether, the altogether, the altogether most remarkable suit of clothes that I have ever seen."

Christened "Little Irving" in honor of the chief of Gilmore's, the statue was enshrined each spring with the first wisp of warm air as part of the store's mall-side cafe. Some of the community's finest men of letters were not averse to marking the occasion with their best "poetry."

Willis Dunbar, from the hallowed halls of academia at

Western Michigan University, took one of the first cracks at capturing the moment with his "Ode to Little Irving" in 1963:

"He is back! He is back!
And he's now all intact
Our pert little, cute Little Irving
Once again on the mall
He's admired by all
For his wonderful derriere curving
With his sly little smile and his stance so demure
And his air of aesthetic distinction
He reminds us of times
When no nuclear bombs and no missiles were threat'n
ing extinction

Tis said even Phidias
Vexed the fastidious
In carving the fair Aphrodite
The Greeks got quite hot
Because he forgot
To clothe her with even a nightie
Our Irving's quite bare
Except for his shoulder upon which a garland is hung
But not even a prude
Could object to this nude
Because after all he's so young."

When the Timi of Ede from Nigeria visited the campus of Western Michigan University in 1965 as part of his country's attempts to establish a system of technical schools, Connable and Jim Miller brought him to the "Little Irving' ceremony.

The Nigerian was dressed in regal robes and his wife was in equally brilliant attire. Connable always wondered what the African was thinking about all of this foolishness. He could only imagine that the Timi was as amazed as those people who were walking down the mall and spotted this kingly African sitting next to a funny-looking statue.

It was at this same gathering that Dunbar crafted possibly his finest composition, "An Ode to Little Irving on the Day of His Apotheosis." Only an academic would know — or care — that apotheosis is defined as the act of raising a mortal to the rank of the gods.

"I must confess
At first I thought all this was dizzy
I thought to cavort here
I was too busy
For Little Irving
Those passing
Must regard this somewhat wacky crew
As slightly touched
To waste their time on a statue
Of Little Irving."

Normally, when fall turned to thoughts of Christmas, city crews whisked "Little Irving" off to his winter quarters in some warehouse. But for the 1968-69 snow season, he was frozen into place, a fact that was cited in a piece of Dunbar prose:

"And so this season he remained in place
At Halloween, Thanksgiving, he did grace
The mall, and Christmastime 'neath mistletoe
The little rascal begged a kiss or so."

Part of the mystery is that none of the downtown celebrants was dead certain of the statue's origins nor of its ultimate fate. Like The Kingston Trio's dirge about the poor fellow riding "The M.T.A.," "Little Irving could be lost forever 'neath the streets of Boston, it's the statue that never returned." Connable swears that Irving found the statue on a trip through France and brought it back to Kalamazoo as part of one of his pranks.

There is no record of the first official spring rite of

"Little Irving," except that the Kalamazoo Mall went into place in 1959. By 1963, "Little Irving's" unrobing, so to speak, was on everybody's social calendar. Unknowingly, the straight-laced Wall Street Journal contributed to the giggles and mirth, with this blurb:

"The (U.S.) Secret Service uses code names for President (Lyndon) Johnson in order to keep secret his future movements. A recent `cover name' was `Little Irving.'"

Connable served as the event's social director, planning the agenda and sending out the invitations. Most of the invitees showed up to pay homage as shoppers wondered what in the Sam Hill was going on. When vandals with no senses of humor desecrated the idol by whacking off one of the arms, the statue was canonized as Kalamazoo's "Venus de Milo." Reattachment surgery became almost an annual project.

Doomsday came after the city convinced downtown merchants that the mall needed refurbishment. A spot for "Little Irving" seemed unlikely. Planners told the fraternity something like "don't call us, we'll call you." The statue disappeared one fall day and never returned.

To Al Connable, the contributions that two families made to his community will never disappear. They weren't statues of stone. They were guardian angels with heart.

KALAMAZOO'S CAPTAINS, KINGS AND CHARACTERS

Throughout the 20th century, the features of Kalamazoo as a community have been sculpted not by a witch's brew of characters and charlatans — although as with any town, it's had its share — but by those who generally stood above all the shenanigans and shortcuts.

Alfred Barnes Connable Jr. traveled in the latter circle, either by right of birth as a child or later in life professionally, socially and culturally. The P. T. Barnums, the shysters, and the in-it-only-for-a-buck crowd rarely entered that circle because they didn't want to stay around long enough to prove their worth as citizens first and profiteers second.

Earlier chapters have covered both in depth or briefly the contributions and endeavors of Dr. W. E. Upjohn, William Lawrence Sr., Irving Gilmore and others who, as captains of industry or barons of business, all served a higher calling as knights of the community.

With the self-admitted caveat that somebody worthy and deserving of mention will be inadvertently forgotten or omitted by lack of foresight, others are now recalled in capsulized commentary, vignettes and anecdotes beginning with Dr. Willis "Bill" Dunbar, who like symphony founder Leta Snow, was born in Hartford.

In 1928, Dunbar was appointed to the history faculty at Kalamazoo College, his alma mater, and worked his way up to a full professorship. History was both Dunbar's academic specialty on campus and his avocation in leisure. His spare moments were dedicated to the pursuit of interesting tales about southwest Michigan's past and about the people who settled its communities. Contemporary historian Larry Massie has built upon his legacy of work. Dunbar's "Kalamazoo and How It Grew" was his perspective of how Connable's home town came into being and developed.

Elevated to a deanship at Kalamazoo College, Dunbar began serving as a news commentator for WKZO, John

Fetzer's 12-year-old radio station and the first in the community, in March of 1943. Eighteen months later, he shelved his career in academia and took the job as program director for Fetzer's two-station stable of operations.

Fetzer was breaking new ground in hiring an academic as program director. Few in the radio field had master's and doctoral degrees — in any discipline for that matter — hanging in their office as Dunbar did in his office on the seventh floor of the old Burdick Hotel. Why did Fetzer do it?

"I had been searching throughout the broadcast industry for a number of years for a certain kind of program director," Fetzer recalled. "I couldn't find that kind of person I required for our operation inside radio. So I selected Willis, a man whose background in other fields was sound. My selection, from the standpoint of good radio at the time, was considered unorthodox. However, I was determined to experiment.

"I believed we should be making the station's community-service and educational programming as interesting as possible," Fetzer said. "Just filling air time with these spots was a waste. A radio station, to my way of thinking, falls

Willis Dunbar enjoys a good laugh with Al at the Gull Lake cottage.

far short of meeting its community responsibility when it merely makes time available to organizations. Unless it goes further and helps translate a message into an interesting radio program, it is doing the organization little good and driving away its own listeners.

"There was a growing number of faculty members at American colleges and universities who were beginning to see the importance of radio as an educational tool," Fetzer said. "Willis was one of them. Naturally, we never saw eye-to-eye on all matters."

Fetzer was roundly hooted at by radio colleagues, especially after Dunbar published an article in an alumni magazine titled, "The Adventures of a Ph. D. in Radioland," in the spring of 1946. Cohorts chided Fetzer that Ph. D. stood for "piled high and deep." Fetzer stood by his selection, who moved up the hierarchy to director of public affairs of the Fetzer Broadcasting Co.

Dunbar hired WKZO's first female announcer and provided the political commentary when the Kalamazoo station did remote broadcasts from the 1948 Republican National Convention in Philadelphia. Dunbar and key Fetzer sidekick, Carl Lee, were sent because one of the favored candidates for the presidential nomination was Michigan's highly respected senator, Arthur Vandenberg. Dunbar interviewed the favored son, members of the Michigan GOP delegation, broadcast giant Edward R. Murrow, and Connable's singing buddy, Thomas Dewey, who won the nomination.

Connable also attended that convention where he saw a Willkie-like idealist, Harold Stassen, take his first stand, and first of many falls. Elected Minnesota's youngest governor in history in 1938 at the age of 31, Stassen was in the middle of his third two-year term when he resigned to join the U.S. Navy. He compiled an impressive war record under Admiral "Bull" Halsey in the Pacific Theater.

If Willkie's "One World" didn't make an impression on Stassen, then the horrors of war did. President Harry Truman appointed Stassen to the U.S. delegation at the founding conference of the United Nations. Stassen became another before-his-time advocate of global village-dom at the 1948, 1952, 1964 and 1968 Republican conventions. Each time his message came up short and his nominations deteriorated into being something of a joke despite a distinguished career as the president of the University of Pennsylvania and as an adviser to President Eisenhower.

Dunbar left the Fetzer holdings in 1951 and joined Western Michigan University. His stature on campus and in the community reached such proportions that an academic building was named in his honor and voters elected him to a pair of terms on the Kalamazoo City Commission. Even in his later years, Dunbar continued to serve as a Fetzer commentator on local elections for both the TV and radio outlets. Dunbar died in August of 1970 at the age of 68, missing the opportunity to interview his son, Robert, upon the latter's election to the city commission.

"Bill Dunbar was one of the most versatile men I have ever known. He was an outstanding historian and teacher, author, public servant, an avid gardener, a pianist who loved jam sessions, a scholar and a witty emcee. He and his wife, Corita, hosted many lively and interesting gatherings in their home. The conversation was only exceeded by the food, much of which came from the Dunbar garden.

"In 1957, I was running for my third eight-year term on the Michigan Board of Regents. It looked like a tough race for our Republican slate of candidates because Gov. `Soapy' Williams and his Democratic Party were at the height of their popularity. However, I had some cross-party support from Democrats because I was regarded as a moderate instead of a zealot. There was even a movement at the Democrats' state convention to support my candidacy, but double endorsement was not possible in Michigan.

"On election night, the returns for the educational and judicial races were slow in being reported, which is always the case. Well past midnight, it looked like a Democratic landslide but there were still no numbers for the regents' race. Bill had finished his night's work at WKZO as a special commentator/analyst and stopped by the house to hold my hand. I didn't think I had a chance, but Bill went to work on the telephone.

"He called the Republican state headquarters, but there was no answer. The show was over. Bill then dialed up the Democrats' control center and reached the party's chair, Neil Staebler, who would later run for governor. Neil gave me the bad news. I was out, with the only consolation being that I had led the Republican ticket across the state.

"Compassionately, Bill stayed with me until the early morning hours, reassuring me that I was not rejected because of my record as a regent. I was the victim of a political landslide. You know how much I love the University of Michigan. I was crushed. Bill Dunbar was a saint that night.

"Bill left his imprint on Kalamazoo in many other ways. The most visible are the historical markers around this community and county. They were researched and written by him during his chairmanship of the Michigan Historical Commission."

Dr. Richard Upjohn Light: "My friend from childhood enjoyed a full life as a surgeon, aviator, photographer, geographer and humanitarian. He nearly circled the world piloting a seaplane when aviation was still in diapers. After

**Dr. Richard Upjohn Light,
Al's friend
since childhood.**

a 20,000-mile aerial mission photographing the African continent, he published what became a classic geography text. Later in life, he spent three weeks in Antarctica, was aboard an aircraft carrier that was delivering aerial strikes into North Vietnam, and was among the first to speak out against the peril of overpopulation on this planet."

Closer to home, it could be said that Light saved Kalamazoo College, or at least was among its main rescuers. When he joined the board of trustees in 1951, the college had racked up 15 straight years of deficit budgets, a deteriorating endowment, and a shrinking enrollment. The son of W. E. Upjohn's oldest daughter reversed all that in his 23 years of service.

"Dick and President Weimer Hicks were a great team. Over that nearly quarter of a century, enrollment quadrupled, the value of the physical plant grew to $20 million from $2 million, and the endowment expanded to 21 times what it had been. They were amazing fund-raisers.

"Yet, their greatest achievement, I believe, was the establishment of Kalamazoo College's program of foreign study for its students, which was probably a first of its kind in the nation. How many colleges and universities these days are trying to catch up on internationalizing their programs and curriculums. Kalamazoo College has been doing it since 1958. Something like 80 percent of the students go overseas. The $2 million to seed the endowment of the foreign-study program came from a trust established by Dick's father, S. Rudolph Light.

"Dr. Richard Light was one of this town's most creative thinkers. When Louis Sutherland was mayor of Kalamazoo, he appointed Dick to head a committee charged with studying aging in the community. On a trip to Sweden, he picked up the idea of people giving memorials to a fund for senior-citizen housing instead of for flowers. That idea germinated into the Senior Citizens Fund. Dick asked me to serve on the first board of directors. John Fetzer's wife, Rhea, and her longtime friend, Lucille Mehaffie, were on the board for years.

"The donations in lieu of flowers, coupled with some fund drives and foundation grants built the Harold and Grace Upjohn Community Nursing Home on Portage Street, the Merrill Residence on Lovell and a third housing complex. In about the late 1980s, Senior Services changed its name to the Heritage Community of Kalamazoo, but it's still part of Dick Light's legacy."

Judge C. H. Mullen: "I became acquainted with Charlie Mullen and his talented wife, Alice, when they first came to town from the University of Michigan Law School in 1947. He's had a distinguished career as a lawyer, banker, corporate trustee, vice mayor of Kalamazoo, symphony supporter, and jurist. As a circuit judge, he ranks in stature with Lucien Sweet, Raymond Fox and, going back to my father's era, Judge George Weimer. With it all, C. H. is famous for his delightful wit and sense of humor. The Broadway lyrics say it best. He's as corny as Kansas in August. That's his home state."

Louis Upton: "He and his brother, Fred, founded the Whirlpool Corp. and have been generous supporters of Kalamazoo College. Lou had a policy of not serving on boards outside of his home area of St. Joseph, but I did quite a sales job on him and convinced him to join the board of the Monroe company. He added great expertise.

"One of his lasting achievements in his home community was establishing the Economic Club of Southwest Michigan. I guess he was paying me back because I helped him organize the club during World War II. I had made some interesting contacts through my work with the Office of Price Administration and Lou was doing the same with the war work he was doing in Washington. That's how we were able to bring some outstanding and controversial speakers out to the hinterlands, so to speak, and establish the club's reputation that continues to this day.

"We'd balance industrial executives against labor leaders, Republicans against Democrats. One of the most con-

Al and his friend Congressman Fred Upton, II, in 1996.

troversial speakers in those early days was Eleanor
Roosevelt, who willingly brought her message to this
region of rock-ribbed Republicanism. It was Lou's philosophy to listen to all points of view.

"Working with him on the speakers committee, we were
trying to recruit Dwight Eisenhower, who had resigned
from the Army to serve as president of Columbia University
beginning in 1948 until his nomination for the presidency. I
had an ulterior motive for our interview with Ike. The
Michigan Board of Regents was interviewing candidates to
be the university's new president and I wanted the general's
opinion.

"Ike was in civvies and from his demeanor, it was obvious he was waiting for a draft movement to run for president. He was most gracious during our interview. I gave him our list of candidates, one of whom was his brother, Milton. Pointing to Milton's name, he said, `Here's your best man, but you are a week too late. He's going to be named president of Penn State.' That was a special moment in my life, particularly since I shared it with such a good friend as Lou Upton."

Robert Brown: "We were at the University of Michigan together where he was the captain of the football team in 1925. His son, Robert M., served as captain of the 1962 squad, which is quite a distinction for a family. Bob senior's wife, Albertine, was a member of the Monroe family. He was on the board of Industrial State Bank for 30 years, served on Michigan's board of regents as I did and was deeply involved in Republican politics as a close ally of George Romney. He even served on the Kalamazoo County Board of Supervisors when that local unit of government existed.

"But to me, the roots of the concept of the Kalamazoo Mall go directly to Bob Brown. As I recall, he and a couple of other fellows were standing on a downtown corner brainstorming. At the time, Bob was a chamber of commerce officer. They took the idea to Irving Gilmore, who told me about it.

"From then on, all of the downtown forces got busy and the Downtown Kalamazoo Association was created. Mike Hindert in our office played a role as did Nathan Rosenfeld, the head of the Jacobson's stores. The mayor was Glenn Allen Jr. and he skillfully carried the political ball.

"A tremendous amount of planning and coordination for the Kalamazoo Mall was done by Elton `Buzz' Ham, who taught political science at Kalamazoo College and became a tremendous resource for the downtown. He was a tireless worker and should be given much credit for the Kalamazoo

Center that opened in the mid-1970s.

"'Buzz' died at an early age, but his wife, Caroline, carried on. Besides being Kalamazoo's first woman mayor, in my opinion, she was one of the most progressive mayors and one of the best. She has been an outstanding community leader and passed that baton on nicely to Marilyn Schlack, the president of Kalamazoo Valley Community College. Like Caroline, Marilyn has that ability to bring people together, reach a consensus for action, and move to improve the community."

Jimmy Foxgrover: "Everybody remembers Jimmy for the way that he dressed. Purple shoes, yellow slacks and a green sports coat were routine daily attire for a super salesman who wanted to be remembered by prospective customers. I think Jimmy was the model for the zoot suit.

"His personality was a combination of Jimmy Cagney and Mickey Rooney. He was the antithesis of Howard Hughes, the inveterate hermit. He was the constant showman, the entertainer looking for a stage. I first got to know Jimmy when he worked for William Lawrence Sr. at Paper Makers Chemical Corp. in Parchment.

"Along the way, he gained the attention and respect of Lewis Calder Sr., one of the giants of America's papermaking industry, for his moxie, spunk and knowledge of the business. When Calder and his son died, Jimmy became president of their company, Perkins-Goodwin, in New York.

"It was through this connection that the Calder Foundation made many grants to Kalamazoo-based programs and in support of the paper-tech program at Western Michigan University. Like Will Rogers, Jimmy never met a person he didn't like and wouldn't talk to.

"While golfing was nearly a year-round passion, the circus came only a ring or three short of matching that fervor with Jimmy, who had somehow made the acquaintance of John Ringling North, the master of the Ringling Brothers, Barnum and Bailey Circus. North frequently visited the Foxgrovers at their home on Gull Lake. In return, for 20 or

30 years, Jimmy would shelve his business life for weeks at a time and run away to the circus, even to Europe. He'd do just about any job — clowning, cleaning up after the elephants, set up tents, anything except being a part of the trapeze act. He just loved people and the circus was full of great people to Jimmy.

"What people forget about him was that he was very hard-working and very generous. He not only donated his own money, but he raised a lot, especially for Western. He was a great salesman for the university's paper program. He and Jim Miller had a great relationship. I was a WMU trustee when Jimmy was given an honorary degree. Not bad for a guy who probably never got past the sixth grade, but who never quit learning."

E. Gifford Upjohn: "His career spanned the evolution of the pharmaceutical industry from a formulator of accepted remedies to the research-oriented producer of innovative drugs. He launched Upjohn's medical division. Another major contribution was in pushing hard to establish the company overseas, which became a big part of Upjohn's market.

"Gifford was the grandson of Dr. Henry Uriah Upjohn, who co-founded the company. When Henry died of typhoid fever in 1887, Dr. Will bought out his widow and her five children for $8,000. Gifford's father, Lawrence, rejoined the company and became president.

"Another line of the family went in other business directions. Henry Upjohn, the father of Burton Upjohn, was in the hardware business. He served on the Kalamazoo Board of Education and was elected vice mayor of the city. Henry was a very conscientious and public-spirited citizen.

"So was Paul Todd Sr. Members of two fine families, they clashed as Kalamazoo city commissioners over the question of providing electricity to the community — should it be a public utility or turned over to private enterprise? Paul favored retaining the municipal power plant, perhaps because his father, Albert Todd, had long champi-

272

oned the municipal ownership of utilities. Henry supported selling it to Consumers Power Co. in the name of efficiency and better service.

"Their rhetoric split the town into two camps. I believe there was a vote and the Consumers side won the day. The debate has gone full circle because the clamor of public ownership seems to be returning.

"Carrying on the family tradition of public service, Paul Todd Jr. ran for Congress in the fall of 1964 and was elected — the first Democrat to serve Kalamazoo in the U.S. House of Representatives since his grandfather made it to Washington in the early part of the century. Paul Jr. has always been a bright intellectual and held in high esteem for his interest in public affairs and humanitarian causes. They and Dick and Tim Light seem cast out of the same mold in that regard.

"With his father, Paul Jr. has managed a highly successful company, Kalsec Inc. on West Main Street, that manufactures a variety of extracts and flavors for companies worldwide. He is a prized friend, possessing a curious mind and a sharp sense of humor."

Karl Sandelin: "He's the classic example of the value of people traveling and having exchanges with residents in other countries. He's why Kalamazoo County should be opening up to new and fresh ideas instead of becoming too inward in its thinking. He's also an example of how a Rotary Club can be such as asset for a community.

Karl came to Kalamazoo from Finland as a young man through a Rotary Club scholarship. He liked the town so well that he enrolled at Western Michigan University, later becoming Paul Todd's right-hand man at Kalsec. His almost religious belief that service to others should come first in a person's life has greatly endeared this native of Finland to his adopted home town. His examples have influenced many people in this community."

Dorothy Dalton: "We served on the WMU Board of Trustees together. When she stepped down in 1972, Gov.

Milliken said she had more empathy with the young than a host of those chronologically closer in age. Was he ever right about that. She wasn't afraid to wear tennis shoes anywhere.

"One of the reasons that Miller Auditorium became such a great showcase and place to go is because of Dorothy's — shall we say — stubbornness. She was an advocate of continental seating in which the center aisle is eliminated and wide rows stretch across the room without a break. The trustees argued long and hard over that one. A center aisle ate up some of the best seats in the house and the long, wide rows allowed the auditorium to be cleared much more quickly. She became quite an expert on the good and bad features of auditoriums. I'm glad we listened to her."

The Burdicks: "There has always been a close associa-

Dr. James Miller posed before the globe in the lobby of the WMU auditorium named in his honor.

274

tion between our two families, even before Larry married my sister. When they took over Fidelity Federal from their father, the twins proved to be good managers until they retired at the age of 65. Neither Larry Jr. nor his brother-in-law, Jim Thorne, were interested in careers in finance. They were interested in other pursuits and I respect them for that. Jim started his own engineering business and Larry Jr. created a restaurant, the Red Lion Inn, that has an outstanding reputation in Vail, Colo.

"They had to go outside the family to find a new president in 1961 and made an excellent choice in bringing in Phil Hatfield from Indiana. His son, David, eventually succeeded him in 1981 so it remained something of a family affair. Larry was elected to the city commission in the 1940s, serving with the likes of Paul Todd Sr., Gifford Upjohn, (Kalamazoo attorney) Henry Ford and Glenn Allen. That was one of the ways you could tell Willis and Larry apart. Willis was the one who wasn't on the commission."

James Gilmore Jr.: "Other than my own elections, I had a fire in my belly for political campaigns three times — for Wendell Willkie's bid for the presidency, for Bill Milliken's run for governor, and for Jim Gilmore's race for Congress in 1980. Well, one out of three isn't bad.

"Not since Willkie's days had I seen such enthusiasm and dedicated hard work from volunteers in all walks of life as was inspired by Jim Gilmore in his race for Congress against Howard Wolpe.

"Many people for the first time learned the importance of rolling up their sleeves and playing a part in the political process. Both our country and our two-party system need this continuous infusion of new people to be effective. Jim had a rare talent for inspiring people. He would have made a great and very effective congressman."

By the mid-1950s, Connable could easily see the handwriting on the wall for the home of his grandparents. The Peck house had continued to serve the community as a museum after its days as a patriarchal residence. Its three floors vibrated and squeaked when visitors explored the exhibits and showcases to get a peek of their past.

So it was something of a bittersweet moment for Connable when, in the spring of 1958, the $1.5 million library/museum complex made its debut on the downtown landscape, taking the place of his grandparents' house.

Inside a 2,000-cubic-inch copper box that was to be stashed inside the building's cornerstone were the typical items that would tell future generations what Kalamazoo was like in the middle of the 20th century.

Yet, there was a nice twist to that tradition. Included were letters written by citizens from all walks of life. One stated:

"We have lived our lives the best we know how and trust you will not judge us too harshly."

Those are words to live by for Kalamazoo's captains, kings and characters.

THE ARTS —
AS BASIC AS THE THREE R'S

Are the arts practical?

If it's practical to have one's spirits lifted, to make people think about the life and times in which they live, to examine the human condition - then the arts are as practical as the hammer and chisel used by the great sculptors who transformed the medium of marble into a message.

The arts for art's sake have served civilizations and their aesthetic natures well for millennia. Artists have delved into anthropology and history because, to know where it's going, humanity must know where it has been.

But the practical benefits people derive from their exposure and involvement in the arts are often minimized or overlooked.

Be it the dance, painting, music, sketching, the theater, carving or sculpting, artistic expression nurtures creativity, ingenuity, discipline, logic, problem-solving, decision-making, teamwork, and most of the other characteristics that employers say they value in prospective workers.

Literacy, the ultimate objective that schools have for their students, is much broader than reading and writing skills. The arts promote literacy's all-encompassing definition — the ability to secure meaning from the wide range of forms that are used in culture to express meaning.

Alfred Barnes Connable Jr. was brought up in an environment where the arts were not regarded as excess baggage, relegated to the ranks of second-class citizen with the rest of the steerage. They were given the status of being one of the hallowed "basics" alongside the classic "three R's" because they teach living and working skills.

In the Connable household at the top of Prospect Hill, the arts were more than enlightenment and enhancement. They were existence. These three E's of the arts were partnered with the three other R's of education — reasoning, responsibility and relevance. Humanity does not live by bread alone. Nor by math and science. It needs a good dose of the arts.

With their musical backgrounds, the senior Connable and his wife, Frances, were in lockstep with the Upjohn family during the first third of the 20th century when seeds of the cultural organizations that have blessed the Kalamazoo area over the years were sown. Soon after their origins, these culturally focused groups had the collective vision to realize they must appeal to the young crowd as well to survive.

The logic was simple. There was enlightened self-interest at both ends. The young folks could demonstrate their artistic talents, gain self-esteem, and find possible career paths, while the arts community was cultivating future patrons. That way, the so-called "greying" of fine-arts audiences could be reversed without a shampoo or two of Grecian Formula.

"I learned years ago there are three kinds of musicians. There's the composer, the performer and the listener. The listener is just as important as the other two. We had all three in our house on the hill. Chamber music abounded.

"Neighbors like the Burdicks would come with their violins, violas and cellos. My mother and sister Ginny would play the piano. Sister Josephine played the violin. Larry Burdick was a violinist and twin brother Willis was a cellist. Larry joined our little gatherings a lot, especially around World War I when he was courting Ginny.

"Remember in those days, radio was hardly around and the movies were silent. People performed in their homes for entertainment. They did lots of reading, and often read to each other. As a child, Larry Burdick wasn't allowed to read the comics in the Sunday newspaper. He had to go over to Irving Gilmore's house to see what the Katzenjammer Kids were up to. We attended the First Presbyterian Church and heard some great music there. Dad was a Sunday School superintendent. But our family certainly wasn't that restrictive when it came to entertainment. We could read the funnies.

"We had a man in our neighborhood, Justin Keyes, who could get one of those player pianos to work with his feet, freeing his hands to play the fiddle. We kids thought that was just about the greatest thing you could ever see.

"Then there was Harry Parker, a local Chrysler automobile dealer. We knew him from out at Gull Lake on the island because he had the fastest racing boats. But that's not why we remember Harry. Before a race, he'd stay up all night working with the mechanics and tuning up the motors. After the race, and probably another win, Harry would go back to his front porch on the island and play his beautiful golden flute. Now that was a very strange combination.

"We were brought up immersed in music. I took piano lessons and singing lessons from Glenn Henderson, who played organ at the First Presbyterian Church and was a founding board member of the Kalamazoo Community Concert Association. After a major fire severely damaged the church in 1926, my parents donated a new organ in honor of my grandparents, Mr. and Mrs. Horace Peck. This was part of a rash of arsons that included the burning of the First Congregational Church in 1925 and the First Methodist Church in 1926. The crimes were never solved and the arsonist was never found."

"Our home was the place to come for Christmas caroling. I think that's where my voice got polished enough to make the University of Michigan Glee Club my freshman year. Willis Burdick made it, too. Of course, we weren't the stars. That was Tom Dewey, who could out-sing us all and was always out front. He wanted to sing in the New York Metropolitan Opera but he ended up smashing the crime rackets in that city and running against presidents Roosevelt and Truman."

In the spring of 1921 when Connable was wrapping up his days as a member of the Culver cadet corps, Leta Packer Snow was working on a dream. The catalyst in the conception, incubation and maturation of the Kalamazoo Symphony Orchestra, she was responsible for enriching

The Kalamazoo Symphony Orchestra, ca. 1938.

Kalamazoo's cultural life by a quantum leap. Connable came to know her over the years as a "very tough-minded, energetic and enthusiastic lady."

Born to Quaker parents in 1880 in the community of Hartford, Leta grew up listening to her guitar-strumming mother's ballads. Mr. Packer owned Van Buren County's first piano and daughter Leta began learning her way around the 88s as a 7 year old. Quaker constraints came into play when young Leta wanted to add the violin to her repertoire. Father equated it to the "fiddle," which translated into "dancing and cavorting around," but a more liberal mother won the day. Once a week, Leta was taken by train to the American Conservatory in Chicago for piano lessons from the family's home, which was then closer to the Windy City in Watervliet.

She married a Paw Paw resident, Harry Snow, who, as a school administrator, headed districts in Indiana, Michigan and Illinois. Leta was also in the education business, teaching music, Latin, German, history and English. When Harry left the profession to become a real-estate broker, the family was living in Wilmette, Il. Ill health convinced Snow that his best interests were back in his home state of Michigan. He moved his wife and three daughters to Kalamazoo in 1917 and nailed up his real-estate shingle.

Leta was crushed at the prospects of the move because she had become well-entrenched in the Chicago area as a concert performer and patron of the arts. Her impression was that Kalamazoo would be a wasteland. Instead, she found the town inhabited by culture vultures just like her.

Within four years, she had moved up the hierarchy of the Kalamazoo Musical Society to become the group's president. The society met weekly in the ballroom of the old Burdick Hotel. At one gathering, the attendees reached a monumental decision. They would send Leta Snow to the convention of the Federation of Music Clubs as their delegate.

In early 1921, Leta trucked off to Davenport, Iowa, and

her place in Kalamazoo destiny. She witnessed a concert by the Tri-City Symphony Orchestra. A concept enveloped her — if three cities can form a symphony orchestra, why can't two such towns as Kalamazoo and Battle Creek?

Back home, she summoned as many musicians as she could think of to her home and served up some tea, crumpets, and an idea. Despite hearing many versions of "You're crazy, Leta," there was enough support for the idea to germinate some action. The Battle Creek angle never materialized, but in May of 1921, Leta assembled 25 musicians for the first rehearsal of the Kalamazoo Symphony Orchestra. The inaugural concert was held the following December in the Masonic Temple on North Rose Street. By that time, Leta's legion had grown to include Alfred Connable Sr. as a member of the society's first board of

Leta Snow at her beloved piano.

directors. Another of the pioneer supporters was Harry Parker, the man with the golden flute.

Over the next nearly three decades, Leta Snow served as the symphony's business manager, the chief go-for, head promoter, and No. 1 choice as a substitute musician. In May of 1942, the Kalamazoo woman made a lasting and national contribution to her form of cultural expression when she spearheaded the founding of the American Symphony Orchestra League, which has grown like topsy since then. Leta served as its president through the war years. She retired from her local post in 1949 and died in 1980, having reached her goal of becoming a centenarian.

While Leta had no active connection with the establishment of the Civic Theater, where she lived in those years did. Sharing living quarters with her in an apartment building in the 300-block of Elm Street were Norman and Louise Carver.

Not knowing that the stock market was going to come down with a lot more destructive force than an opening-night curtain, the Carvers joined in 1929 with Dorothy Dalton, Howard Chenery, Larry Burdick, the presidents of Kalamazoo College and what is now WMU, and others to give birth to community theater in Kalamazoo. Like the symphony, it, too, has gone on to carve out a national reputation.

After his cadet and college years, the closest that Connable ever got to the roar of the crowd and the smell of the greasepaint were the occasions he was mistaken for actor Franchot Tone, but sister "Ginny" frequently graced Civic productions in its first decades.

"Leta Snow knew what she wanted for the community and she wanted it first class. I used to go to her house and watch her teach music to youngsters. She was an excellent teacher. Her driving force made the symphony a reality. She called on community leaders to get them interested and financially involved. Of course, my parents were an easy sell. So were all of our friends.

Willis Dunbar (center), Al (right), and other Kalamazoo Symphony Orchestra board members gathered at Dunbar's home, ca. 1965.

"My dad was the board's chair early on. I also held that post in 1947-48 and again about a dozen years later. I served on the board of the American Symphony Orchestra League that Leta started and I chaired its 20th annual convention in Chicago. The Burdick twins played in the symphony in its early years. So did my sister, Josephine Rood — for 25 years. Nieces and nephews have played in the Kalamazoo Junior Symphony. They've carried on the tradition of support. Ginny's daughter, Mary Thorne, and her husband, Jim, have both been members of the symphony's board. Jim has served as chair, too. In 1985, the Connable, Rood and Burdick families created an endowment fund for the symphony's principal viola chair.

"The symphony grew and prospered as a quality orchestra because of that kind of community support, participation and leadership. Another reason was that the music departments at Kalamazoo College and Western Michigan University attracted some outstanding musicians through the years. They, too, supported the symphony, making it a highly unique institution.

"Of course, this may be one of those chicken-and-the-egg questions. Were they attracted to Kalamazoo because of the good atmosphere nurtured by the likes of Irving Gilmore, or did people like Harper Maybee, Henry Overley and Lawrence Barr create the outstanding cultural environment in the first place? I guess they kind of feed on each other.

"Whatever the origins, Irving may have been the greatest patron of all. In many ways, he helped develop Kalamazoo's many musical organizations, making certain they had all of the right instruments and boosting the music education of promising students. He bought students the best instruments and supported them in their professional careers. One of them, an opera singer, sang at Irving's memorial service. Irving was singularly responsible for that wonderful Starlight Symphony series of concerts on July nights in the 1960s on the roof of his store's parking ramp.

Because of his support, tickets were easily affordable for families."

The first one in 1962 featured the George Gershwin composition of "Rhapsody in Blue," which matched how patrons looked that night on an unseasonably chilly evening. Between 3,000 and 4,000 music-lovers would be packed together on the top floor of the ramp at tables with candles or in bleachers to listen to some of the greatest contemporary performers in the country, ranging from Duke Ellington to Peter Nero to a more-than-slightly inebriated jazz saxophonist Stan Getz.

Connable, C. H. Mullen, Bill Lawrence, Joseph Brogger, Thorne and other symphony leaders served on the planning committees that organized the annual series. It died before the arrival of the 1970s. Booking four-star performers became more difficult and costly because they were

Left to right, Al, Bill Lawrence and Irving Gilmore present an award to Judge C. H. Mullen at a Starlight Symphony concert ca. 1967.

looking for solid, long-running gigs instead of one-night road shows.

"It just collapsed from its own weight," said Alice Mullen, involved with the symphony for five decades as a performer, decision-maker and supporter. "That was regrettable. The committee decided to end the series and never personally told Irving, who had been such an important part of the entire effort. I think he was hurt by that. He also believed the decision was wrong because the concerts gave downtown Kalamazoo some high-level prestige on those Wednesday nights.

"Irving was very generous to the symphony," she said. "He paid for the personalities who were booked for the fashion show that the Women's Symphony League staged as a fund-raiser. God bless the first families in this community. They were willing to put their money back into the town and its people. They didn't take their profits and scoot."

Al and Kalamazoo Symphony Orchestra Music Director and Conductor Yoshimi Takeda.

The Connable clan rated as one of those "first families."

"I was deeply touched when Irving and I were made honorary trustees of the symphony. Dorothy Dalton and Genevieve Gilmore had received that honor a few years before. It happened at the board's annual meeting. I was taken completely by surprise. It was a memorable moment in my life because I know how much my parents loved symphonic music."

At the height of the popularity of the Starlight Symphony series came another measure of the orchestra's stature on a national scale. The Ford Foundation awarded the Kalamazoo Symphony a $500,000 matching grant in 1965. Only the Detroit Symphony equaled that feat in Michigan. Coming with the approval was the possibility of another $100,000 in assistance if the grant could be matched locally.

If? Could Wolfgang Amadeus Mozart write music? The mechanics of the application were assembled by a committee headed by contractor Cameron Davis and Gregory Millar, the symphony's conductor. Connable's comrade in culture, WMU President James Miller, ran the capital campaign that raised the local match as easily as Tom Dewey doing do-re-mi. And, of course, Connable did his part in the fund-raising as a committee member.

Spurred by a growing range of community leaders, support extended in the 1930s, '40s and '50s to more specialized groups — the Kalamazoo Concert Band, the Kalamazoo Chamber Music Society, the Bach Festival, the Society for Old Music, the Fontana Ensemble, and the Kalamazoo Community Concert Association. In the 1960s, Life magazine did a feature story on "The Culture Kick in Kalamazoo." One former business manager of the Kalamazoo Symphony referred to the cultural competition as "a shootout in Little New York."

But to Al Connable, the more the merrier, and more kept coming.

A la Professor Harold Hill in Meredith Willson's "The

Music Man," Leta Snow and Edna Stanley were friendly rivals for the title of Kalamazoo's "Music Woman." Edna logged in excess of 40 years as one of the guiding lights of an association founded in 1932 on the premise that a community such as Kalamazoo needed first-class musical performances of all ilks at a third-class price.

Even though the nation was locked in The Great Depression, the grim times didn't warp the yearning for good music. A fellow by the name of Ward French, an impresario in the Sol Hurok tradition, combed the country forming local associations to serve as focal points for quality music.

In Kalamazoo, his gaze fell upon the wife of attorney Fred Stanley. The residents of Henderson Drive were neighbors of Alfred and Frances Connable. The game plan was to schedule an outstanding line-up of concerts by marquee performers and then sell season tickets or memberships at very reasonable prices. Members of the Kalamazoo Community Concert Association's first board of directors included Henderson, Mrs. Alfred Curtenius, Harper Maybee, and Irving Gilmore.

Over the years, the series brought to Kalamazoo such stalwarts of the stage as Nelson Eddy, Marian Anderson, Lawrence Tibbett, Lily Pons, Vladimir Horowitz, Helen Trauble, Jascha Heifetz, James Melton, Yehudi Menuhin, Paul Robeson, Rise Stevens, Eugene Ormandy, Ezio Pinza, Van Cliburn and Marcel Marceau, as well as some of the best symphonic and philharmonic orchestras in the world.

This caliber of cultural climate must have fertilized the innate music talents of Kalamazoo-born Thomas Schippers. The local symphony was only in its ninth year when Schippers, bound for international stardom, was born in 1930. His childhood would be nurtured by the quality of Edna Stanley's concert series.

A 4-year-old piano prodigy, Schippers enjoyed a connection to the likes of Brahms and Liszt. One of his teachers, then 90 years old, knew the great composers. By

December of 1940, he was a boy soprano in the St. Luke's Episcopal Church Choir. The following fall he was studying the organ under Henry Overley, chairman of the Kalamazoo College Department of Music and originator of the community's Bach Festival.

Schippers finished high school at age 14, departing Kalamazoo Central for the Curtis Institute of Music in Philadelphia. Two years later, he was coaching singers at New York's Metropolitan Opera. Schippers was knighted as the golden boy of classical music in April 1955 when he became the youngest conductor to take the baton at the famed La Scala Opera House in Milan, Italy. The "youngest-ever" tag followed Schippers to just about ever legendary orchestra and philharmonic.

In 1966, Vogue magazine listed him among the seven greatest living conductors. Life magazine branded him the "The Matinee Idol Maestro." He and his wife, "Nonie" were jet-set copy for New York's society pages. In 1970, Schippers accepted the position of music director of the Cincinnati Symphony, grasping an opportunity to flee from his popular image.

Once that happened, Edna Stanley was on the telephone to her booking organization in New York. The Cincinnati Symphony normally didn't tour, but if that tradition ever wavered, Kalamazoo had to be one of the stops to bring "the golden boy" home. The forces of change did take hold and Cincinnati's symphony was scheduled to go on the road.

The itinerary was all set when personal tragedy entered Schippers' life. His wife died of cancer in 1975 and the conductor decided to cancel the entire tour. But Edna Stanley had a special feeling for this man and his music. She believed that conducting his great orchestra in his home town would be an elixir of life during depressing times. She conveyed her sentiments to the maestro's parents who still lived in Kalamazoo. Schippers' mother interceded and the Cincinnati Symphony came to Kalamazoo. The homecoming concert was a smashing success, rating as another gem in Kalamazoo's cultural crown. A little more than two years later, Schippers himself was dead, a victim of lung cancer at age 47.

Five years before encountering Schippers, Overley had joined the Kalamazoo College faculty in 1936 to launch the school's music program. He brought with him a love of the music of Johann Sebastian Bach and a belief that those who shared his passion would welcome the opportunity to hear it performed live and well. At about the time that Connable was relocating his family from Ann Arbor to his home town, Overley staged the first Kalamazoo Bach Festival in 1947, a three-day event with a $2,000 budget. It also is going strong 50 years later.

Connable's first wife, Dorothy, was no shrinking violet in local cultural circles, either. Once entrenched in the community, she founded the Kalamazoo Chamber Music Society in 1955. She became its executive director three years later and served in that capacity until the early 1970s. She was also one of the early strong supporters of the Bach Festival with Edna Stanley and Lawrence Barr. The Connable household on the Grand Avenue hill hosted many of the greatest classical musicians of this century.

Dorothy also rallied to the strange cause of Neill Sanders and Anne Meade, who decided to showcase their love of chamber music not in the relatively cosmopolitan cities of Kalamazoo or Grand Rapids — but in a rural hamlet about halfway between the two. Their chosen venue was a run-down, former general store and post office in the crossroads Allegan County town of Shelbyville.

The amazing chapter in the story of this couple from the British Isles comes from their roots. Sanders joined the Western Michigan University Department of Music in 1977 with the reputation of possibly being the best French hornist in the world with credits that included playing for the likes of The Beatles and Bing Crosby. Meade had operated an art gallery in one of the most picturesque parts of Spain. But in Shelbyville, Mich.?

After selling their Kalamazoo home in 1979, the couple moved lock, stock, easels and French horn to Shelbyville and bivouacked in a building that came out of the ground in 1881. Five months of cleaning, refurbishing and modernizing fixtures prepared the way for their new quarters upstairs and for the Shelbyville Art Emporium on the ground floor.

Sanders was a founder-member of the famous Melos Ensemble, in London, which emerged as one of the finest of the larger chamber music groups in the world after its organization in 1950. It was as a Melos member that Sanders first came to Kalamazoo for a concert in November of 1969 at WMU. Soon he was a member of the music faculty.

Sanders never abandoned his love of chamber music and he soon discovered that the old store's acoustics would complement a Melos-type group. With the art emporium starting to roll, Sanders fell back to old habits and he began associating with chamber-music aficionados, including Dorothy Connable.

"Dorothy and the Kalamazoo Chamber Music Society

Neill Sanders and Anne Meade at their Shelbyville art and music mecca.

gave me great encouragement to pursue whatever wild dream I had," Sanders said. "I even received a $1,000 faculty-research grant from Western. I had to quit talking and start working."

For decades, Shelbyville residents were serenaded to sleep on warm summer nights by a cricket symphony. Beginning in July of 1980, thanks to a cross-country selling job by Sanders to attract quality musicians and organize the Fontana Ensemble, the Shelbyville crickets had to share air time with the best of Beethoven, Stravinsky, Mozart and Brahms coming from the open doors of the emporium. With the support of Dorothy Connable and others, Meade and Sanders proved that champagne and a jar of pickles can be just as lovely a tandem of bedfellows as art and chamber music.

After Dorothy died in October of 1981 at the age of 77, the Kalamazoo Chamber Music Society's opening concert for its 26th season two weeks later was dedicated to "her generosity, intelligence, energy and taste." Reported the Kalamazoo Gazette in its review of that concert: "She will surely be remembered as the single most important factor in the development of a sophisticated audience for this most intimate art form."

Even before the Fontana Ensemble put a regional twist on the family's support of the arts, Connable had been asked to provide leadership on a statewide basis when Gov. William Milliken appointed him to the Michigan Council for the Arts in July of 1969. He subsequently was renamed to that board for two additional four-year terms.

"During my years on the council, it changed from a loosely formed organization supporting the arts to one that was highly structured. The idea came from Gov. George Romney who appointed a study committee that included Genevieve Gilmore. The committee concluded that it was perfectly proper for state funds to be used to support the arts. Public support of the arts had been routine in Europe for centuries. I guess just about every little Italian village has its own opera house supported by the public. That was a foreign concept in the United States.

"When I was appointed to the council, the chair was Woody Varner, president of Oakland University. We were able to convince the Michigan Legislature that state funds should be allocated for the arts. Naturally, as the word spread, the struggle began for the dollars and, just like everything else, it boiled down to Detroit versus outstate. We did a lot of homework to come up with the right answers when it came to fair allocations. That problem still crops up.

"It was under the able leadership of Gov. Milliken's wife, Helen, that the council was able to send the Michigan Artrain down the tracks to take some of the greatest works of art to smaller communities in the state. The Millikens invited a large Kalamazoo delegation, including me, to the May 1971 dedication of the Michigan Artrain in their home town of Traverse City. It was quite the gala event."

The Michigan Artrain was the state council's response to the findings of a research project financed by the Rockefeller Fund — 95 percent of Americans surveyed had no experience with the performing arts and 90 percent had no experience with the visual arts. In effect, the report gave the nation a cultural black-eye.

Beginning with the Traverse City dedication, the Artrain went on a five-year quest to take the arts to communities across the state. The Michigan itinerary for the traveling museum of art that first year included stops in Sault Ste. Marie, Manistique, Escanaba, Menominee, Ironwood, Marquette, Houghton, Iron Mountain, St. Ignace, Cheybogan, Gaylord, Mount Pleasant, and Kalamazoo to coincide with a major community art festival held there that year. Packaged inside its three cars and caboose were authentic works of art, artifacts, and multi-media exhibits that illustrated humanity's 25-century love affair with the arts. Were they practical or nothing but frills?

"I think that was a great achievement because it carried some of the great art treasures to smaller communities. The

Michigan Artrain was exceedingly well done. The exhibits were constantly being freshened. It was so good that Michigan was asked to loan the train to other state councils. We saw the Artrain in Pittsburgh while visiting family."

Connable feels fortunate to have grown up and lived in a town that belies the statistics in the Rockefeller survey that spawned the Artrain. "I have lived in three cities — Cambridge, Mass., for two years, 20 years in Ann Arbor, and the rest in Kalamazoo. Each is 'Town and Gown,' the perfect mixture of the academic and professional-business life. The result has been all of the things I've talked about in this chapter and so much more, like the New Vic and the Barn theaters.

"I can remember many a warm spring morning walking on South Street from home toward my downtown office and I'd hear the beautiful sounds of piano music coming out of Irving Gilmore's open windows. He was having his usual morning culture-workout. Classical, popular, jazz, he loved all kinds of music and kept his windows open so passersby could enjoy his playing.

"Then we would walk to work together, past the Civic Theater, through Bronson Park, he to the Gilmore store and I to my office in the American National Bank Building. We often talked about the wonders of music and of our home-town of Kalamazoo. He loved them both and so did I.

"And what a legacy he has left us all in the International Keyboard Festival sponsored by his foundation. For a week, Kalamazoo becomes the keyboard capital of the world and our community is blessed with hearing and watching not only the best pianists on the planet but those young people with unlimited potential.

"All I can say is wow, and thanks, Irving."

A few kudos are due to Mr. Alfred Barnes Connable Jr. as well. They came in 1994 when the Arts Council of Greater Kalamazoo presented him the Theodore Cooper Award for the life-long energy he has supplied to power the culture kick in Kalamazoo.

THE ADMIRAL AND
"THE GOOD SHIP ABC"

To the casual observer, it was just another pontoon boat, said to be the first of its kind to ply the waters of Gull Lake.

But to Admiral Al Connable and the men who shipped out on her, "The Barge" (also known as the SS ABC as in Alfred Barnes Connable), was "The Love Boat," a floating island for fun and games, a place to get away from it all, a retreat to celebrate the joys of living with friends.

Gull Lake's first float boat arrived in the spring of 1960 without much fanfare, having been purchased from a dealer in this new kind of watercraft at Pine Lake near Plainwell.

Connable credits Fred Ashby with masterminding its conversion into "The Barge." Ashby, a legendary graphic artist with a genius for humor, is more than a shirt-tail relative. Ashby married a niece, Ellen Rood, daughter of Connable's sister, Josephine.

It was Ashby who installed special rigging, lighting and nautical trappings. He equipped it with a treasure chest to store the ship's log and "an adequate supply of grog for weary and exhausted sailors."

After its inaugural voyages in the summer of 1961, "The Barge" started to attract a wild and wacky crew, not too much different from the magnetic qualities of Frank Sinatra and his famous "Rat Pack" of followers.

With Connable carrying the rank of admiral and Ashby the commodore, the ranks of honorary captains began to swell — Connable's son, Alfred III, brother Horace, Kalamazoo Symphony Orchestra conductor Gregory Millar, C. H. Mullen (who later displayed his captain's certificate in his chambers when he served as a Kalamazoo County Circuit Court judge), Western Michigan University history professor Willis Dunbar, and Ned Wooley, who ran the Lew Hubbard's men's clothing store in downtown Kalamazoo. In Dr. Robert Hume, "The Barge" even had a surgeon general.

Al and good friend Dr. Robert Hume, who served as surgeon aboard The Barge.

"Sometimes a person just drifts into your life and becomes indispensable. Bob Hume was one of them. He answered a late-night emergency call at Bronson Hospital and found me in the operating room with acute appendicitis. After he introduced himself as Dr. Hume, I asked where he had received his medical training. When he said it came at the University of Michigan, that was good enough for me. We've been great friends ever since. He's always calling to check on my health. He trained at Michigan under Dr. Fred Collar, chairman of the surgery department. I knew Fred very well when I lived in Ann Arbor."

All of them had to be shipboard alert because Ashby was the master of practical jokes. When Hollywood produced "It's a Mad, Mad, Mad, Mad World," it could have been based on some of Fred's good-natured stunts at the expense of "friends." Like these deeply plotted schemes:

* Seeing may be believing, but imagining is much more powerful. Every so often, Fred would file a fraction of an inch off the front legs of a chair used by a fellow graphic designer. The difference was never so much that it could be noticed from day to day. Slowly but surely, his comrade sank toward the floor, causing him concern that his body was shrinking . . .until Fred admitted the dastardly deed.

* To drive a photography buddy batty at work, Fred drilled a tiny hole in the floor of the darkroom. As photos were being developed, he built a small fire out of old wire and insulation, inserted a long plastic tube into the hole, and directed wisps of smoke into the darkroom. The beleaguered photographer smelled the burning rubber and rationally concluded that there was a short in some wiring, all of which prompted major meetings with maintenance people each time Fred did his thing. Finally, just before crews were about to rip up the darkroom, Fred fessed up.

Mother Nature had her way with fun and games, too.

The seaworthiness of "The Barge" was put to the test over the Fourth of July weekend in 1963 when a squall turned Gull Lake into a junior version of an ugly Lake Michigan. Seven people and two dogs were on board, according to the log. "Force 3 winds" were kicking up white caps as the SS ABC moved past the Gull Lake Country Club.

When the gale picked up the deck mat and sent it to Davy Jones' locker, there was some concern, but not as much as when the anchor line was washed overboard and fouled in the propeller. "The Barge" was dead in some very alive water. Connable's son found a snorkel and went over the side to clear the fouled prop. These "fun and games" were becoming perilous.

The log captured the drama, albeit in a rather cavalier manner:

"At 17:09 (shortly after 5 p.m.), with Grassy Island on the starboard beam, the SS ABC began taking on water, and the commanding officer ordered the speed reduced to five knots. At 17:11, the winds reached Force 7 and were described variously by the civilian observers as being all the way from typhoon class to a brisk breeze. The heavy seas again carried away the anchor line, which was again fouled in the propeller.

"A passing fishing trawler was hailed alongside and furnished cutting equipment, with which Honorary Captain Alfred III again cleared the fouled propeller."

It was time to end the adventure. A course was steered to the Gull Harbor Inn where the landlubbers were put ashore. The admiral and his crew then headed for a safe mooring at "Connable's Landing" where, after a few sighs of relief, appropriate citations for valor were awarded and toasted.

In the best tradition of Winston Churchill, "The Barge's" finest hour came during a rescue mission of its

A typical crew gathered at the Connables' Gull Lake cottage prior to launching The Barge, ca. 1970.

299

own. Joe Brogger's regular Sunday-morning race took on elements of danger when "a sudden tropical storm" snapped his jib and broke the rudder.

"It was blowing like hell," Brogger recalls. "When we started to take on water, I began hailing for help and who should be cruising around but the admiral and his barge. He attached a couple of strong lines and towed us to shore, where we could bail her out and do some repairs."

"Joe still remembers that I saved his life. At least, he said I did. At any rate, I awarded myself The Connable Cross."

When "The Barge" was launched each season with the aid of WMU students John Ochocki and Bill Liaskas, the first stop was always Bill Lawrence's dock for tea, crumpets and other goodies. Lawrence would dress in tie and tails — and a pair of shorts — while wife Dorie would welcome the crew in her maid's costume.

Other rituals were added to the schedule. Like the annual pilgrimage to what became known as "The Bible Belt." "The Barge" would anchor off shore where a summer camp with religious overtones was located. "I don't know if the people on shore were all that enthused, but we certainly enjoyed Fred's rendition of `Onward Christian Soldiers" on the tuba."

"The Barge" and its crew of honorary captains could also frequently be spotted near the dam where the level of Gull Lake is controlled. It may appear to be a channel to most people, but to Connable's mates, it was a tropical stream and a perfect place for cooking steaks.

"That's where we took kids a lot of time. We had them believing that there would be monkeys by that tropical stream." Instead there was a little supervised monkey business for the youngsters and a local history lesson, if they paid attention. Connable's ancestor built that dam and operated lumber and grist mills at the site in the 19th century.

Gull Lake's famous island became an annual port of call, too. That's where Father Neptune, alias Kalamazoo

In remembrance of The Barge,
Fred Ashby fashioned a nautical trophy
for Al's 70th birthday.

banker Harold Jacobson, would welcome Connable's crew for some swimming, sunning and refreshments.

"Jake had a great sense of humor. He'd be in a Hawaiian costume banging a tin drum. We made him the official harbor master, awarding him a certificate. Hell, just about everybody had a certificate or a ranking."

All of the island's inhabitants would come down to welcome the men of 'The Barge,' reminiscent of when Captain Cook first visited the Hawaiian Islands. Father Neptune routinely welcomed his guests with offerings of a social beverage or two. Greetings were also issued by Dave Howard's family who had taken possession of the cottage on the point.

"Strange things happened when people were caught up in the 'Spirit of the Barge.' To be a barger, one had to be partially nuts. Nobody knows how it all started. It just did. There was no formal process. We played it by ear."

By the late 1960s. "The Barge" was feeling the pressure of societal change. Instead of urging his crew to "Man that anchor rope, boys," the admiral had to sing a new tune: "Person that rope, folks."

"We thought separate but equal was the way to go, even with the ominous rumblings of the Women's Liberation Movement. While 'The Barge' did give women tours of Gull Lake, none of our spouses was allowed on our special cruises. We allowed them to fix the goodies but they were not on board when we launched. We held out for three seasons."

In 1969, female spouses and significant others were first given their own ship — a "Barge-ette." It was provided to "The Mermaids" (who frequently dressed that way) by sailors extraordinare, Bob and Annie Cain, who in later years would navigate their schooner across oceans and around the world.

"We finally saw the error of our ways and let them on board. After all, we were all advanced thinkers. Our co-ed status on 'The Barge' actually predated the U.S. Navy's action in that direction. And it certainly was a lot more fun."

"The Barge" always carried plenty of rescue rigging, extra cans of gasoline for stranded boats, scores of life jackets, and an ample supply of rum in the event sailors were in a bad way. When people from other countries visited Gull Lake, "The Barge" gave them the grand tour.

No fooling! It even served as a training ship for local Naval Reserve cadets who were under the command of Ashby, a retired naval officer.

"It sounds corny today, but in those days, 'The Barge' was truly something special. Take Ned Wooley, for example. He loved `The Barge.' When he was admitted to Bronson Hospital with pneumonia and was dying, his doctor wouldn't allow any visitors.

"The next morning, when the doctor visited Ned's room, Ned was wearing on his pajamas his badge as an honorary captain of `The Barge.' The doctor called me on the telephone and kind of chewed me out because he had ordered no visitors. Of course, I denied going to the hospital, but I did tell the doctor that Ned had earned his badge and that he wanted to die with it on. Which is exactly what happened. 'The Barge' meant that much to him."

After Connable moved away from Gull Lake in the 1970s, "The Barge" became only happy memories for the crew members. It returned to Pine Lake — a gift to the institute located there that helps rehabilitate veterans.

"I don't think we could recapture that spirit today. The boat traffic on Gull Lake is too heavy with speedboats and jet skis. They would constantly be disrupting the ambiance of a ship like 'The Barge.' It just wouldn't be the same."

HE'S A TRAVELIN' MAN

Long before Abe Sapperstein and his clown-around basketball team, Al Connable was a globetrotter.

Family affluence and a bit of gumption dispatched him on a compendium of mind-enriching journeys during his childhood, teen and college years, exposing him to different people, intriguing places and historic events in the best that experiential learning has to offer. Reading about the Marginot Line is fascinating. Seeing it gives a chapter in 20th century history a searing relevancy.

Well into his 80s, Connable retained his zest for travel and the power for life-long learning that it possessed. Equally as vital was the potency of humor. To Connable, a hearty laugh carries much more punch than a placebo effect. That penchant once took him to the brink of serious trouble

**During his European rambles in 1923 Al explored a
WWI German bunker at Aisne.**

with authorities who were not in the mood for a laugh.

In retrospect, Connable never blamed them for their lack of a sense of humor because he frankly misjudged the seriousness of the moment.

To understand, one must consider the tenor of the times when unthinkable acts were becoming almost daily headlines — "Olympic athletes killed in Munich," "Terrorists hijack Dutch airliner," "Bomb blows plane out of the sky," "50 killed in shooting spree at Frankfurt airport." Prior to those brain-numbing events, people walked from their parked cars at the airport, through the terminal, showed a ticket, and went aboard a plane.

The only security one needed for travel by flight was the common sense a person had between his or her ears. That is, until zealots began applying the tool of terror to advance their cause and chose the cramped quarters of airliners as the medium to gain high-profile news coverage.

The response was fairly quick, serious and intense — security guards, electronic detectors, and no-nonsense questions. That's how Connable got into his little jam, and right in his own home-town airport. He made the mistake of joking about having something possibly dangerous in his carry-on bag, and the guards were not in a joking mood. Only some heart-to-heart talking in an apologetic tone kept him on schedule and out of the slammer. Never again. In retrospect, it was about as smart as making comments about German U-boats during Atlantic crossings during World War I and II would have been.

His business life took him to Europe many times. Public service in the role of a WMU trustee sent him to Africa. Nostalgia and the 55th reunion of his class at the Harvard University Graduate School of Business in 1984 was parlayed into an excursion through upper New England into Canada's maritime provinces of New Brunswick and Nova Scotia. The ultimate destinations were Cape Breton Island and Halifax as a fleet of "tall ships" from all over the world gathered to observe the 350th anniversary of Jacques Cartier's landing and exploration of the Gulf of St.

Lawrence.

Appreciation of the arts put him and Dorothy on a plane for Puerto Rico for a 1957 festival built around the genius of cellist conductor Pablo Casals. A heart attack sent the 80-year-old Casals to the sidelines, but he lived another 16 years to play again.

"Once I got out of college and started working in Detroit, my amount of travel greatly decreased. I was too busy with my career. We did have family vacations. Like my father, I took the kids out to the Rockies. Estes Park in Colorado was a favorite destination. So was Puget Sound in Washington and Vancouver in British Columbia.

"Then came the war. It wasn't until I went back to Kalamazoo that my passport became important again. I

Al and Tenho at their wedding celebration on November 11, 1972.

306

didn't get back to Europe until my Monroe connection when we settled on opening a plant in Amsterdam. Whenever their schedules allowed, I took Nancy and young Al with me.

"When we started building up our sales organization throughout Europe, I rented a car in the summer of 1952 and called on our dealers in Holland, Belgium, France, Switzerland and Italy. Nancy and Al accompanied me that summer. They were in their early 20s. It was great showing them where I had visited back in the 1920s.

"As Nancy and I headed off for such places as Paris, Geneva and Zurich, we dropped Al off in Rome where he stayed at the home of Stan Swinton, head of the Associated Press Bureau there and an old U of M colleague. Al had aspirations of becoming a journalist, as I once did, and he wanted to see the foreign correspondents in action while working in the AP's Rome bureau."

Earlier that year, Connable had interrupted his own winter vacation in Phoenix to do a favor for a friend. Alfred E. Curtenius Sr. had among his treasured family heirlooms a Dutch catechism written in 1790 by one of his ancestors, Petrus Curtenius. When he learned that Queen Juliana and Prince Bernhard of The Netherlands would be visiting the

Al and Tenho enjoyed a visit to Lac Mariposas during a trip to Mexico.

307

University of Michigan campus to receive an honorary degree, he made a casual remark about how great it would be if she would autograph the 160-year-old manuscript.

The remark reached Connable's attention. Then a member of the University of Michigan Board of Regents and the chairman of a company doing business in post-war Holland, Connable had not been intending to interrupt his Arizona vacation to attend ceremonies for the royal couple in Ann Arbor — until he learned about his friend's wish. He arranged to have the catechism mailed to him, bought a plane ticket for Detroit, took part in the welcoming, and had the family heirloom signed. Then it was back to the desert to continue his vacation.

Mexico was the ultimate destination for him and Tenho the spring following their marriage on Nov. 11, 1972. The target was Guadalajara and the area around Lake Chapala near the Pacific Coast in the country's midsection. As the crow flies, it's quite a trip, but this time they weren't flying "Crow Airlines." They weren't flying at all. The chosen mode of travel was automobile and off they went for Florida and Captiva Island near Fort Meyers on the Gulf Coast. That's where they would find Ginny and Larry Burdick in their winter quarters.

Another family stop was next, following a drive across the Florida Panhandle, through New Orleans, and into Texas. The newlyweds headed down the coastline bound for McAllen where Connable's brother, H. P., lived with his wife, Geno, overlooking the Rio Grande River and the Mexican border. After recharging their mechanical, mental and bodily batteries, they crossed into America's often-troubled neighbor to the south.

"Mexico has always been one of my favorite places to visit and that postponed honeymoon was my best trip there. Instead of taking what was then a new four-lane highway toward Mexico City, we drove the old Pan American route that skirts the Sierra Madres and goes through many small and colorful villages. In most cases, we found the accommodations clean and the food tasty, especially the soups."

The Sierra Madres these days for tourism purposes are billed as "Copper Canyon Country" because its complex of gorges is said to rival that of the Grand Canyon. Those who

**Returning from their Mexican trip in 1972,
the Connables stopped off at Salt Lake City.**

live in the vicinity called the region, with its mile-deep cuts, "Las Grandes Barrancas de la Tarahumara."

The Tarahumara Indians of north central Mexico sparked memories of Connable's trip to South America and the tales he heard about the Quichuans of Ecuador. In their dialect, the word "Tarahumara" means "foot runner." A better translation would be "long runner" — "really, really long runner." To these people, a marathon is a jog around the block.

The Tarahumara have been known to catch deer to fill their stomach by running after the four-footers for days. At the end, the prey is exhausted and the hunters are fresh enough for a few more laps.

The stark grandeur of the Tarahumara homeland makes their feats of running even more amazing. The Boston Marathon, for example, is a grueling endeavor with probably a hill or two to ascend. Can you imagine a race up and down a course in the Grand Canyon? Plus, the Tarahumara often add a wrinkle — one specialty race features each of the runners kicking a wooden ball ahead as they make their way up and over the mountains from sunrise to sunset.

Their races are not against the clock, but are measured against the evolution of heavenly bodies. A fairly short contest is 12 hours. Routine is an event that extends three days and nights, covering hundreds of miles. Pine torches line the course so that the runners can see their way in the dangerous darkness. They also wear rattles to help stay awake when the distance reaches triple digits.

When Americans think of the Sierra Madres, coming into focus are images of Humphrey Bogart, Walter Huston and Tim Holt seeking a treasure of gold and instead finding the motherlode of human greed. The film didn't do justice to the rugged terrain that overwhelms most visitors and delivers a much-needed dose of humility to homo sapiens.

"Crossing the mountains in an early-morning fog was an eerie and breath-taking experience. The road was narrow and was, as the Clint Eastwood movie would say, `every which way but loose' and sometimes it was loose. Farmers and Indians with their donkeys walked along the edge with no fear of falling or of you. Occasionally, the fog would lift and we could see down into the deep, green valleys several thousand feet below. While we were glad to get to the other side, it was a thrilling and unforgettable experience.

"If any one city in Mexico is our favorite, it's Morelia, which is due west of Mexico City and reminiscent of Kalamazoo in that it is the home of a good university and is a cultural and sports center. I had spent a week there before with my sister, Josephine, and her husband, Paul. Their son, Jon Rood, and his wife, Hazel, lived two months in the hills above Morelia writing papers on the research in animal behavior they had conducted in Africa and Argentina.

"Our host this time was the family of Arturo Schmidt, whom I had met earlier through the Roods. Arturo was one of the finest tennis players in Mexico and was coaching the sport as well as managing the Morelia Country Club. Like most Mexicans, they were very warm and hospital people."

The journey continued westward to Lake Chapala, which reminded Connable of Lake Geneva without the Swiss Alps in the background. Found on its northwest shores and about a 45-minute ride south from Guadalajara — Mexico's second largest city — is Ajijic, a half-a-millennium-old fishing village with a rich cultural and artistic heritage.

Since the 1950s, Ajijic (which is pronounced as if you are trying to hold back a sneeze — "Ah-hee-heek") and its Garden-of-Eden-like weather have reigned as the artistic hub of what is called the Chapala Riviera, so named because the lake is the largest in Mexico (65 miles long and nearly 17 miles wide) and is shaped like the Mediterranean. A haven for "arteests" of all forms of creativity, the Chapala Riviera attracts its share of celebrities. When Elizabeth Taylor was filming "The Night of the Iguana" in Puerto Vallarta to the west, she frequently took the short flight there across the mountains to escape the paparazzi.

The trip back through villages made famous during the Mexican Revolution took the Connables to the streets of Laredo and then up into San Antonio. He remembered the Alamo, but he also remembered the interesting riverfront developments there that would later serve as a model for Kalamazoo's Arcadia Creek venture.

North of the border beckoned later and again they did the driving themselves, up through the Upper Peninsula and then west. The Connables stayed a couple of nights with Jim Miller and his wife at their lakeside cottage in northern Minnesota near the community of Blackduck — population 700 on a good day.

In 1977, the Connables visited Tenho's ancestral home in Konevesi, Finland.

Another Western Michigan University connection for the Kalamazooans came during a week's stay at a Wyoming ranch with Myron "Barney" Coulter, a former WMU administrator and acting president who had taken a college position out west. The ranch served as a jumping-off point for excursions to Yellowstone National Park, Glacier National Park and the Canadian Rockies.

"We never got as far as Alaska per se. We drove up into British Columbia as far as Prince Rupert, which is just south of the inland passage to Alaska. We drove our car onto the ferry there and returned to Vancouver, one of the great cities of the world. We came home by the Canadian National Railroad, a truly remarkable trip. We had been on the road for two months."

A fifth-anniversary gift was a trip to Tenho's roots in Finland. Joining the Connables on the voyage across the

**Al and brothers H.P. and Harold enjoyed a sail in
Grand Traverse Bay, ca. 1975.**

Atlantic aboard the Queen Elizabeth II was the Texas branch of the family. After a couple of days in London, H. P. and Geno headed for Scotland while Al and Tenho flew to Helsinki to begin a three-week adventure through the southern and central portions of Finland.

When Scandinavia was again booked, their traveling companions were brother Hal. Connable and his wife Becky. From Oslo, Norway, the Kalamazoo Connables leased a car to drive through fjord country while the other half of the quartet viewed the coastal regions by mail boat.

"We took a three-day trip on a canal boat that starts in Goteborg. That's how you can get across Sweden to reach Stockholm, passing through a series of rivers, lakes and ancient locks. Some of the locks date back to the Napoleon years and are hand-cranked. The entire waterway is called the Gota Canal.

Traveling played something of a role in Connable being able to retain a 50-year affiliation with the Kalamazoo Rotary Club, of which his father served as the second president of the service organization in 1917-18. Uncle Ralph was a Toronto Rotarian.

Early on in his business career, Connable was often too busy in the office and found it difficult to keep his Rotary commitment. Later on, as the pressure eased and the office began to grow, increased travel gave him the opportunity to attend Rotary meetings at chapters around the country and the world — in Texas, Mexico, Hawaii and in Nigeria, for example.

The three Connable brothers evolved into something of a legend at Rotary chapters in Michigan's Upper Peninsula. "Once a year, Hal would visit us from the Hawaiian Islands, bringing with him each time the wildest Hawaiian shirts he could find. When the three of us vacationed in the Upper Peninsula, we'd make our Rotary meetings up there. We'd wear those gorgeous shirts and became known as 'The Hula Triplets.'"

"You can learn so much by traveling. I don't understand

people who don't like to travel. It's so important for one's education and you encounter so many different kinds of people. You quickly learn how we are so different, yet also how we are so similar.

"On one Fourth of July, we were in Venice. That evening our party went to St. Mark's Square and we heard a familiar, yet out-of-place piece of music. Just around the corner were about 300 American students who were singing the Star-Spangled Banner. They sang one patriotic song after another and we joined in."

Their Indonesian adventure was truly a "once-in-a-lifetime" experience. And they mean it. Too hot. Far, far too hot.

Included in the package was a two-week cruise around Sumatra and Java with fellow passengers hailing from Australia, France, Germany, and other nations. It helped to be bi-lingual, but all instructions and lectures on the ship were delivered in three languages. One of the ports of call took the travelers across central Java to see the sights by rail, followed by a flight over that part of the world's active volcanoes.

"The temples and the dances were magnificent, but I don't think I'd want to go back again. Singapore must be the cleanest place in the world and the safest place in the world, but it is also the hottest place in the world. By 10 in the morning, we were done. All we wanted to do was get back inside our air-conditioned hotel."

Deep inside, all Al Connable has ever wanted to do was get back safe and sound to Kalamazoo. There are thousands of interesting, exciting and adventurous places to visit on this planet. After enjoying most of them, for Al Connable there is not a better place to return to than Kalamazoo.

ONE MAN'S FAMILY

Once outside the womb, there are no guarantees.

Life can be beautiful. It can be gut-wrenching, twisting one's innards into knots.

Family homesteads can crumble under the wrecking ball, shattering recollections of special suppers and sing-alongs. Marriages can blossom and wither. Children can die before parents. Business ventures can sour.

Song lyrics say it best for Al Connable — pick yourself up, dust yourself off, and start all over again. One must move on.

The Connable home on Prospect Hill was eventually given to Kalamazoo College and torn down. His marriage to Dorothy lasted 45 years, ending in divorce in 1972. She died in October of 1981.

They buried a son, John Lee, in November of 1973, who fell to his death at the age of 39 from the 14th floor of American National Bank building. He had been undergoing treatment for a mental condition at the Kalamazoo State Hospital and was in the building to keep a dental appointment.

When a couple is blessed by children, as the Connables were in 1929, 1931 and 1934, those kinds of thoughts and probabilities never enter the minds of proud, new parents. Later in life, even the hard, sad times can be blotted out, replaced by the shared thrills of climbing mountains, by traveling the country to extend horizons, and by experiencing the arts.

Nancy, Alfred III and John all followed their parents' proclivity for cultural expression and pursued studies in the performing arts in New York and on the East Coast.

When Nancy was 21, she was off to New York City to study dancing at the Henry Street Settlement. The University High School graduate put her dancing shoes on the shelf in 1953, trading in all those brightly colored costumes for Army fatigues. She enlisted in the Women's

Army Corps and a proud father flew to Fort Lee, Va., for her graduation from basic training.

About the same time, Alfred III headed for Fort Knox, Ky., to begin his Army indoctrination after graduating from the University of Michigan. As the city editor of the Michigan Daily and a political science major, he received Sigma Delta Chi's national journalism award for reporting and also showed great promise as a creative writer, winning several literary contests including the prestigious Hopwood Award.

Al and daughter Nancy in Ann Arbor, ca. 1942.

During one of his summer breaks at Ann Arbor, he was able to sample some hands-on learning with pros in the field — way out in the field. Alfred Jr. dropped his son off in Rome where he was able to link up with Stan Swinton, a U of M colleague who headed the Associated Press Bureau in Italy.

"He got what amounted to an internship in the summer of 1952. Working with hard-core veterans of the foreign press corps was a tremendous learning experience. You can't buy that kind of education. Stan was willing to take him on because Stan had been the editor of the Michigan Daily himself. He was also very fond of Al III.

"Stan became a famous war correspondent for `Stars and Stripes.' His big story was the capture of Mussolini. The Germans had been hiding `Il Duce' in northern Italy, but the Italian underground was able to ferret him out. Even though the lines of communications had broken down, Stan heard through the grapevine that something big was going on in Milan. He drove his jeep through enemy lines to get the story. He was the only war correspondent there as Mussolini and his mistress were killed by the mob and strung up by their feet. Stan had the scoop and received a major award from the Associated Press. As I said, one can't get that kind of learning in a classroom."

The following summer Alfred III experienced a different kind of regimentation as a private in the U.S. Army, spending some of his military time at the Aberdeen Proving Ground in Maryland and later in Hershey, Pa., in a public-information outfit.

Following his discharge, Alfred III was back in Ann Arbor as a graduate student and seeking his old identity. It was as "Barnes Connable" that he accepted a prestigious campus award for a one-act play.

He was still Barnes Connable in his third year at the Yale Drama School in 1957 when he was awarded a $1,000 fellowship in playwriting. The award had been endowed by the widow of Robert Anderson, author of "Tea and Symphony." Alfred III was studying under instructors who had schooled such stalwarts of the stage as Tennessee Williams and Arthur Miller.

"Shadows in the Court" by Barnes Connable was performed by student actors in New Haven in May of 1958. Based on his knowledge of the lives of newspaper reporters, the play had in its starring role a former Miss Illinois who was studying theater at Yale.

Armed with a master's from Yale, Alfred III continued to write plays, did some free-lance writing for such publications as The Magazine of Fantasy and Science Fiction, and began writing books. He also did some work for NBC

Alfred Connable, III and wife Roma, ca. 1970.

News, the New York Times, United Press, and the Carnegie Endowment for International Peace.

"One of his books,`The Tigers of Tammany: Nine Men Who Ran New York' is about the politics of city hall in New York City. He did a tremendous amount of research on seven consecutive bosses and chronicled their lives, their clout, their accomplishments, and their excesses. The book dramatizes why our American political scene periodically needs to be reformed and why it is so important that people stay involved."

Co-authored in 1967 with New York Herald Tribune political reporter Edward Silberfarb, it was called "lively politics and absorbing history" in a New York Times book

Alfred Connable, III's international espionage thriller appeared in 1971.

320

review, probably because Connable knew of what he was writing. He had an insider's view, working as an aide to New York Mayor Robert Wagner. No moderate Republican like his father, Alfred III worked as a press officer for Eugene "Clean Gene" McCarthy in 1968 and later wrote speeches for the Democratic presidential campaign of Edmund Muskie of Maine.

He was married in May of 1962 to a writing soulmate. Roma Lipsky had served as the editorial director at the Michigan Daily, worked on the staff of former New York Gov. Averell Harriman, and was a partner in a public relations firm in New York. She, too, had been published in the New York Times and, at the time of her marriage, was on the staff of the Federal Housing and Home Finance Agency. Al served as his son's best man and Irving Gilmore attended.

In 1972, the New York-based Alfred III returned to his home territory to promote his suspense novel about espionage, "Twelve Trains to Babylon." At one time, it was being considered as movie material. These days, Alfred III lives in Long Island and does his writing for the president of Columbia University.

John Lee followed his older brother to a prep school in Dublin, N. H. As a freshman and English major at Rollins College in Winter Park, Fla., he flashed the quality of his singing voice with a role in one of Puccini's operatic forces. Over the next four years at Rollins, John Lee sang in the community's Bach choir and the college's choral group, and landed leading roles in several drama productions, including "The Crucible," "Pygmalion," "Born Yesterday," and "Romeo and Juliet." During the summers, he continued learning his craft back home in productions at the Kalamazoo Civic and the Barn Theater near Augusta.

In March of 1958, he and Joan Brand, a theater arts major and sophomore at Rollins, exchanged wedding vows. The duo had starred in a campus production of Thornton Wilder's "Our Town." He would die 15 year later in "His Town."

Al and his second wife, Tenho, divided their time between two residences — the one in downtown Kalamazoo at the Hinman Skyrise and the other on Guernsey Lake Road just north of Gull Lake in Barry County. The University of Michigan's first female engineering graduate, she also earned a master's majoring in computer science from WMU in 1972 where she also taught for 15 years. They were married in 1972

In 1937, the former Tenho Sihvonen's freshman year in Ann Arbor, female engineering students were a rarity. When she was denied admission in the School of Engineering, she did a flanking movement, checked in as a literature major, earned some dynamite grades, and convinced the fathers of university engineering to integrate their good-old-boys club with a few daughters.

The delay, however, cost her some time and she wasn't able to graduate with her engineering degree until February

Tenho Sihvonen (Connable) became the first woman graduate of U of M's Chemical Engineering Department in February 1942.

1942, just in time for World War II. "Because of the war and the fact that I wasn't draftable," she said, "I had my pick of jobs. Doors that had been closed to a woman engineer suddenly opened very wide. That's why I often tell young people to do what they want and to not worry about the job market."

Formerly married to Connable's deceased and longtime partner, Michael Hindert, she parlayed her Finnish ancestry and love of donning a set of blades into founding the Kalamazoo Figure Skating Club in the early 1960s at the city's ice rink, which was located near Upjohn Park and the old Sears store.

"Tenho helped start dozens of things around the community, but she's pretty tight-lipped about it. The Finnish have a word — sisu. It means pride in yourself, your country and your independence. That's Tenho. She has sisu. Even before I ever met her, I had always admired two countries other than my own — Finland and Israel. They have the guts to stand up for themselves. Finland did its own fighting in World War II, stood up to the Russians, and was the only country to pay off its war debts. That's sisu."

They're able to regularly see Nancy, who never married, because she has stayed close to Kalamazoo. After hanging up her WAC uniform, she eventually took a job among the administrative staff of opera singer Beverly Sills and was instrumental in arranging for Sills' visit and performance in Kalamazoo in July of 1970.

"The Admiral" added greatly to his crew with his marriage to Tenho. Her four children and their spouses brought with them quite the brain trust — eight undergraduate and nine graduate degrees hang on the walls of their respective homes.

Pat Hindert, born in 1948, majored in history at Harvard and added a law degree from his mother's alma mater, the University of Michigan. A former French teacher and tennis coach at the Cranbrook Academy, he is president of Benefit Designs Inc. of Cincinnati. He and his wife,

Louise, are the parents of two teens.

Dan is a year younger. He received his bachelor's at Williams College and advanced degrees in law from Vanderbilt University and Eastman Kodak's institute. He's a trial lawyer with a Utah law firm. His wife, Carol, heads a family-practice clinic in Salt Lake City. They are the parents of two children. An adventurer, Dan has experienced a wide range of exploits, from teaching Outward Bound courses to driving a cab in New York City.

Kristina Hindert Nehring is married to a circuit judge in Utah. After studying geology for two years at Middlebury College, she enrolled at the University of Utah and went on to earn her medical degree with a post-graduate emphasis on child psychiatry. The mother of three children, she has served as an executive director of the Children's Center in

Al posed with new U of M President Lee Bollinger at commencement in June, 1997.

her adopted state. She was born in 1951.

The youngest of the Hinderts, Thomas, was born in 1954. He has undergraduate and graduate degrees in architecture and urban planning from Michigan. Now vice president of the Mills Corp. in Arlington, Va., he and his wife, Tania, have three children, including twin teen-age sons.

Following in the Finnish tradition of athletics as their mother has, collectively the four Hinderts have run for school track teams, participated in the Boston Marathon, been involved in Outward Bound experiences, and engaged in extensive mountain climbing in the United States, Canada and Europe.

Because he's within walking distance of his office while residing in the Skyrise, Connable stays in pretty close touch with what's going on. That's also his passport to the past.

Gracing his walls are dozens of photos of presidents, governors, relatives, political "wanna-bees," family members, captains of industry, and even one of his pet poodle, Fauvette.

He has stories about all of them — the cuff links that Jerry Ford sent to him during Ford's sojourn in the White House as the Michigan man tried to heal the nation after Watergate.

Fauvette's photo was a gag shot that was set up as part of the opening of a new American National Bank branch. It shows the poodle on a chair, shaking "paws" with Glen Smith Jr. as one of the bank's first depositors.

One of his fondest keepsakes is a grandfather clock that dates back to the late 19th century. "I heard that thing ticking when I was a kid. It tells the time, the weather, and every other darn thing you want to know. It needs a little doctoring now and then, but it still works."

And so does Al Connable in his 90s, laughing all the way.

A Michigan Man and proud of it.

SOURCES CONSULTED

Balls, Ethel & Lassfolk, Marie. Living in Kalamazoo. Kalamazoo, 1958.

Bordin, Ruth. The University of Michigan. A Pictorial History. Ann Arbor, [1967].

Brannon, W.T. "Yellow Kid" Weil. Chicago, [1948].

Carlisle, Robert D.B. A Century of Caring. The Upjohn Story. [Elmsford, N.Y., 1987].

Catalogue of the Officers & Students of the University of Michigan. 1855-1856. Ann Arbor, 1856.

"A Century Marches By" Jackson County Centennial. [Jackson, 1936].

Dunbar, Willis. Financial Progress in Kalamazoo County Since 1834. Kalamazoo, [1966].

Dunbar, Willis. Kalamazoo & How It Grew & Grew. Kalamazoo, 1969.

[Durant, Samuel W.] History of Kalamazoo County, Michigan... Philadelphia, 1880.

Fisher, David & Little, Frank, eds. Compendium of History & Biography of Kalamazoo County, Michigan. Chicago, [1906].

Gilmore Bros. 1881-1944. [Kalamazoo, 1944].

Gould, Jean & Hickok, Lorena. Walter Reuther Labor's Rugged Individualist. New York, [1972].

Green, James J. compiler. A Historical Brief: Allegan Michigan 1838-1963. N.P., 1963.

Gull Lake Its History, Location & Advantages... Cleveland, [1904].

Gunther, John & Quint, Bernard. Days to Remember: America 1945-1955. New York, [1956].

[Jarvis, Nancy H., ed.] Historical Glimpses Petoskey. [Petoskey, 1986].

Kalamazoo City Directory. Kalamazoo 1890-1990. (Titles Vary).

Knauss, James O. The First Fifty Years. A History of Western Michigan College of Education 1903-1953. [Crawfordsville, Indiana.] 1953.

Massie, Larry B. Michigan Memories. Allegan, 1994.

Massie, Larry B. Potawatomi Tears & Petticoat Pioneers. Allegan, 1992.

Massie, Larry B. & Schmitt, Peter J. Kalamazoo: The Place Behind the Products. [Woodland Hills, CA., 1981]

Michigan Manual 1941-1985. Lansing, V.D.

Offical Program. October 27, 1934. Illinois vs. Michigan. Ann Arbor, 1934.

Orcutt, William Dana. Burrows of Michigan & the Republican Party. 2 Vols. New York, 1917.

Personalities at WKZO, Kalamazoo, & the Columbia Broadcasting System. Peoria, Ill., 1940.

Picturesque Kalamazoo... Chicago, N.D.

Quaife, Milo, M. This Is Detroit. 1701-1951. Two Hundred & Fifty Years in Pictures. Detroit, 1951.

Rowe, Ford F. Kalamazoo the Debt-Free City. The Reason Why. [Kalamazoo, 1939].

Schubert, Phil, ed. The Best of Encore Magazine. [Kalamazoo, 1989].

Smith, Richard Norton. Thomas E. Dewey & His Times. New York, [1982].

Stine, Leo C. Western - A Twentieth Century University. Kalamazoo, [1980].

The Story of K.V.P. East Aurora, N.Y., 1927.

Weissert, Charles A., ed. An Account of Kalamazoo County... N.P., [1926].

Your City & Its Government. A Twenty Year Story of City Manager Government in Kalamazoo 1918-1938. [Kalamazoo] N.D.

INDEX

330